"If anyone is qualified to write on leadership in a global age of crisis, it is Michael Bassous. Drawing on his experience of growing up and living in the chaos that has often surrounded his home country of Lebanon, Michael offers deep wisdom on life and leadership. This is the fruit of long reflection and engagement with one of the most challenging environments, in which he has learned to offer leadership that can radiate calm and inspire hope."

—GRAHAM TOMLIN, president, St Mellitus College

"I find the author's idea original—namely, exploring what Jesus can still tell us about leadership in the crises of today's world, an issue with which we are all confronted both at a personal and societal level. His considerations, based on his own experience in a land challenged with a long period of war and his analysis of different positions, are stimulating and open new perspectives for living our own responsibilities toward others."

—GABRIELE CACCIA, permanent observer of the Holy See
to the United Nations

"To speak about leadership in crisis is something, and to speak out of personal experience is something else. Bassous shares life illustrations and invites you to a journey full of courage, credibility, and practicality. It exposes the hidden corners of what it means to lead in crisis and provides principles of leadership that help leaders to embrace the extraordinary. This book is a valuable gift for Middle Eastern and worldwide leaders."

—NAJLA KASSAB, president, World Communion of Reformed Churches

"Bassous's incredible life story and deep leadership wisdom make this book stand out among the many 'armchair-wrestling' leadership books on the market! He offers a refreshing perspective to recalibrate how we think about leadership. His inside-out approach advocates for the nurturing of inner qualities and character, coming alive through powerful, transformational leadership practices. . . . This book is a crucial read!"

—MARCO BLANKENBURGH, international director, KnowledgeWorkx

"I find this work to be an excellent reflection on the crises facing individual leaders in the Middle East and at large. Bassous invites us to ask the question of 'how' rather than 'if' crisis will end. The book is infused with strong biblical values, which are coupled with an ecumenical spirit, global perspectives, and inclusive approaches. It concludes with the most appropriate leadership model in history, that of our Lord Jesus Christ."

—ANBA ANGAELOS, Coptic Orthodox archbishop of London

"I know few people as qualified as Michael Bassous to write this book. He has shown incredible skills guiding ministries through some of the most horrendous times any country has experienced. . . . Those who have the opportunity to read this book will find, I am sure, their ability to lead in crisis enhanced and made much more effective by reading this book."

—BOB HOSKINS, founder, OneHope

"*Leadership . . . in Crisis* has come out from a person who has literally been enmeshed in one crisis after another, on a global scale and also on a personal level, and therefore Bassous could boldly pen, 'Leadership is one of the most used, misused, and abused terms in the Western hemisphere.' . . . After so brilliantly setting out the different ramifications of this topic, he has also brought out new insights on the leadership role of Jesus Christ."

—ROBERT CUNVILLE, president, United Bible Societies

Leadership ... in Crisis

Leadership...in Crisis

A Global Perspective on Building Resilience,
Stamina, Agility, and Confrontation

Michael G. Bassous

Foreword by Gene Habecker

RESOURCE *Publications* · Eugene, Oregon

LEADERSHIP . . . IN CRISIS
A Global Perspective on Building Resilience, Stamina, Agility, and Confrontation

Resource Publications
An Imprint of Wipf and Stock Publishers
199 W. 8th Ave., Suite 3
Eugene, OR 97401

www.wipfandstock.com

PAPERBACK ISBN: 978-1-6667-4322-7
HARDCOVER ISBN: 978-1-6667-4323-4
EBOOK ISBN: 978-1-6667-4324-1

Contents

Foreword

RECENT ESTIMATES (FORBES) SUGGEST that leadership development is now a $350 billion global industry. Amazon now handles more than 50,000 books in all formats that include the word "leadership" in the title. Conservative reports place the number of leadership books published each year at more than 1000. So, what gives? Why are people obsessed with leadership training and leadership development? Michael Bassous' book provides a partial answer—because *leadership . . . is in crisis*, globally. And people are chasing after solutions that might help improve their reality. No matter which part of the world one calls "home," there are numerous examples of leadership dysfunction, if not failure.

There are multiple reasons why this book is so timely: its author, the blend of research coupled with practical application, and the leadership context. First, the author himself is well-trained and experienced as a global leader. Holding both an MBA and a PhD, he is able to engage the research literature with facility. Accordingly, the book is very well researched. The multiple footnotes themselves are a veritable source of books and articles on leadership theory and practice. His education and training are then combined with a strong experiential foundation which has included more than 35 years of experience in both the for-profit and non-profit worlds. He just doesn't discuss leadership as a theory but, as an experienced practitioner, he is able to apply theory to practice. His leadership context is global. Because the Middle East has been his long-term home, he has first-hand experience about leading in crisis. His regular travel to all parts of the globe has given him expertise in the contextual understandings which are so often absent in the literature and practice of leadership development.

Some of the strengths of the book are the multiple stories it references, stories of leadership failure and success; stories of triumph and defeat; stories of learning, unlearning, and relearning. Many of the stories shared illustrate in practical ways the ways Bassous has attempted to combine leadership theory with leadership practice. Importantly, the foundation for Bassous' book is a vibrant Christian faith coupled with strong ethical commitments.

The leadership topics addressed are timely and all are relevant to the contemporary leadership context. He notes the importance of resiliency, stamina, and agility as important leadership essentials. Of special importance, he references the need for leaders to develop the ability to confront, whether difficult issues or people. Much of the dysfunction we witness in leadership is because this leadership skill has never been mastered or it has been poorly applied.

Leaders have multiple choices when it comes to selecting books and articles on leadership. Those who make *Leadership ... in Crisis* one of those choices will be on the pathway to becoming better and more effective in their leadership.

Dr. Gene Habecker, PhD, JD
Senior Fellow, Sagamore Institute; Chair Emeritus, Board of Directors, Christianity Today; President Emeritus, Taylor University; and author, *The Softer Side of Leadership: Essential Soft Skills that Transform Leaders and the People they Lead.*

Introduction

"WHAT DOES IT TAKE to be a good leader?" asked the young lady in the audio message on my phone. She was applying for a managerial role at a partner Christian organization. *"I have applied and progressed in the job application because of my commitment to the organization and its mission, but I have never led or managed a small team. Can I call you for some tips?"* This short conversation reflects what people may consider it takes to become a "good" leader—a short phone conversation! Even though it may have worked on some occasions for certain organizations, leadership is not a quality so quickly learned and easily demonstrated in a job interview.

Leadership is one of the most used, misused, and abused terms in the Western hemisphere, corporate and organizational worlds. We tend to use the word without any consideration of its value, weight, and impact. *Senior leadership, executive leadership, team leadership, organizational leadership, corporate leadership, administrative leadership . . .* are just a few examples of how this term has penetrated our vocabulary. It seems to add value—an intangible, altruistic value—to any role that entails responsibility. The question is: How do we measure this value?

Are you a leader? A question that I have asked and been asked many times by different stakeholders. We tend to associate a certain level of pride and superiority to someone who is labeled a *leader. "My son is a leader in his basketball team"* says a proud dad; *"my daughter leads the team at her office"* resonates a gratified mom; *"my wife is a leader in her field of expertise"* adds a delighted husband; *"I have inherited my dad's leadership skills"* claims a young woman. What is so important about this concept that we race to attach ourselves to it? Can we add a concrete substance to this label? More importantly, do we need to?

The mere association to such verbs and terms—*lead, leader, leader-ship*—appears to add unique value to what that person does, who s/he is,

1

why they do what they do, and how they go about doing it. Elusive, yet powerful. Obscure, but prestigious. Immaterial, but of great value. How and when did this association infiltrate our jargon, creating stratified classes of those with and those without *leadership skills*? Why and where did we draw the line that differentiates our contextual perception and understanding of what a leader is or is not, how s/he should behave, and what constitutes leadership attributes? This manuscript aims to address some of these existential questions on leadership.

I am writing this introduction of what I hope to be a fresh look into the essence of leadership from my hometown just outside Beirut, Lebanon—a tiny country in the Middle East. My apparent leadership preferences would probably be influenced by decades of conflict, crises, patriarchal/tribal, and emergent environments. My only sibling, a sister who has lived most of her life in Midwest USA, would perhaps have different—even conflicting—views of leadership due to her own experiences and situations. Similarly, my three millennial sons, all leading professional careers in cosmopolitan cities around the globe, would probably defy my leadership understanding. Friends and colleagues from the Far East may offer a substitute model, different from the Global South of mainly African and Latin American perspectives, who in turn may be confronted with European and Nordic interpretations of leadership.

A wide variety of books and research have attempted to capture the concept of leadership. For example, in 1999, more than 2,000 books were published on the topic of leadership.[1] About two decades ago, the Library of Congress in the USA recorded more than 8,000 leadership books in its database.[2] Now that number has increased to more than 43,000.[3] There are more than 80 kinds of leadership *brands* available in the global market; these *brands* allegedly base their concepts and training tools on established leadership theories, models, and phenomena.[4]

With this vast availability of leadership resources and materials, scholars and practitioners are still struggling with adopting a unified, common, and established understanding of the essence of leadership. The reason for the non-existence of one coherent understanding is that leadership is a dynamic concept, a nucleus of energy, developing and changing along

1. Martin and Ernst, *Leadership,* 82–94.
2. Higgs, *Sense of Leadership,* 273–84.
3. Library of Congress, *Leadership.*
4. Rubenstein, *Evolution of Leadership,* 41–49.

with eras, relationships, environments, circumstances, contexts, and structures. A dictator in one country may be considered a leader as opposed to a high school student-union elected leader. Throughout history and across civilizations, the definition of leadership as well as the classification of leadership understanding, have evolved through different intervals, and they keep doing so even now.[5]

So, why another book about leadership? When the proposal to write yet another book on leadership was presented to me based on my experiences and research, I immediately dismissed the idea. Do we actually need another book on leadership? Don't we have enough in the global libraries that, if emerging leaders adopted even 10 percent of their concepts, we wouldn't be having this conversation? I have spent the last 35 years of my professional career adopting, living, applying, practicing, teaching, modeling, and advocating an apparently effective leadership model, yet I have also failed to uphold these transcendent principles many times. Because . . .

Leadership . . . is in crisis

I came to the conclusion that *leadership . . . is in crisis.* The concept of leadership as we would like to perceive it, regardless of our differing interpretations, is in a predicament. We elect political leaders based on their economic growth policies rather than their moral compass; examples include the US presidential elections, Brexit aftermath, reinstatement of dictators in several Arab Spring countries, North Korea's supreme leader . . . Most of our political leadership inclinations are based on what resonates with our future goals and objectives, rather than the greater good of humanity. And unfortunately so.

We choose our preferred business and organizational leaders based on the predicted return on investments (ROI) without much consideration of the side effects, such as global warming, environmental damage, sweat factories, child labor, or human rights violations. It is as if the feudal Machiavelli's mantra *"The end justifies the means"* is still prevalent after five centuries of its introduction.[6] Over the past two decades, we have witnessed some of the largest frauds, scandals, and deceptions of our lifetimes (e.g., USA's Enron, WorldCom, and Bernard Madoff's Ponzi scheme; South Korea's Samsung CEO and heir Lee Jae-Yong's bribery, Iceland's three banks

5. Leonard, *Leadership Development,* 3–14.
6. Machiavelli, *The Prince.*

that triggered the financial crises in 2008: Kaupthing, Landsbanki, Glitnir
. . .). When the ROI was doing well, no one questioned those leaders about
their obscure trading, but when they failed, everyone—governments, financial institutions, investors—probed for reasons why they were allowed
such powers!

Similarly, we provide excuses to cover up Christian leaders' abuses
of power—pedophilia, embezzlement, power struggles, sexual harassment,
etc.—to safeguard our denominations. Post-modern Christian organizations and charities lobby, politicize, and manipulate governing practices to
serve their own "leadership" agendas. We now mold our leadership package to satisfy our plans, propaganda, and those of our key stakeholders.
Some traditional church bodies are experts in these "democratic" practices
while other emerging and contemporary churches claim pious language
to justify irrational decision-making processes. This is perhaps one of the
worst depictions of failed Christian leadership models, which I will revert
to later in this book.

Leadership . . . is in crisis when it shifts from inclusivity to exclusivity,
from comprehensiveness to separatists. Rather than catering to the widest
possible audience of influenced members, leaders have found it easier, and
sometimes more gratifying, to cater to their own groups rather than the
greater good, thereby dismissing one of the highest levels of leadership behavior: *servanthood.*[7] This is usually depicted through the leader-member
exchange model with what is described as "in-group" versus "out-group."
The first is the informal "in-group" members who enjoy high-quality relationships with the leader, preferential treatment with respect to strategic
advice, support, feedback, decision-making freedom, and opportunities for
growth, which may result in higher commitment and cooperation. The second is a formal low leader-member exchange, also known as "out-group"
members, limited to their structure and surroundings—low visibility, and
little potential or growth.[8] Such groupings challenge the mere existence of
leadership and alternate it with a tribal model.

Leadership . . . is in crisis when it allows external factors and environmental changes to dictate new sets of principles and practices. Have
you heard the term "slippery fish"? I heard this phrase when discussing the
character of a prominent Christian leader in the context that one cannot
get a straight answer, position, or decision from that leader. There is always

7. Prewitt, *Integral Leadership*, 327–33.

8. Sparrowe and Liden, *Integrating Leader-Member Exchange*, 505–35.

a gray area, a compromising space, where some leaders are accustomed to linger for a short time. It *is* a short time before the next more powerful forced change blows in another direction, and it is quite unfortunate that such leaders tend to bend, like a palm tree, to the strongest winds rather than be steadfast and rooted, like a cedar tree.

More than a century ago, when migrant workers were flocking toward West Africa to look for entrepreneurial work opportunities, and as the ships coming from the Mediterranean or around the Cape of Good Hope were approaching the seashores of the mineral-rich continent, travelers would occasionally pick up stranded monkeys swimming out toward the Atlantic Ocean. Some monkeys were saved; others perished in the open water. No one understood this predicament. Why were these monkeys swimming out to nowhere and toward their certain death? Research indicated that such primates would be swinging on branches on the seashore, slip and fall into the seawater. When they floated again, they tended to swim head-on in the direction in which they emerged from the water, without considering that the safety of the shores was only a few meters or yards to their left or right side or even behind them.

Such is the dilemma of leadership when in crisis. It loses focus, route, moral direction, credibility, inclusivity, and impact. But what about leading through crisis?

Leadership . . . in crisis

What about *leadership . . . in crisis*? When you walk into a room, what do you see? A quick assessment may emphasize the risks—and the opportunities—available in that room. The ability to transform certain circumstances to benefit the greater good is exactly what people are looking for in the next generation of leaders. Gen Z is keen on finding purpose in their work as they tackle new and challenging working environment of the "next normal" following the COVID-19 pandemic.

I have become accustomed to risk assessment. The civil war in Lebanon started when I was nine-years-old and ended three months after I got married—15 years later! Most of my development, growth, and adulthood years were trenched with inconsistent and sporadic warlike activities that almost incapacitated my future. As a follower of Christ, and despite the personal calamity that engulfed most of my childhood and teenage years, there were enough opportunities to extend a saving arm to a drowning candidate. And many of my cohorts did drown, as they did not strive to search for that window of opportunity in the midst of crises.

So instead of focusing on the crises that leadership is actually in, I decided to realign this book to emphasize leading in times of crisis. Authentic and credible leadership is often tested during turbulent, inconsistent, and unpredictable times rather than through stable and steady phases. The focus is on those leaders that learned valuable lessons from various crises they experienced and adapted accordingly. Rather than be swayed by external circumstances, it is time to lead, to become the rudder—offering direction and opportunities—rather than the sails—being wavered by the winds.

To illustrate, almost two decades ago, I was asked to conduct regional workshops with an international Christian organization in Istanbul, Turkey—a city I love to visit. My itinerary included a 48-hours layover before traveling to Bangkok, Thailand, for another meeting, so I had to choose red-eye flights to make it happen. Upon my arrival in Istanbul and checking into the venue, a huge explosion rocked the neighborhood. Two huge truck-bomb explosions wrecked the British Consulate and a British bank on November 20, 2003, killing at least 27 people and wounding 450 in an assault that coincided with President Bush's state visit to London. All participating trainees—and some trainers—wanted to get on the first flight back home.

This is a normal reaction to a crisis: reactive, panic, halting the planned activities, and wanting to return to our safety net or comfort zone. Although I must admit that some of the regional participants came from countries that did not offer much 'peace of mind', the evil they were used to was better than the evil they did not know. *Leadership in crisis is a matter of perspective*, of what we can control and what is out of our control. Under these circumstances of conducting workshops outside our familiar landscape, heightened tension lingered among participants, trainers, and organizers.

It took a few hours before we could calmly and objectively propose a plan forward: all participants would take a day off for relaxation and recreation before restarting the training program. Dispatching all the trainees to return home was simply wasting resources and opportunities rather than cultivating additional prospects. Interestingly, the Istanbul 2003 cohort held together and reflected positively in their feedback and relationships. Crises bring people together if leadership is proactive in offering an alternative plan. Incidentally, my red-eye flight from Istanbul to Bangkok was even more challenging yet gratifying.

Leadership . . . in crisis requires the adoption of different competencies and traits than other types of leadership to create a pathway for hope moving forward.[9] It is not "business as usual" and it is not about following the same patterns that have proved successful in the past. In the Bible, specifically in Luke's gospel chapter 5, the prospective apostles, who were professional fishermen, stayed out all night out in Lake of Gennesaret trying to navigate their livelihood . . . and failed. An unknown carpenter called Jesus of Nazareth, who had no knowledge of the fishing profession nor the lake's conditions, strolled down in broad daylight and asked the exhausted and frustrated fishermen to go out one more time and throw their nets in the water.

Fishing is usually done during nighttime in the Middle East due to the cooler weather conditions. Those poor fishermen had tried all night and failed to get their catch. Their nets were washed and hanging to dry; their boats docked and resting. And here comes this carpenter-teacher telling them to go back out to the open waters . . . one more time! What was the expectation when we seem to be trying the unfamiliar, or even the impossible, of what our gut feeling and experiences tell us? There are only two possible outcomes of this story. One that we know: they conceded to try this new proposed pathway and in doing so, changed their history as 'fishers of people'. The second outcome would pan out like the rich man who walked away from Jesus sad, as noted in the synoptic gospels[10]—a wasted opportunity to make history.

Leadership . . . in crisis is an invitation to step away from the ordinary and embrace the extraordinary. It is about seizing opportunities when few are ready or willing to do so. Such clutching opportunities, although may seem unwise to many, actually cater the way forward for others to follow. My wife often asks me why I still accept invitations to travel to riskier parts of this world to be with friends and colleagues (I will not mention some of the places I have traveled to in the past decade or so, in full respect for our friends and colleagues who consider these places their home). My repetitive response to this question is simple: I usually go out there with the purpose of instilling hope, but I return home full of hope instilled by these friends

---

9. Demiroz and Kapucu, *Role of Leadership*, 91–101.

10. Matthew 19, Mark 10, Luke 18.

and colleagues. Assumptions are overturned, perspectives are aligned, and hope perseveres when we lead . . . in crisis.

Dr. Eugene B. Habecker, leader, author, and my mentor, who also wrote the Foreword for this book, shared with me this crucial leadership philosophy that was also mentioned in the opening pages of his latest book.[11] *"Leaders absorb chaos, radiate calm, inspire hope."* This was quoted by an unknown source, yet these seven words echo significant principles. The leadership task during crises requires the adoption of three proactive stances.

First, *absorb the chaos* brought about by the uncertainties associated with a specific crisis. People react differently to calamities, simply because their planned activities were abruptly interrupted. The ultimate result is panic, reactive behavior, and unrealistic decisions coupled with clouded judgments. *Leadership . . . in crisis* is invited to absorb the chaos usually caused by people rather than circumstances, assess the damage, isolate fake data from reality, and take it all in.

I recall the Beirut Blast on August 4, 2020. My wife and I had just arrived on the island of Cyprus for a short vacation and we actually heard the explosion on the 200-kilometers faraway island in the Mediterranean Sea. Our minds immediately raced to our youngest son who had landed in Lebanon from Ireland a week before to spend his summer vacation. We were also concerned for the safety of our staff, families, friends, acquaintances . . . In reality, this was not the first explosion, car bomb, or terrorist attack we had experienced, but the same cold sweat feeling crept down our necks. Our son called us immediately to let us know he was safe. I then proceeded through a checklist to ensure that others were also safe.

The second step is to promote a *balanced realistic objective attitude,* thereby calming the chaotic situation. This is not to undermine the calamity of the crisis or the losses incurred, but rather to evaluate the real damages and start the planning process for handling the situation. Although this may sound cold and insensitive, *leadership . . . in crisis* must hold their ground and *radiate calm* to ease those around them. Jesuit Father and author, Dr. Anthony D'Souza introduced the matrix of realism versus optimism more than two decades ago, in which leaders are invited to adopt a realistic-optimist stance in any situation.[12]

---

11. Habecker, *Softer Side of Leadership,* 16–24.

12. D'Souza, *Empowered Leadership,* 212–15.

Back to the blast, and having absorbed the chaos, it was now time to assess the damages caused by the explosion. Staff who lived closest to our office building were asked to make their way over the debris to the premises. Every single window panel was broken, false ceiling on the ground, books off the shelves, dust and smoke filled every room. They proceeded to secure the building entrance with wood panels and nylon screens to isolate the vulnerable part of the office building. Although I was not physically with the team, the longtime training in crisis management paid off, and I am proud of each one of them who participated in the month-long reconstruction process.

The third step is to transmit a *hopeful vision of the future* beyond the chaotic present. The most appropriate question to ask upon the onset of a crisis is not *"When will all this end?"* but rather *"How will all this end?"* There is a window of opportunity and hope in every dark situation. Instead of focusing on the *when* let us focus on the *how!* Lessons learned during any crisis situation are the most valuable and uplifting lessons, *inspiring hope.*

One of the biggest non-nuclear explosions in history, the Beirut Blast left 200+ dead, 6,500+ injured, and 300,000+ people homeless. We lost close friends but also participated in the rebuilding of homes, lives, and a city. That same evening of the blast, I was receiving and answering hundreds of messages, phone calls, and emails from around the globe asking about us and enquiring how they could help. Such gratifying solidarity from fellow humans. As a result, we launched one of our largest reconstruction campaigns—*Reconstruct your Home based on God's Word*—in the midst of . . . chaos!

Therefore, instead of focusing inwardly on where and why *leadership . . . is in crisis*, we should focus on the main task of *leadership . . . in crisis*, or leading in crisis. Futurists predict that the next decade will present new and unprecedented crises that global humanity has never considered before. In the charity work, global humanitarian NGO World Vision researched five global crises in 2021: Food insecurity, refugees, climate change, gender discrimination, and child labor.[13] In the business world, PWC offered an advisory resilience roadmap to their clients based on the concept that disruptive creativity may serve up to 20 percent of global organizations.[14] And the public sector and governments are subsidizing most small businesses. In Australia, the federal government covered the minimum wage

13. World Vision, *5 Global Crises.*
14. PWC, *Global Crisis Survey.*

of all privately-salaried employees for 12 months during the pandemic lockdown.[15] According to experts, this will take about two generations to recover the debt initiated by this action.

There has rarely been a time in history when such a necessity for authentic *leadership . . . in crisis* is emphasized. This is NOT another book on leadership. It is a genuine critique of the current state of leadership vis-à-vis what is sought and needed for the "next normal." This book attempts to deconstruct some of the false and dilute leadership concepts that have infiltrated our corporate, educational, Christian, nonprofit, and public organizations over the past few decades to offer new stimulating and provocative leadership models based on real-life experiences, research-based studies, and a journey of faith.

About this book

In addition to the introduction, this book comprises five subsections divided equally into two chapters per subsection, and a concluding segment. The first two chapters introduce the notions of global leadership and leading through crises. Chapters 3 and 4 address the new hype-phrase of building resilience, followed by two chapters on composing stamina and two on agility. The final two chapters address one of my favorite topics—that of *confrontational leadership* as illustrated through the leadership model of Jesus Christ.

Following is a short introduction to each subsection.

Globalization and global leadership were particularly popular a few years ago. Multitudes of books and research were published to endorse the notion of the global youth generation, world citizenship, and leaders with global skills. However, this concept soon failed as the world—also nicknamed the "global village"—retrenched into secularized ghettos, separatism, and partisan exclusive solutions. Slogans such as "America First" (or any other country, for that matter!) became prevalent. In the meantime, crises swept across communities, nationalities, religions, and regions. Addressing these crises depicted selective approaches rather than inclusive ones.

In chapters 1 and 2, we will revisit the concept of global leadership to evaluate if it was still a valid model. For example, Carlos Ghosn—once Chairman of the global Renault-Nissan-Mitsubishi alliance and now a

15. Institute for Government, *Supported the Unemployed.*

fugitive from the Japanese juridical system—was the ultimate embodiment of a global leader. The success and failure of this global leadership model and similar leadership models of global standings will provide valuable lessons as to what works and what should be discarded when leading global teams through times of crisis. Adjacently, we will explore the impact of crises on leadership deliverables, mainly focusing on the impact of the CO-VID-19 pandemic and projected new crises, and why human crises became a dividing factor rather than a form of global unity.

While the first two chapters are more of a situational analysis, the remainder of the book focuses on the skill-set required to lead, globally and throughout any foreseeable crisis, by offering practical and research-based recommendations on *leadership . . . in crisis*. The four precepts that require constructing—*resilience, stamina, agility*, and *confrontation*—will be elaborated and reinforced with real-life examples and experiences.

Resilience is a term that has also infiltrated most corporate and organizational settings. It does not quite translate into all languages nor carry the same weight in different cultures, yet it seems to indicate a certain vibe that is required to thrive in this era. Where does resilience come from, and how can we accumulate enough resilience equity to ensure smooth sailing during crises? Chapter 3 attempts to compare resilience to constructing a wall, one brick at a time, to achieve the necessary height that safeguards stakeholders' interests during crises. One of the colloquial translations of the term resilience is that of "thick skin," meaning that people accumulate ample experience and soft skills that enable them to *absorb the chaos* and handle crises with a certain level of objectivity.

Chapter 4 continues to explore the opportunities available in any crisis, and how these opportunities can serve as a launching pad to introduce windows and breakthroughs in an enclaving context. I recall the multiple crises that I faced, alone and with the family. The reaction to each crisis left its imprint on our future (ironically, not on our past). For example, when my uncle died at the young age of 47 due to a shrapnel that penetrated his lung on the last day of the 15-year-long civil war in Lebanon, my reaction was that of hatred, resentment, and revenge. What did I gain from my reaction? Nothing really. Let's look for the opportunity and not ponder on the unfortunate circumstances.

Stamina is an adjective borrowed from the sports world, indicating a high level of tolerance and endurance. This term was mainly used in organizational settings to describe highly motivated and hardworking individuals that were driven to achieve personal and organizational goals. It may also be confused with workaholism—or in some settings, "ministriholic" or "missionholic" individuals—that may result in burnout and chronic depression. That is not the leadership stamina that will be explored; rather, the model that marathon runners endure and accumulate over time to reach their goals. As a marathon runner, I will share some of these endurance techniques and how they may apply in organizational settings of *leadership . . . in crisis.*

Chapter 6 addresses factors of perseverance that best fit leadership stamina during crises. Preserving energy (aka slack funds, synergizing resources, diversifying investments . . .), regulating breathing (aka continuous communication, reallocation of tasks, transcendent goals . . .), and accelerating pace (aka lead the momentum, rapid decision-making, fast-tracking processes . . .) are some of the tools that *leadership . . . in crisis* could use to *radiate calm.* Case studies related to successful and failed responses to crises in secular and Christian organizations using "riding the wave" and "sailing through hardships" strategies will be examined.

The timing, format, context, and response to any crisis are crucial. If the response is too early, it may backfire, and if the response is too late, it may be . . . too late! Some leaders choose to jump ahead and lead the initiative during a crisis, which could scorch their efforts due to premature and miscalculated assessments. I have seen such responses in many crises, where leaders rush into so-called bailouts without proper evaluation of the situation, thereby losing much more than the industry average. Other extremes include leaders who wait for the circumstances to change, and when they realize the crisis is here to stay, it may well be overdue. I call this latter model the "Ostrich Syndrome Leader," not aware of, or uninterested in, the surrounding warning signals.

The suggested stance is to be in second place when a crisis is imminent. Despite all the literature that claims the primacy of early adopters, wise leaders may want to stay in second place until just before the finish line. This is what bikers do in the famous Tour de France. Taking the lead means fighting the wind factor, facing the unknown slopes and curves, and incurring mistakes, whereas the closest rival is gliding behind within the wind advantage, dodging road dangers, and learning from others' errors.

This is where *agility* comes into action in chapters 7 and 8. Agility is the ability to be aware of the surrounding circumstances, to be alert to the available alternatives, and to be quick in the responsiveness process.

Flexibility is required to navigate through uncertain landscapes toward the shores of safety. Managing change is necessary to *inspire hope. Leadership . . . in crisis* requires a level of Wisdom Quotient (WQ), in addition to the well-known Intelligence Quotient (IQ), Emotional Quotient (EQ), and emotional resilience, to glide through times of crisis.

The final two chapters offer what most leadership theories, philosophies, models, styles, and behaviors ignore: *Confrontational Leadership.* Diplomacy in leading organizations and ministries, compromising solutions, and overuse of tactical actions have completely diluted basic leadership principles. Confronting realities, addressing diversions, facing problems, and simply "biting the bullet" are no longer the fad for leaders. Neo leaders prefer the 'popularity' scale rather than the 'reality' scale. They prefer to procrastinate, dodge, sway, or ignore confrontation to gain approval ratings and enhance their 'popularity', as if leadership is a beauty contest, all while sacrificing the overall stakeholders' good over narrow interests and personal comfort.

My 35+ years of leadership experience in regional and global roles in business, Christian, nonprofit, and public entities have witnessed several examples of evading confrontation. I have seen tens of unproductive employees holding their positions because their supervisors (I would not label them as 'leaders') refused to confront them with their unacceptable performance, always citing excuses justifying their continued service. For those business leaders, ignoring such inefficient workers is deceitful toward shareholders. For those Christian and nonprofit leaders, it is bad stewardship of donors' resources. For public servants, this attitude is wasting taxpayers' contributions. There is absolutely no excuse for justifying their continued employment, even for humane reasons, in which case the leader should personally contribute toward sustaining their humane needs—if genuine—rather than use positional power to justify their constant drainage of organizational resources.

Chapter 10 provides several scenarios of probable team-members' lagging performance, particularly during crises, and how to address such situations. Overall, members may fall into one or more of the following snares when faced with overwhelming crises: *Disloyalty, Denial, Doubt, and/or Disappointment.* I call them the 4D's. A review of Jesus Christ's leadership model, in addition to case studies from the business, public, and faith-based sectors will be examined and assessed. But more importantly, how should *leadership . . . in crisis* be addressing these unfortunate conducts is the crucial part. I have developed a confrontational model that each leader should examine, and hopefully adopt, that tackles the 4D's with 3C's: *Confront, Construct,* and *Consolidate.*

As human beings, we avoid confronting people, especially those closest to us. We fear that *confrontation* may result in losing those dearest to us, so we avoid it. Some of my best friends and supporters are those I confronted and even argued with over matters in the past. And I look back with a smile over the seemingly trivial discussions we had that led our friendship to move to the next level: *construction.* Now that we have expressed our stances, it is time to construct our social contracts based on these new givens. There is no turning back to the era of non-confrontations. And this is topped off with a *consolidation* factor that unites outlooks and aligns efforts. I simply love confrontation despite its apparent negative connotation, and while there are several lost opportunities encountered in my professional tenure due to confrontational positions, I prefer it anytime, any day, over lukewarm diplomatic compromises.

Takeaways

I am hoping that every reader will be able to identify and implement at least three takeaways from this reading:

1. *Accountable leadership.* Every person in a leadership position must be accountable to certain circles of stakeholders. Leadership does not exist in vacuum. If you feel no one is holding you accountable for your leadership decisions, find someone! The ultimate place for leadership executive accountability is the Board of Directors, Trustees, Managers, etc. Without proper grounds for effective governance and accountability, leadership can easily be confused with dictatorship.

2. *Healthier leadership.* We will examine several models of toxic leadership to better identify effective leadership practices. Dealing with members' trauma care, hurts, and injuries because of bad leadership practices is key to building healthier organizational cultures. Leaders are invited to transform their people from injury to health, hurt to forgiveness, vulnerability to resilience, and despair to joy as indicated in the leadership journey of Jesus Christ.

3. *Courageous leadership.* Leaders are invited to have courageous conversations and confrontations with those they care most for. This is

something not currently being done, nor is it encouraged within leadership circles. The takeaway of "how to" have these conversations is crucial for successful *leadership . . . in crisis.*

Enjoy the challenges and confrontations that will accompany your leadership journey through this book.

Chapter I

Assess the Global Impact
of Leadership . . . in Crisis

Leadership is one of the most observed
and least understood phenomena on earth.

(JAMES MACGREGOR BURNS)[1]

IN 2015, I HAD the privilege to design and deliver a course for Honors students at Taylor University (IN) entitled: *Global Paradigms of Leadership.* The course was a first attempt to provide an international perspective for Christian Liberal Arts learners to apply leadership skills, theories, and practices in a global context. The course should have been accompanied by a Spring Break trip to Dubai, UAE, one of the most diverse business cities in the world, with 200+ nationalities constituting its workforce.[2] The learners would have gained a comprehensive understanding of the essential elements for international human resources, knowledge, change, and content management.

The course was delivered; however, the field trip did not materialize, as many of the students' parents, mainly from the Midwest USA, were worried about their children making a trip to the Middle East. For those of us who have traveled to Dubai, we may find this excuse almost absurd, as Dubai is safe and one of the most modern and cosmopolitan places on earth, with a

1. Burns, *Leadership*, 2.
2. UAE, *Fact Sheet.*

far-fetched resemblance to any Middle Eastern perceived context. The un-founded parental "concern" was one indication of the generational gap in the understanding of globalization and world citizenship. What was once considered to be a "global village" has actually accelerated the shift toward our own familiarity, exclusivity, and separatism rather than fostering open-ness, acceptance, and inclusivity.

In this chapter, we will examine the definition and understanding of global leadership, cultural considerations, and transnational strategies, as-sessing how some of these principles have failed in upholding a universal set of agreed-upon global leadership traits and behaviors. I will share some observations on specific well-known cases of supposedly "world leaders" and how crisis infiltrated their global leadership model. The chapter con-cludes with practical recommendations for sustaining and upholding the main principles of global *leadership . . . in crisis.*

Global leadership defined

Let us start with a definition of global leadership. Mendenhall and col-leagues defined global leadership as:

> . . . *individuals who effect significant positive change in organizations by building communities through the development of trust and the arrangement of organizational structures and processes in a context involving multiple cross-boundary stakeholders, multiple sources of external cross-boundary authority, and multiple cultures under con-ditions of temporal, geographical, and cultural complexity.*[3]

The first half part of the above definition could fit any leadership or managerial role, but the latter part is crucial, as the terms used—some more than once—include: *multiple . . . cross-boundary . . . external . . . cultures . . . temporal . . . geographical . . . complexity.* Let's unpack these seven words:

- *Multiple* is the opposite of singular, meaning there are several layers or tiers of issues to address simultaneously.

- *Cross-boundary* indicates going beyond the known limitations and margins toward unfamiliar territory.

- *External* is the outside environment that requires careful scanning and monitoring, usually beyond the control of the leader.

---

3. Mendenhall et al., *Global Leadership*, 394.

- *Cultures* are the set of values, beliefs, and norms that bring people together as a community.

- *Temporal* refers to the timeframe and process for understanding the other within a set of tangible and intangible criteria.

- *Geographical* indicates the physical space and borders that tend to assign, align, or divide humanity.

- *Complexity* is the true challenge of global leaders, requiring understanding and practicing new and unaccustomed knowledge, skills, and abilities.

Hassanzadeh and colleagues adapted Mendenhall et al.'s 20+ definitions of global leadership, mainly to ascertain that there is no unified definition of global leadership, similar to the lack of consensus on the definition of generic leadership.[4] There is also confusion between global leadership and undertaking global assignments. Some leaders may absorb a temporary international assignment and check it (been there, done that . . .) as a global leadership experience. But it takes more than a brief visit or relocation to an international position while maintaining a cultural attachment to the homeland and even recreating a cultural island in the new location. Even international missionary work has fallen into this trap. This is not global leadership. Global leadership is about attempting to understand the other—the culture, personality, and practices.

I recall hosting a Christian publishing house delegation from Branson, Missouri, in Beirut, Lebanon more than a decade ago. We have only a handful of things to be proud of in the Lebanese culture due to all our crises, but our cuisine—a combination of refined Ottoman-Turkish and French influenced dishes—is definitely one of our prides. The leader of the delegation was an American friend, highly cultured, and lived in many parts of the world, including the south of France. He managed his language skills, a combination of English and French, to network with all our stakeholders, making an impact on all who met him.

Among the delegation were two American staff members, a couple who have rarely traveled outside the USA and were on the verge of retirement. The leader of the delegation wanted to honor their service by inviting them on an international trip before their retirement. This couple was a hosting nightmare! Instead of exploring new and unfamiliar experiences,

---

4. Hassanzadeh et al., *Effective Global Leadership*, 14–24.

they retrenched into their familiarity zone. They refused to try any kind of foods except for "pasta" and "French fries," spent most of their time in their hotel rooms rather than enjoy the biblical tour of Lebanon, and simply had a miserable time on my scale.

This is the exact opposite behavior of my first trip to China in 2012, where I explored and experienced every food, drink, tradition, practice, and interaction with our Chinese hosts. By the end of the second week, I had more friends in China than in any other country. To qualify as a global leader, you have to make your host community feel you are willing to try and experience everything about their culture, regardless of whether you like what you tried or not. In fact, they tend to appreciate you more if you shrug or feel sick from trying one of their extravagant foods or practices. But the key is in trying!

Understanding global leadership

To better understand who is labeled as a global leader, let us examine some of the existing literature. Osland provides three different prototypes of global leaders: Mahatma Gandhi as a political leader, Alexander the Great as a military leader, and Mother Teresa as a spiritual leader.[5] I can add three more to the list: Carlos Ghosn as a business leader, Greta Thunberg as an environmental leader, and Jesus Christ as a humanity leader. And you, as a co-author/reader, can add more names based on your own perspectives, philosophies, and perceptions.

The key is to identify fundamental characteristics to qualify the label: *Global leader*. There is a wealth of research and literature that attempts to identify the basic functions of global leadership. I would narrow them down to seven competencies: *linguistic, cultural, geographic, empathic, inquisitive, risk-taking*, and *relational* tendencies. The first three competencies are explicit knowledge that can be acquired, whereas the latter four pertain to the leader's personal preferences. A brief elaboration of each competency is pertinent.

The knowledge and acquisition of *linguistic* skills enhance global competencies. Although language fluency does not necessarily equate to global competencies,[6] it offers a gateway to a better understanding of some cultural practices of similar language groups. My first trip to France was

5. Hassanzadeh et al., *Effective Global Leadership*, 14–24.

6. Hammer, *Intercultural Effectiveness*, 382–93.

in 2003. French was my third language, which I struggled with and mostly tried to evade studying. It was only when I walked through the streets of Paris that I realized the cultural similarities it holds with a big part of my home country's heritage. Lebanon was under French mandate for some 25 years, although the French language outlived the mandate by magnitudes. Language matters. Even though there are an estimated 7,000 languages and dialects globally,[7] learning more than your mother tongue is an enriching experience.

Sometimes I like to play a game alone while traveling in airports or sitting in airport lounges. I try to listen to people around me and guess, from their language, phonetics, tone, and/or body gestures, what language they are speaking. It is always a victorious feeling to get a glimpse of their passports and find out that I guessed right. Languages are grouped (e.g., Latin-based), and matching the verbal language with the nationality is a gratifying experience.

Cultural competency is a vast discipline. Intercultural competence and intelligence are required tools to be actors on the global stage. I am a certified Inter-Cultural Intelligence (ICI) practitioner—a certification program offered by Knowledgeworkx, a global company founded in Dubai, UAE.[8] This program allows leaders to enhance their cultural agility and have a better understanding of people from diverse cultures (I will be exploring this program in more detail in the next section). Basic cultural communication competences, skills, relationships, and situations are required for global interaction.[9]

The array of *geographic* knowledge and internal compass is necessary for global aptitude. I have visited five continents and traveled to more than 60 countries and regions worldwide. Although the number sounds impressive, it only represents about 30 percent of the countries/regions in the world, and considering that every country has multiple cultures, the figure represents a humble exposure to what is out there. My second son Daniel, who currently lives and works in Boston, MA, and tries to keep up with my international travels, bought me a world scratch map one Christmas. To relieve myself from the tedious task of scratching all the countries I had already visited, my son was "commissioned" to scratch the visited countries with my commitment to continue then after. Looking at the scratch map

7. Lewis, *Ethnologue*.

8. KnowledgeWorkx, *Inter-Cultural Intelligence*.

9. Bennett, *Cultivating Intercultural Competence*, 121–40.

on my office wall, it is not very impressive! Between 70 percent of the world map covering the oceans and 30 percent of countries traveled, the scratched areas covered almost 10 percent of the map and were far from remarkable; hence, I cannot objectively claim to be a geographically competent global leader.

But being able to have a general geographic knowledge of the countries' proximities—Global South, Global North, East, West, seasons, time zones . . .—is a basic acquired competence. The situation today is far different from the eighties when I lived in the USA and most of my American friends had never obtained a passport or traveled abroad. With airline connections to thousands of destinations and traveling facilities, geographic competence can be an intentional added skill for those purposefully seeking to gain global exposure.

The remaining four areas are personal skills of empathy, inquisitiveness, risk-taking, and relational abilities. Cognitive *empathy* is the ability to put yourself in someone else's place; this is also known as *perspective-taking* or accepting an alternative point of view.[10] It may sound simpler in theory than in practice. We tend to exercise temporary cognitive empathy if we are out on a field trip for a few days, whether to help in building an orphanage in a deprived African nation or to serve in feeding refugees in a camp somewhere in the Middle East . . . then return to a safe haven of a five-star hotel in transit back to the security of our home country. I have personally traveled to Iraq with Christian relief agencies, "sacrificed" a few days of hardships, then cleaned it off at some hotel/spa in Amman, Jordan. Similar to the time my wife and I visited an orphanage in Cuenca, Ecuador, and enjoyed interacting with the hosts and children for half a day. Then . . .

This is not real empathy. We have all been part of this paradox with the intention of being more global in our relationships. Real empathy is the ability to put ourselves long-term in another's shoes—understand their context, sufferings, hopes, and dreams. On one of my many field trips to Iraq, and while visiting another refugee camp in Koya, Kurdistan, I decided to break away from the formal delegation and gather around a few boys and talk about their dreams. As most of them wanted to become professional football (soccer) players, we soon started playing football. Quickly, the competition became fierce, as almost half of the children in the camp joined the growing opposing teams in this senseless competition. Time was frozen as I exchanged childhood moments with these children, from my

10. Galinsky et al., *Perspective Taking and Empathy*, 378–84.

own childhood having lived in a 15-year-long civil war playing football on the streets. The empathy span was very brief, but the impact was longstanding. I will never forget these special moments.

Inquisitiveness goes beyond cognitive empathy by trying to understand the "why" behind the behavior or practice. Marco Blankenburgh, the entrepreneur behind Inter-Cultural Intelligence (ICI), identified a cultural learner as a person who is curious and inquisitive, trying to discover the other.[11] As a cultural learner, a global leader would always seek to ask questions to better understand the other and not just put themselves in their place, which creates cultural synergy.

There is a funny story of a curious young girl who was helping her mother in the kitchen to cook a gigot (leg of mutton). The mother was struggling to break the bone in half before putting the meat in the oven to slow-cook for hours. The young girl asked the mother why she was trying to break the bone, and the mother responded, "I don't know . . . your grandmother always cooked it like this." So next time the mother and daughter went to visit grandma at her place, the inquisitive girl asked her grandmother the same question: "My mother cooked it that way" was the response. Finally, all three generations managed to make a visit to Great-grandmother at her senior home and the question was posed again by the girl. "I broke the bone" said the elderly lady, "because it did not fit into my tiny pot!" Only by inquiring about certain practices are we be able to truly understand the reasoning behind them—if ever.

The *risk-taking* part of global leadership is an obvious required skill. Risk-taking was one of the contingent traits identified in Project GLOBE (Global Leadership & Organizational Behavior Effectiveness) Leadership Traits that received input from 17,000 global leaders in 62 countries.[12] Similar results appeared in Wills and Barham's assessment of holistic core competencies: risk acceptance.[13] The Global Competence Aptitude Assessment (GCAA) also identified the willingness to take risks as one of the eight "readiness" factors for international assignments.[14] The level of risk tolerance comes with experience, crisis leadership, and willingness to test the waters. It is not an invitation to blindly walk into a jungle without preparation, but rather to calculate the risk and weigh in the outcomes.

11. Blankenburgh, *Inter-Cultural Intelligence*, 11.

12. Den Hartog et al., *Cultural Specific*, 219–56.

13. Wills and Barham, *Being an International Manager*, 49–58.

14. Hunter et al., *Globally Competent*, 267–85.

For example, I have never refused an invitation to visit colleagues in riskier countries/regions if they were living there permanently and extended the invitation. Just imagine what kind of devastating behavior would surface if you turned down an invitation to participate in meetings, workshops, or even field trips purely based on risk assessments from your corner of the globe. I have been subject to multiple disappointments when some leader-friends from the Western or Northern hemispheres canceled their participation in meetings in our region due to "risk" factors. The first comparison that comes to mind . . . "Are their lives more important than ours?" Calculated risk-taking and dependency on local intelligence is a prerequisite.

Finally, *relational* skills. The relational aspect refers to the flow of interaction with others who are culturally, ethnically, and geographically different.[15] It can also mean building mutual trust, willingness to share knowledge, collaboration, and respect.[16] These attributes relate to how we express ourselves. If we know someone, we tend to be open in our expressions, whereas we tend to conceal our expressions with people we just met. But if you are like me, sometimes we meet a person and immediately "click," as if we had known each other for years, thereby enabling the relational expression to be open, honest, and transparent almost immediately.

Now imagine the above scenario with a person you have just met who comes from the exact opposite cultural spectrum. Let's say a Nordic and a Chinese. Generally speaking, the latter express themselves softly, indirectly, and respectfully, whereas the former is direct and firm. The relational compromise can only take place when both find a safe zone or third space to express themselves, such as talking about technology or sports. When the discussion subject is over, they may both retrench to their familiar relational turfs.

I once heard of a Western woman visiting China who offended her Chinese hosts over a dinner invitation simply by turning her wine glass upside down and claiming: "I never touch this stuff." The hosts were offended and immediately terminated the dinner and the exchange proposal that was supposed to be the focal point of the dinner. Although one should respect her personal choice toward drinking alcohol, the expressive gesture offended the hosts' generosity and was certain to break the relational aspect (she could have easily accepted the wine in her glass but not drink it).

15. Mendenhall et al., *'Global' in Global Leadership*, 493–503.
16. Taylor, *Creating Social Capital*, 336–54.

Cultural competencies

As noted earlier in this chapter, it is imperative to sharpen cultural proficiency and knowledge as a prerequisite for any globally-engaging setting. In fact, what differentiates, segments, and partitions humanity is not just geography, history, language, nationality, or religion; there is an added complexity and diversity when adding the vast and dynamic concept of cultures. There are an estimated 4,000 distinct types of cultures recorded in Price's Atlas of Ethnographic Societies,[17] which anthropologists consider to be an underestimation, as new cultures are emerging as we speak.

But what is culture and how does it fuse into global *leadership . . . in crisis*? Cambridge Dictionary offers a simple definition . . . *"the way of life, especially the general customs and beliefs, of a particular group of people at a particular time."*[18] Merriam-Webster dictionary offers multiple definitions of the word "culture"; I selected the one that best fits into leadership perspectives. Culture is *"the integrated pattern of human knowledge, belief, and behavior that depends upon the capacity for learning and transmitting knowledge to succeeding generations."*[19] Let's unpack these two definitions.

The first definition assumes that culture is a pattern that dictates certain manners for a particular community. Understanding these patterns and behaviors allows the leader to interact more effectively within that specific culture. It also assumes that culture changes over time, hence requiring regular updating. The second definition is more elaborative, as it undertakes a form of knowledge management, mainly tacit knowledge, from one generation to another. The leadership implications for better cultural understanding include monitoring behavioral patterns, engaging in the learning process, and transferring tacit knowledge to explicit.

According to the UNESCO Universal Declaration of Cultural Diversity, Article 1, *"cultural diversity is as necessary for humankind as biodiversity is for nature."*[20] It is a human right, a source of creativity, an opportunity for learning and accepting the other, and a heritage to honor and uphold. As the term *cultural diversity* is gaining ground in the recruitment process of many organizations, local and international, it is important to identify the role of the global leader. Simply put, it is not to seek the unification and

17. Price, *Atlas of World Cultures.*
18. Cambridge Dictionary, *Culture.*
19. Merriam-Webster, *Culture.*
20. UNESCO, *Declaration of Cultural Diversity*, 1.

assimilation of culturally-diverse teams into a higher agreed-upon organizational culture, but rather to celebrate the wealth of diversity and create an environment of tolerance.

I have witnessed many organizations, in their quest to uphold this "diversity," align their recruitment standards to ensure a culturally-diverse workforce, particularly on the senior level. This was evident in several CEOs' search assignments, police departments, hospitals, corporations, NGOs, ministries, and para-church organizations. Despite the good intentions toward diversity, many have failed because the entire organizational structure was still a mono-cultural one. Meaning that the attempt to insert diversity into certain positions did not infiltrate the embedded single or dual cultures that reigned over these enterprises. Hence, diversity of cultures requires enhanced environmental conditions to accept and adopt real diversity.[21]

For any reader willing to engage on a global level, I highly recommend the Inter-Cultural Intelligence (ICI) certification program offered by Knowledgeworkx.[22] Although I considered myself to be culturally and globally equipped, I found this certification program to be extremely helpful. And now I am an ICI certified practitioner, Foundational Stage 2 Champion. It is an invitation to switch from being a cultural critic to a cultural learner by adopting the cultural learner behaviors.[23] One of them is to create a third cultural space for effective adaptability.

The ICI program offers Self Cultural Analysis tests and questionnaires that emphasize three worldview drivers: *Guilt/Innocence, Honor/Shame,* and *Power/Fear.*[24] By identifying and understanding your own mix of cultural worldview drivers and recognizing the drivers of your closest team members, which may be different from your own, you will be able to connect more effectively with these differing worldviews. Noting that people shift their worldviews as they progress through life, we mainly practice all three with different intensities in certain contexts and at various intervals.

The ICI certification program also includes extensive research on the 12 behavioral dimensions of cultures with opposing conducts on the following aspects: *Growth, Relationships, Outlook, Destiny, Context, Connecting, Expression, Decision-making, Planning, Communication, Accountability,*

21. Foley and Lahr, *Diversity of Cultures*, 14.

22. KnowledgeWorkx, *Inter-Cultural Intelligence.*

23. Blankenburgh, *Inter-Cultural Intelligence*, 11–4.

24. Blankenburgh, *Inter-Cultural Intelligence*, 18–24.

and *Status*.[25] By identifying your own preferences and scale on these dimensions vis-à-vis your team's, it offers a preview of the span of behaviors that exist within the same team, organization, or context. This is called the Cultural Mapping Inventory (CMI), introducing a *"new way of understanding people, enabling us to become perceptive on many levels, more flexible and adaptable in new territory and ultimately to excel in intercultural settings."*[26]

In this era, the need for cultural agility is a necessity as more communities are closing in rather than building bridges. The task of global *leadership . . . in crisis* is to seek to close the gap of an ever-growing schism among cultures, religions, communities, and regions. A cultural learner leadership model coupled with humility and understanding is needed to set the stage for the new culturally-diverse workforce of the "next normal."

Transnational strategies

A few words about transnational strategies. It simply means adopting strategies that work locally as well as globally. The balancing act between global and local has created the new term: *Glocal!*[27] A few years ago, researchers were determined that a global worldview and hybrid culture would take over new generations, estimating that a global youth culture with universal outlook would prevail.[28] This was not the case. Even HSBC, one of the largest banks in the world, dropped their well-known mantra *"The world's local bank"* in 2016—a brand they had picked up back in 2002.[29]

Transnational strategies could work when a leader is able to balance domestic and global needs, but they often fail, as the needs are so different. One of the examples of failed transnational strategies is Euro Disney, a case study I usually include in my International Marketing course.[30] The almost century-old company tried to duplicate Disney's California and Florida structures in France, thinking they could attract most of Europe's vacationers to include Euro Disney Paris as part of their regular holiday program. Instead, they were faced with different cultural and lifestyle patterns amongst the Europeans. For example, many families chose to camp

25. Blankenburgh, *Inter-Cultural Intelligence*, 25–32.

26. Blankenburgh, *Inter-Cultural Intelligence*, 33.

27. Lexico, *Glocal*.

28. Kahn and Kellner, *Global Youth Culture*, 2–5.

29. Gibbs, *World's Local Bank*.

30. Cateora et al., *International Marketing*, Case 2.1.

outside the site rather than use the Disneyland hotel. It took years before the operation of Euro Disney was altered to better fit European taste and turn their red figures to black!

I have selected three different transnational strategies to examine and assess their global impact. They are *marketing, capacity building,* and community *services.*

Transnational *marketing* strategies include a unified approach toward the 4P's (product, price, placement, and promotion) where "one size fits all."[31] The *product* or service aspect is universal, common, and consumable (e.g., Pepsi). The *price* standards are unified and globally agreed upon, such as iPhone prices. The *placement* and distribution channels are known, established, and regular (e.g., Nestle water bottles). And the *promotion* campaigns, advertising, sales offers, and e-commerce are internationally accessible, such a major airlines ticketing offerings via multiple platforms.[32] Although the 4P's may succeed in some transnational strategies, a more contextual approach can yield much better results. Global leaders are invited to assess their transnational marketing strategies and the effectiveness of the 4P's across national borders, even amongst Christian organizations and mission work.

Capacity building across borders is also subject to cultural and appropriate presentations. While many capacity strengthening programs are global in nature, it is important to consider local settings. Some cultures emphasize high work ethics; others are lenient on time management; capitalism vs. socialism, anarchism vs. communism, theocracy vs. democracy, etc. Such concepts influence our understanding of what capacities are lacking transnationally. For example, I have done transnational capacity building training workshops, sometimes with simultaneous tri-lingual interpretation (English, French and Spanish), time zones ranging from Ecuador to Mongolia (a 13-hour time zone difference), yet the standardized approach proved to have varying outcomes and long-term sustainability based mainly on the participants' context and location.[33] For instance, the learning outcomes of colleagues from Africa was different from their European cohorts, also different from the Asia-Pacific participants. It is therefore crucial to identify the changes required for capacity building programs to better fit the context of the participants.

31. Shams and Hasan, *Capacity Building for Transnationalisation,* 466.

32. Stafford and Taylor, *Transnational Education,* 625–36.

33. Mitchell et al., *Power and Irrelevance,* 174.

According to Mitchell and colleagues, there are four types of trans-national NGO *services* that are contingent on their structure.[34] The first is *unitary*, meaning that the NGO functions as a single unit, top-down, same services and activities across the globe. The second is a *federation*, consisting of national entities under the oversight of a centralized headquarters, thereby allowing some freedom in altering services as long as they meet the clearly set criteria. The third is a *global membership organization* consisting of interdependent members with a common purpose who come together and establish a coordinating secretariat; such a structure has room for diversely-implemented services based on the members' needs and contexts. The final one is the *confederation*, with the largest margin of flexibility and autonomy in the services rendered. The spectrum—from top-down to autonomy—is important to understand, as these different transnational structures affect operational outcomes and impact, and are pertinent for global leadership, particularly in times of crisis.

Case studies of global leadership . . . in crisis

Let us examine a few case studies that resonate with the challenges and crises facing global leadership. The following illustrations are not meant to demean anyone, but rather to recognize the lessons learned for future global leaders, if any. I will start with examples from our turf, the Christian church, with a few cases stemming from faith-based entities in all three traditions: Protestant/Evangelical, Catholic, and Orthodox. Recent examples include the late Ravi Zacharias' harassment charges in North America. The Indian-born Canadian-American international evangelist founded the Ravi Zacharias International Ministry (RZIM) in 1984, which employed dozens of people and had an annual budget of $25 million.[35] A few months after his passing away in May 2020, an independent investigation revealed multiple sexual harassment cases related to the evangelist-author's co-owned spa female staff. This appeared to be the tip of the iceberg, as several claimants came forward to discredit one of the most influential global evangelical leaders in the world with 30+ books credited to his name.

Also, one of the highest-ranking Vatican officials, Secretary of the Economy, and Australia's Archbishop of Melbourne and Sydney, Cardinal George Pell, faced sexual abuse accusations for several years before being

34. Mitchell et al., *Power and Irrelevance*, 153–68.
35. Guidestar, *Ravi Zacharias International Ministries*.

acquitted of these charges in 2020—a rich history of interfaith and scientific positions, coupled with continuous child sexual abuse and court cases. Although his cases were acquitted by the High Court of Australia, it is only a matter of time to establish the damage these accusations would have had on devoted followers.

The political schism in 2018 between the Orthodox churches of Russia and Ukraine was an evident stance to further the power struggle between Moscow and Constantinople. This came as a consequence of the failed Pan-Orthodox Council of Crete in 2016, which could have been the first council for the Orthodox churches since the eighth century. In return, on 15 October 2018, the Holy Synod of the Russian Orthodox Church, meeting in Minsk, decided to cut all ties with the Constantinople Patriarchate. Politics and regional tug-wars were prevalent in the formation of this twenty-first-century schism, followed by heightened tensions now evident in the Russia-Ukraine conflict. All these three illustrations from the Christian world are examples of failed global leadership.

In the corporate world, the name of Carlos Ghosn made headlines and entered global leadership academic books and research about two decades ago. He also made the headlines in 2018 as an internationally wanted fugitive! Born in Brazil to Lebanese parents, Ghosn moved to Beirut to study at the prestigious Jesuit school where our three boys attended, and continued higher education at the infamous École Polytechnique and École des Mines de Paris, France.[36] Holding three nationalities, living in four continents, and mastering four global languages—French, Portuguese, English, Arabic, and later Japanese—Ghosn joined the mother French Tire company, Michelin, and moved into various positions including COO of the Brazilian subsidiary, eventually becoming Michelin's North America CEO. In 1996, he shifted careers to join French automaker Renault as VP, and was eventually named the CEO of Renault and Nissan and Chairman of the Nissan-Renault Alliance in 1999.[37]

As the first non-Japanese CEO of Nissan and not fully accustomed to the Japanese culture, analysts predicted that he would fail in recovering the faltering Nissan. Instead, Ghosn proved to be a globally-cultured leader, altering Nissan's course into a profitable company, and becoming a hero figure in Japan.[38] Ghosn would get a standing ovation when walking into

36. Millikin and Fu, *Ghosn at Nissan*, 122–25.

37. Millikin and Fu, *Ghosn at Nissan*, 125.

38. Mendenhall et al., *Global Leadership*, 179.

a restaurant in Tokyo, in recognition of his efforts to turn around one of Japan's national brands: Nissan. With Renault's helm in his other hand, he became the first CEO to run two Fortune 500 companies.[39] By 2016, Ghosn added Mitsubishi to the alliance, thereby creating the world's fourth-largest auto group.[40] This global crescendo all ended on November 19, 2018, when Ghosn was arrested upon his arrival on a private jet to Tokyo over allegations of false accounting.[41]

The freefall of this global leadership model shocked the world. Several questions come to mind. *Did the Japanese system and culture realize that a non-Japanese should never have such powers? Was Ghosn actually guilty of withholding income tax declarations? Did we stop recognizing global leadership skills after the fall of globalization? Have we now retrenched to our ghettos? Have we failed to recognize competencies and rather prefer leaders that represent our culture/context?*

I had the opportunity to meet Carlos Ghosn back in 2015 when he was a guest speaker at one of the universities that I taught at. His interview was truly genuine and humbling, providing tips and advice on how to succeed globally. After the event, I had a short chat with him, explaining that he was a key person in the Global Leadership course that I was teaching at another university. He expressed his appreciation and voiced that he is a continual learner, and will never reach the destination. Regardless of his words, his tenure was proof of a successful leadership track record, as actions speak louder than words, followed by an incredible fall.

Ghosn, having escaped the rigid Japanese juridical system, is now an international fugitive living in Lebanon, defensively waiting to clear his name or be indicted. He was stripped of all his operational titles, responsibilities, and authorities, and is currently undergoing investigations by several entities/countries. Such a downfall of global *leadership . . . in crisis* begs the question: Was this case a changed mindset of a failed leadership model?

Despite the above illustrations, the following are three recommendations for sustaining and upholding the main principles of global *leadership . . . in crisis.*

---

39. Taylor, *Ghosn fix GM.*
40. Greimel, *Mitsubishi with Ghosn.*
41. Fortune, *Arrested in Tokyo.*

Respect the culture

Regardless of the level of intercultural competency and intelligence a person may think they possess, there are always hidden, intangible, and undeclared forces in any culture. A global leader should never assume that they know all that it takes to survive or thrive in multiple cultural settings. This is further complicated when dealing with multilayered cultures, such as an organizational culture functioning within a national or local culture, as in the case of Carlos Ghosn's integration of French and Japanese corporate and national cultures. As noted by Ghosn himself, *"no one leader should try to impose his/her culture on another person who was not ready to try the culture with an open mind and heart."*[42] The question is how much time can we offer others to *try the culture with an open mind and heart*? And the answer is: *indefinitely.*

Respect the structure

Every setting has its own unique structure. Understanding the formal and informal structures is necessary to navigate through, and avoid landmines. There is an aspect of change management involved in any global leadership assignment; therefore, respecting the structure prior to suggesting changes to it may be detrimental. Structure is part of life and provides security. When suggesting changes to a well-accustomed structure, leaders may be shaking the very foundations of the success criteria of an entity. I have witnessed multiple organizations' restructuring activities, including Christian entities, mission work, and NGOs; many of them ended up where they used to be a few years ago! Change for the sake of change is not legitimate. When all primary stakeholders agree that a structural change is necessary, the global leader is then invited to lead the organization toward a new sustainable structure.

Respect the people

Both cultures and structures are made up of people. We often tend to ignore the power of people in leading global teams. Not everyone is prone to cope with global leadership and is able to lead people globally. Kets de Vries and Florent-Treacy identified four criteria for nurturing globally-tolerant

42. Millikin and Fu, *Ghosn at Nissan*, 128.

people: (1) growing up in mixed-cultural homes, (2) attending international schools, (3) exposing to international and exchange higher education programs, and (4) having a supportive base for experimenting and exploring global assignments.[43] Such prerequisites mostly revolve around interaction with people at various levels and settings. Therefore, attention to people's needs and respecting their journeys, particularly during crises times, is necessary for sustaining global *leadership . . . in crisis.*

To conclude, this first chapter focused on the components of global leadership and the elements required to lead globally during times of crisis. Competencies such as *linguistic, cultural, geographic, empathic, inquisitive, risk-taking,* and *relational* tendencies were discussed, in addition to cultural intelligence and diversity. Understanding the three global worldviews and 12 behavioral dimensions of cultures is key to enhancing global leaders' Inter-Cultural Intelligence (ICI). The chapter further explored three trans-national strategies relating to *marketing, capacity building,* and community *services.* Examples and cases of global leaders' tenures were presented as experiential illustrations, concluding with three recommendations to respect the *structure, culture,* and *people.* The next chapter will examine the need for *leadership . . . in crisis.*

Recommended action points:

- Adopt the necessary global competencies to lead and impact in times of crisis.

- Build your cultural agility to become a cultural learner, practitioner, and champion.

- Practice humility in understanding and respecting the other.

---

43. Kets de Vries and Florent-Treacy, *Global Leadership from A to Z,* 295–309.

Chapter II

Lead (or Sway) in Times of Crisis

Bold leaders view these [crisis] times as opportunities to go beyond
simple damage control and look for ways to emerge from the crisis
stronger, better, and more resilient.

(ROY WOOD)[1]

ON NOVEMBER 1, 2012, I was woken up by multiple messages on my mobile
phone from all over the world. Two of our colleagues went missing in Syria
while traveling inland from Damascus to Aleppo on a bus. Another well-
meaning colleague posted a prayer for them on her social media page when
she found out that they did not disembark the bus at its arrival destination.
Based on different time zones, some messages were sent from people about
to go to bed, while others were waking up to this news. My first task that
early morning was a fact-finding mission, to separate the fake from the real
news. It was true. The two were kidnapped just outside Aleppo city limit,
when a bunch of armed militias stopped the bus and asked the "Christian"
passengers to step off the bus. Three males disembarked the bus and the
rest were released on their way.

The second task was to enforce a total communication blackout, by
asking the goodhearted colleague to remove her post from social media
immediately and not respond to any queries. I assumed responsibility
for coordinating the communication hub, releasing only need-to-know

1. Wood, *Crisis Leadership*, 9.

information confidentially, and ensuring that all references to their ab-
duction were removed. I proceeded to communicate with the colleagues'
families to establish a contact person to play the role of negotiator with the
abductors while I remained the shadow negotiator. Similar to all international NGOs, our organization refuses to negotiate with kidnappers or pay
ransoms. In the meantime, tens of local, regional, and international press
agencies tried to contact us for a comment, but we evaded most of them.
The reason for the blackout was for the safety of our colleagues; had they
been identified as workers in an international organization, their release
conditions would have been outrageously difficult.

By that time, I realized that my trip to China on November 5 would
have to be canceled, as the situation required hands-on crisis management.
The next step was the negotiations, a delicate task given their families'
emotional state and the kidnappers' demands. Although I cannot reveal the
details of their release for the sake of all those who were involved, the first
staff was released on November 8 as a goodwill gesture due to his need for
daily medications, while it took another week to secure the release of the
second staff on November 15, safe and unharmed.

The most important outcome of this experience was the lessons
learned. A small group of global leaders (I was Vice-Chair of our international organization's Global Board at that time) held a meeting after the
ordeal to evaluate the steps taken and see if anything could have been done
differently, including revisiting the standard policies and procedures. I then
proceeded to communicate to all stakeholders, first offering my apologies
for the communication blackout, explaining the reasons, and revealing the
outcome of the case. Needless to say, all those who reacted to the commu-
niqué expressed their full support for all the steps taken.

In this chapter, we will discuss what constitutes a crisis, identify the
phases of a crisis, and how leaders should be attentive to the pre-crisis signals that are usually out there but remain undetected by many. We will
then examine some of the leadership models that have been established
by practitioners to offer multiple proposals to lead in times of uncertainty
based on their own experiences. The chapter will conclude by exploring
three leadership strategies as additional pragmatic approaches for tackling
crises situations and *lead (or sway) in times of crisis.*

What constitutes a crisis?

At the onset of teaching physical-presence courses, I always engage with the learners in a short discussion: *What is the difference between an emergency and an urgency?* This question is not a philosophical one, but rather a practical one to determine the learners' legitimate absence from course sessions. Their responses are usually varying but mostly serious in their definitions. In concluding the discussion, we usually have a consensus that an emergency is a sudden situation that is out of the hands and control of the learner, such as sickness, flat tire, accident . . . and an urgency is, simply put, bad time management! And I usually add this example, *". . . and if you missed the session because you had to pick your sibling from the airport, it is NOT an emergency and you could have easily pre-managed this situation . . ."*

A crisis is beyond an emergency, as in the latter case, leaders still have tools to work with: take medicine to attend to your sickness, replace the flat tire with a spare, buy insurance to deal with an accident . . . Crises usually resonate a sense of helplessness. A crisis is an event or phase that causes a turning point or core changes to an individual or organization's planned activities.[2] For example, the COVID-19 pandemic disrupted travel plans, weddings, events, and even our basic normal human behavior, thereby bringing entire industries down on their knees. Getting a hotel reservation in Manhattan during Christmas 2020 for less than $100 a night was one indicator of the damage caused by this pandemic to certain industries. It is estimated that world economies shrank by 4.3 percent in 2020[3]—that is, 4.3 percent of $88 trillion, which is about $3.8 trillion in one year!

A crisis is commonly unexpected, disruptive, a single event or multiple occurrences, and could lead to either positive or negative results. Although there are signals that a crisis is looming, these signals are not always evident to many. *"We did not see this coming"* is a usual phrase to justify our inability to sense the warning signs around us. This "blind spot" could be attributed to two reasons. First is our own self-ego that may blind us from seeing what is happening around us, especially when things are going well. Financial crises are the best examples, as the bubble growth in markets is usually followed by a huge tumble. The second reason is our introverted busyness that keeps our heads lowered without looking at the horizons ahead. I have witnessed my share of wars and warfare conflicts in my life, and although

2. Veil, *Learning in Crisis Management*, 117.
3. The Economist, *Economic Cost of COVID-19*.

I did not see many of their signals ahead of time, looking back and assessing their reasons indicated that there were signs that went undetected and therefore caused unnecessary loss of lives.

A crisis can be attributed to humans or nature—the latter usually referred to by insurance companies as an "Act of God," a natural hazard outside human control.[4] I do not particularly endorse this phrase, as God is not in the business of inflicting crises on His creation and creatures. In some religions, this may be the case, but in Christianity, God is love, and love cannot possibly inflict disaster as a matter of discipline or revenge. Nature-caused crises are better known as "force majeure," a French term to indicate an external uncontrolled force behind the crisis, which is rarely predictable and usually outside the control of humans. Human-caused crises are numerous ranging from technological sabotage, financial recessions, or mergers/acquisitions[5] to as simple as a partner stepping out of a relationship, thus disrupting planned activities. Regardless of their source, crises are undesirable circumstances that require leaders to address and offer a secure path through the waves of uncertainty toward the shores of safety.

Finally, *a crisis* brings out core leadership attributes. It is quite easy to portray effective leadership skills, models, and styles during normal circumstances despite the usual fierce competition and daily challenges, but scratching the surface may unravel the other side of the coin, thereby exposing real core values. In 2002, while I was participating in a leadership development program in Singapore, all cohorts were asked to evaluate their instructors. Amongst them was the late Jesuit Father Dr. Anthony D'Souza, who was an incredible author and teacher (and I have used all his books in my daily practices, research, and in this book). However, I was forced to mention one negative aspect in evaluating this outstanding teacher and leader. As a Jesuit priest who is devoted to the Society of Jesus vows of poverty, chastity, and obedience,[6] he was not subjected to the same aspects of crises as the rest of us, whether in juggling married life, children's needs, job, and social demands. The perspectives are different when dealing with multiple crises in the real world versus those of a convent community or a monastic order.

4. Demiroz and Kapucu, *Role of Leadership*, 93.
5. Bhaduri, *Leadership in Crisis Management*, 535.
6. The Jesuits, *About Us*.

So, what kind of leader are you—the type that embraces crises head-on or is swayed by their winds? In the epic movie *The Passion of the Christ*, there is an imaginary scene emphasized by director Mel Gibson in which the Christ is embracing the cross he is carrying while Simon of Cyrene is mocking him for accepting his dilemma, simply because Jesus Christ was aware of the positive outcome of the crisis he was facing: salvation to humanity through his sacrificial crucifixion and resurrection. Similarly, leaders should embrace a crisis and lead others through the various phases of a crisis toward a safe path that offers deliverance.

Phases of a crisis

Before discussing the phases that crises usually pass through, several practitioners have attempted to identify the types of crises.[7] Bernstein and Bonafede mentioned three types: *creeping, slow-burning,* and *sudden crises.*[8] The first one is usually undetected, creeping up until it explodes in its full capacity without obvious warning signs. These usually resemble financial crises that many do not see coming, and when they do manifest their aftermath, impacted stakeholders would run to governments for bailouts. The second is the *slow-burning,* resembling the well-known experiment of heating water on the stove with a frog swimming in the pot enjoying the warmth and not realizing that at a certain kindling point, the frog would lose its life. Many armed conflicts are slow-burning, such as the negotiations between Ethiopia, Sudan, and Egypt over the Nile River dam, which could explode at any time into a regional crisis. The third is the *sudden crisis,* such as the 2004 tsunami, 2010 Haiti earthquake, multiple coal-mines collapses, 2021 Colorado avalanche . . .

Other practitioners, such as Dezenhall and Weber, divide crises into two categories: *sniper-fire* and *character-driven* crises, indicating an external force versus an internal one.[9] Others have also differentiated between externally- and internally-led crises, although it could be difficult to differentiate between the two. For example, the 2004 tsunami could have been avoided if meteorologists had warned the affected parameters of the upcoming tidal waves following the earthquake. Now we regularly hear on the news of a possible tsunami that may hit affected island shores well ahead of

7. Frandsen and Johansen, *Communicating During Crisis,* 260–73.
8. Bernstein and Bonafede, *Guide to Crisis Management.*
9. Dezenhall and Weber, *Damage Control.*

time, although their tidal waves are usually mediocre. Therefore, it is safe to assume that most types of crises are a combination of internal and external factors.

Normally, every crisis goes through three generic phases: *pre-crisis, crisis,* and *post-crisis.*[10] When conducting workshops on Crisis Leadership, I always emphasize that at any point in time, we are in a pre-crisis phase and should be getting ready for the next crisis. In fact, human history is a series of crises, and humanity is juggling between these three phases interchangeably. For example, while many may think we are in the post-pandemic crisis, we are actually in a pre-crisis for the next big thing, such as the energy crisis resulting from the Russia-Ukraine conflict, although it is not quite clear what it may look like when fully manifested. Hence, we are continuously navigating through these phases at different intensities, meanwhile learning valuable lessons in preparation for the next one.

Other literature identified five stages of a crisis: *signal detection, preparation/prevention, contamination/damage limitation, recovery,* and *learning.*[11] This is a more elaborate model that offers two additional phases: *preparation* and *learning. Preparation* is the vast field of crisis management. Multiple books have been written on this subject. Crisis Management is as old as humanity; we have always tried to find solutions to unexpected events. Although the phrase "Crisis Management" has entered contemporary vocabulary in recent decades, in fact, it has been unconsciously practiced by humankind since early civilizations.[12] As a teenager growing up in war-torn Lebanon, I vividly recall how my parents attempted to keep my sister and I focused on our studies throughout the civil war (I may have failed them much more than my sister!). But looking back at those 15 years, my parents' preparation and prevention efforts have made all the difference.

And *learning* is a process that should infiltrate all levels of crisis phases, to foster better preparation for the upcoming crises. It offers an opportunity to lessen the burden of the next crisis, and build contingency plans to address unpredictable situations. As noted in the introduction of this book, the question is not *"When will all this end?"* but rather *"How will all this end?"* I have learned the most valuable lessons through all the crises encountered in my life, whether they pertained to bankruptcies,

---

10. Veil, *Learning in Crisis Management,* 119–21.

11. Bhaduri, *Leadership in Crisis Management,* 538–40.

12. Zamoun and Gorpe, *Crisis Management,* 206.

broken relationships, financial meltdowns, disappointments, or warlike conflicts. The question every leader should ask: *What have I learned from this situation?*

Regardless of the various phases, cycles, and stages, crises typically cause anxiety and uncertainty to individuals, organizations, and entities at large; it is an undesirable situation most leaders would want to avoid. But can we genuinely avoid crises through attentive monitoring of the warning signs?

Pre-crisis signals

A legitimate question: If every crisis sends pre-crisis warning signals, why aren't we better prepared to face any crisis? For example, did the COVID-19 pandemic send warning signs that went unnoticed? Certainly not, and not every crisis, particularly sudden crises, have clearly identifiable indicators. But we can agree that some countries managed the pandemic much better and faster than others, which questions their abilities for preparedness based on hypothetical identical scenarios. Warning signals are always there—over-populated globe, aging demographics, trespassing urban and rural terrains . . .—but we just do not always see them.

It is virtually impossible to predict with any sort of precision when and where a crisis will strike. At the same time, there may be barriers that prohibit leaders from detecting the warning signs, thereby rendering them unable to lessen the impact of the crisis. These include our busyness in day-to-day operations that prohibit us from sensing the signs, lack of long-term strategic vision and direction, inwardly focused on our problems, reliance on past success (aka, we have been through this before and survived), and dependency on external factors, such as the 2008 bailout of motor and other giant companies in the USA. According to Veil, *"To catch the early warnings of trouble, we must be alert to new information, to subtle deviations from the way things typically go."*[13] This requires the deployment of all our senses to catch the vibes of possible deviances.

Because I am accustomed to living and working in multiple-crises situations, catching early warning signs of trouble is a natural (but unpleasant) behavior. In the summer of 2006, when Israeli jetfighters bombed Beirut International Airport and grounded all flight activities, I was "stuck" with three international guests who needed to get to their homes in North

13. Veil, *Learning in Crisis Management*, 136.

Africa and Europe. The natural contingency plan would have been to transfer them by land to Damascus International Airport for a safe passage, but knowing that such a plan would already be saturated, I planned ahead and ensured their safe exit to Queen Alia International Airport in Amman, Jordan (an additional three-hours land trip) where few others would have adopted this plan. Flights were easily available for them to reach their destinations by the weekend.

In contrast, my close friend who works for a conglomerate giant in the USA and has all the proper insurance coverage and contingencies for such "incidents" was visiting his family in Lebanon when the airport closed. It took a few days (and a few tens of thousands of dollars) to get him evacuated with an exhausted driver to Damascus, where he boarded a plane and headed home through multiple transit stops and a few days' delay. Regardless of the outcome, the leader who senses the warning signs and acts accordingly and promptly, eventually would lessen the impact of the crisis on the stakeholders. Dependency on external factors to change favorably is not an option in a crisis.

Pre-crisis signals may reduce the risks that are created by the crisis and assist the leader in being better prepared, strategically and tactically, to face that crisis. In the signal detection phase, it is vital to filter out the right signals from the wrong ones; otherwise, the leader would be calling "wolf" too many times without proper cause. Hence, acquiring the appropriate information and knowledge is vital.[14] Today, we are facing serious issues with filtering out fake news. Media agencies are politicized, social media platforms are open to viral news, and scoops seem to capture the largest attention spans of audiences. The number of contradictory news flashes related to, let's say COVID-19 vaccinations, was incredible. It shaped the minds of communities and molded people's attitudes. Only time will assess the true damage of the wrong signals that were transmitted.

To *lead (or sway) in times of crisis* demands two prerequisites to accelerate the detection of pre-crisis signals: *Organizational structure* and *leadership skills*. If the structure is flexible, the organization is more apt to sense warning signs and deal with internal and external crises. Rigid and bureaucratic structures hamper the detection of pre-crisis warning signals. This has nothing to do with the size of the organization but rather its agility. One global example of a rigid structure dealing with a crisis was the 2010 British Petroleum (BP) oil spill in the Gulf of Mexico. It was believed that

14. Bhaduri, *Leadership in Crisis Management*, 541–42.

BP could have avoided the crisis if they had been more alert to the obvious warning signs, which were ignored by contractors and workers, thereby causing an unavoidable environmental crisis.[15]

Similarly, some leadership skills may better enable the detection process, such as sense-making, sharing perspectives among organizational members, promoting interaction, and helping with problem identification.[16] In fact, organizations that "prepare for crises systematically and continuously search for potential breaks before they are too big to fix" are successful in averting crises.[17] These concepts will be further unpacked while addressing the four pillars—*resilience, stamina, agility,* and *confrontation*—necessary for *leadership . . . in crisis.*

Crisis leadership models

There are vast resources that portray multiple crisis leadership models, although I am not convinced that any model is applicable across the board. Practitioners and consultants have drafted these leadership models based on their own experiences, but these models are mostly not research-based nor apt for generalization in similar or future crises. That is why I will list some of the models here, with the full knowledge that you, as a crisis leader, will need to understand these models, yet craft your own crisis leadership model relevant to your context, stakeholders' needs, and situation.

I once asked my dear German friend, Dr. Felix Breidenstein, why most German organizations had dual leaders and a two-tiered governance model, where organizations with 2000+ employees would designate half the members on the Board of Directors as employee-representatives. Imagine that Mercedes-Benz's Board of Directors includes half of its members representing the staff, workers, and the labor force of the company. This is known as the theory of co-determination, or *Mitbestimmung.*[18] Felix responded to my question calmly and with his usual smile: that the word "leader" in German is best translated as "Führer," meaning a single authoritarian leader, thus the reason why most organizations opted to appoint two equal heads in leadership following World War II. In fact, rarely do we hear media news about a single CEO of a German-run company—although

15. Cappiello and Weber, *Withholding 'Critical' Spill Data.*
16. Bhaduri, *Leadership in Crisis Management,* 541.
17. Bhaduri, *Leadership in Crisis Management,* 541.
18. Nordberg, *Corporate Governance,* 74.

there are several large global companies—simply because of the dual-tier system of leadership. Unlike the CEOs of most American corporations (e.g., Bill Gates, Jeff Bezos, Mark Zuckerberg, etc.).

Likewise, crisis leaders should not be soloists without their orchestra. Crisis leadership models are really about team and group work. The leadership skills required to lead before, during, and after the crisis requires a distinct set of skills for each phase.[19] Following are samples of crisis leadership strategies and behaviors compiled over the last two decades:

Authors and practitioners	Strategies and behaviors
Klann (2003)[20] offered several leadership skills, traits, and perspectives required in crises, such as:	*Consistent communication, clarity of vision, caring, role modeling, character, competence, courage,* and *decisiveness*
Slater (2009)[21] provided a set of leadership behaviors required to overcome a crisis situation, ranging from:	*Casting a compelling vision, team building, positive spirit, destination-oriented,* and *continuous team encouragement*
Haley (2009)[22] advised leaders to:	*Set the direction, plan and prepare (rehearse) for the future,* and *develop other leaders*
Mitut (2011)[23] emphasized the following qualities:	*Managerial competence, promotion of confidence, proper motivation, objective assessment of subordinates' work results,* and *communication*
Boin et al. (2013)[24] listed the following 10 tasks for effective crisis leadership:	*Early Recognition, Sensemaking, Making Critical Decisions, Orchestrating Vertical and Horizontal Coordination, Coupling and Decoupling, Meaning Making, Communication, Rendering Accountability, Learning,* and *Enhancing Resilience*
Stern (2013)[25] emphasized:	*Organizing and Selecting; Planning (To Improvise); Educating, Training, and Exercising;* and *Cultivating Vigilance and Protecting Preparedness*
Wood (2013)[26] simplified the strategies to basic skills, such as:	*Doing the right thing, being wise and bold, remaining poised,* and *celebrating the victory*

19. Demiroz and Kapucu, *Role of Leadership*, 95–99.

20. Klann, *What is Crisis Leadership?*, 11–26.

21. Slater, *Leading People*, 15.

22. Haley, *Leading in a Crisis*, 14.

23. Mitut, *Management of Crisis*, 21–24.

24. Boin et al., *Times of Crisis*, 82–87.

25. Stern, *Task of Leadership*, 52–54.

26. Wood, *Crisis Leadership*, 7–9.

Authors and practitioners	Strategies and behaviors
Kaschner (2017)[27] provided four steps in the process:	*Prepare in peacetime, get familiar with supplements and anticipate failures, KISS (keep it short and simple),* and *use the crisis log*
Agnes (2019)[28] provided fours steps:	*Identify and understand your risk, develop strong emotional intelligence, proactively find opportunities to consistently build trust,* and *choose to embed a crisis-ready culture*
Bhaduri (2019)[29] integrated organizational culture into leadership strategies and styles to include:	*Holistic approach toward crisis preparedness; Building crisis management competencies; Standardizing learning in crisis management;* and *Engaging stakeholders in the planning process*

Despite the numerous crisis management, disaster response, and leadership skills advices offered by consultants, experts, and practitioners, this book poses the following three leadership strategies as additional pragmatic approaches for tackling crisis situations.

1. Embrace a realistic-optimist attitude

During a crisis, it is imperative that the leader maintains an objective balanced outlook. This goes far beyond having a positive attitude during uncertain phases. It requires gathering data, analyzing it, providing alternatives, and transmitting a realistic future stance. In this era, accessing absolute truthful facts versus relative truth is a challenge. We tend to believe the insignificant relative news transmitted by social media, friends, or multiple conspiracy theories over fact- and research-based truths. For example, the speaker at my commencement ceremony at Long Island University on May 17, 1987, Dr. Carl Sagan, the Cornell University astronomer and Pulitzer Prize-winning author, cited researchers who estimated that by 1990, one out of every three people we know would be infected with HIV/AIDS. Such speculative information based on immediate patterns is often untrue and relative.

Embracing a realistic-optimist position particularly during crises is a crucial leadership ability. It requires the aptitude to see beyond the current situations, hence providing prompt decision-making and problem-solving tools.[30] In general, realistic optimists are people who "construct

27. Kaschner, *Crisis Decision-Making*, 33–34.

28. Agnes, *Becoming Crisis Ready*, 8.

29. Bhaduri, *Leadership in Crisis Management*, 545–46.

30. Rogers, *Optimism or Positivity*, 19.

positive ways to persevere through the storms of life."[31] Such advocates for progressive forward-looking leaders should not be mistaken for unrealistic optimists. Jesuit Father Anthony D'Souza in his book *Empowered Leadership* argues that optimistic leaders refuse the concept of helplessness and position crisis as a temporary setback and not a permanent situation, unlike their pessimistic opposites. He further provides the following (recreated and abridged) matrix that summarizes four possible leadership outlooks:[32]

FIGURE 1

	Pessimist	
U N R E A L I S T I C	**Unrealistic Pessimist** Tends to over-estimate negative reality Believes things are terrible and they will get worse Foresees doom Avoids reality Makes excuses Lives in self-defense =>Despair	**Realistic Pessimist** Sees both positive and negative aspects of reality Tends to focus only on the negative Lacks self-confidence and believes s/he is trapped Emphasizes only the negative and sees no solution Lives in the status quo and feels like a victim of circumstances =>Carries morale downhill
O P T I M I S T I C	**Unrealistic Optimist** Tends to under-estimate negative reality Ignores problems Or sees no problems Does not face the issues or situation squarely Runs away from reality Creates a period of temporary well-being in the group =>This may be followed by disaster	**Realistic Optimist** Faces reality and sees both positive and negative parts Tends to focus on the positive strengths & resources Has positive self-regard/confidence Sees every problem as a challenge Looks for alternative solutions and searches for best Acts on the best alternative solution or seeks new ways Faces every challenge with new solutions or new ways =>Leads to change, growth and progress
	Optimist	

Adapted from D'Souza[33]

The quest for realistic-optimist leadership is to dismiss negative thoughts or images, focus on the positive aspects of any situation, and choose thoughts and ideas that may change the current status. It is not an invitation to be blindly optimistic without considering the facts.[34] In summary, "optimistic leaders frame difficulties in a way that is empowering,

31. Rogers, *Realistic Optimism,* 7.

32. D'Souza, *Empowered Leadership,* 212–15.

33. D'Souza, *Empowered Leadership,* 214.

34. Fox, *Realistic Optimism,* 8.

encouraging, and enabling"[35] rather than being swayed by rumors, speculations, and unwarranted myths. Research indicates that over 90 percent of the things we worry about never happen.

I still recall my high school years in war-torn Lebanon, how I was barely passing from one class to another, struggling to retain any of the formal curricular education due to multiple distractions of non-consistent academic years. The situation is very similar to the COVID-19 pandemic disruption of our education system in 2020 and beyond. A very pessimistic and hopeless future was looming on my horizon, so I hardly cared about anything—studies, future plans, career . . .

And then in the summer of 1983, accompanied by my mother, I took a boat trip to Cyprus to spend a couple of weeks with my uncle, when full-scale war broke throughout Lebanon. I wanted to come back home to be with my comrades in arms (I was already trained by militias to "protect" our region), but it was impossible to return. Having no real choice, my uncle accompanied me to the nearest college in Nicosia, Cyprus, where I was admitted on probation pending the submission of my high school diploma, grades, etc. To make a long story short, that first semester, I landed on the honors list, and the rest is history. With the changed context and the mere age of 17, I realized the importance of optimism and positive attitude, and adopted a realistic approach thereafter. Sadly, many of my school-aged friends never survived the pessimistic attitude. This is a personal choice, not an externally-dictated karma on your life. Choose to be *a realistic-optimist.*

2. Adopt your own plan—Don't copy others

The Chinese character for the word "crisis" combines two words: *Danger* and *Opportunity.* In every crisis situation, there are imminent dangers hovering over individuals, organizations, and entities; yet based on their own different contexts, such situations could provide unique opportunities for growth and success. Hence, the leader must adopt relevant contingency plan(s) specific to the entity's context as identified in its internal and external environments, mainly SWOT, PESTLE, Porter's Five Forces, and Stakeholder analyses.[36]

Ask the question . . . *what works for me, us, my family, the organization, industry, country . . . ?* Following my successful college semesters in

35. Rogers, *Realistic Optimism,* 7.

36. Kaschner, *Crisis Decision-Making,* 29–30.

Cyprus, I was faced with the reality that a degree from a small college on the island will probably not match my future plans. Hence, I had to craft my own plan, despite the many hindrances and obstacles that were present in the mid-eighties: financial, inflation, visa restrictions, cultural barriers, and family margins. Yet I managed to transfer my credits to a respectable university in New York State, work night and day to make ends meet, and finally graduate with my first higher-education degree. Adopting my own plan, not duplicating my sister's tenure or my closest friends' paths, made all the difference.

There is a tendency to adopt an existing well-proofed contingency plan from a similar crisis/organization/situation. Several leaders prefer the option of copying a plan already implemented or duplicating another organization or country's contingency plan. This rarely works. Leaders must engage with their stakeholders in developing innovative solutions *relevant* to their own contexts. The contingency plan must have reason and meaning for the specific setting coupled with good knowledge of the individual or organization's environment.[37]

Some leaders prefer to play it safe. They tend to wait and see how others will react and under what pretenses. They withdraw from being on the frontlines and simply copy others in their reactive approaches. While moving to second place is not always a bad strategy, you must still adopt your own plan. Craft your path as recited in Robert Frost's poem *The Road Not Taken*: "Two roads diverged in a wood, and I—I took the one less traveled by, and that has made all the difference." Stakeholders will remember those leaders that carved their own tracks, not those that copied others'.

3. Review contingency plan(s) constantly

The argument to develop and adopt your own plan(s) should not be confused with the leader's abilities to continuously review, adapt, and modify their own contingency plan(s). There is always a tendency to do nothing new, lay back, depend on the known and tested plans, and adopt a defensive strategy. Several concepts may hinder us from moving away from the familiar, such as *denial, lack of capacity to get to where we want to go, stuck in the middle, relationship risks, building arrogance,* and *scapegoating others.*[38]

---

37. Zamoun and Gorpe, *Crisis Management*, 210.
38. Dotlich et al., *Navigating through Complexity*, 37–39.

The inclination is to review, review, and continuously review the plans even during the assumed peak of the crisis.

Researchers emphasize the need to avoid irreversible decisions during a crisis and engage in continuous communication.[39] Effective communication strategies are required to amend and adopt changes in contingency plans.[40] The main task of crisis leadership is preparing—preparing alternative plans (Plan Z, not just Plan B or C) to address crises such as the Boston Marathon bombings (unlike New York, Madrid, and London—cities with a history of terror attacks) and other natural disasters.[41] This should not be ignored, as doing so lies solely at the leaders' peril.

My university years in the USA were very fruitful, but they were not *my* plans for the future, unlike many of my peers during that phase. Equipped with a prominent university degree, I headed back to [still] war-torn Lebanon to engage in my first business venture and was able to enroll in the prestigious MBA program at the American University of Beirut. I kept "reviewing" my plans amidst continued civil commotion until I was finally able to finish the MBA—now married and graduating with a year-old son on my arm. That was the result of my reviewed plan.

In every contingency plan, there is a trade-off component. In my case, it was a trade-off to leave the safe USA context (as a student) and head back to my homeland, where I could make an impact. Leaders should seek the right information as they make crucial decisions that involve complex trade-offs.[42] Some examples of trade-offs include safety vs. output, differentiation vs. integration, short- vs. long-term, profitability vs. social responsibility . . . Each plan involves constant trade-offs balancing one good over another.[43] Leaders should be aware that the continuous dynamic reviewing process of contingency plans will affect trade-off criteria and place one good over another good. This obviously involves a sacrifice and balancing act among stakeholders' needs, which I gladly embraced back in 1987.

To conclude this chapter, to *lead (or sway) in times of crisis* is one of the most challenging tasks for the school of leadership. Many individuals and organizations may claim to possess crisis management, risk assessment,

39. Ansell and Boin, *Taming Deep Uncertainty*, 1089.

40. Zamoun and Gorpe, *Crisis Management*, 205.

41. Stern, *Task of Leadership*, 51.

42. Ansell and Boin, *Taming Deep Uncertainty*, 1094.

43. Dotlich et al., *Navigating through Complexity*, 101.

disaster response, and trouble-shooting experiences; however, research indicates that unless leaders have first-hand knowledge of overcoming the dangers associated with crises and focus on opportunities, they tend to maintain the status quo—if not even fall behind. This chapter reviewed the multitude of practitioner literature pertaining to this discipline, and offered three additional pragmatic leadership strategies to overcome such crises—which are a part of everyday life—and choose the path less traveled by.

Recommended action points:

- Be attentive and alert to pre-crises warning signals out there.
- Stay focused on the valuable lessons learned from crises and *how will all this end* for you.
- Adopt a realistic-optimist and forward-looking stance during a crisis.

Chapter III

Build the Resilience Wall

That which does not kill us makes us stronger.

(FRIEDRICH NIETZSCHE)[1]

IT WAS SOMETIME IN April 1976. My father's job at the British Bank of the Middle East (known today as HSBC), relocated its headquarters from Beirut, Lebanon to Nicosia, Cyprus, due to the ongoing civil war in Lebanon that had started the year before. As a nine-year-old, I was excited to make my first ever international trip—by boat—to Cyprus, as Beirut International Airport was closed. The warlike activities in Lebanon were intriguing in my childhood, such as encountering a disruptive school year, camp-life style, and nights in the shelter that were full of board and card games. I never really grasped the seriousness of the situation.

Setting off that early morning from Jounieh Bay on a private yacht that was altered to host 45+ commercial passengers to Larnaca was, to say the least, exciting. The 8-hour-long sea trip was thrilling for the first few minutes, but then turned ugly as my stomach could not hold back the motion sickness that I had never encountered before. Dizzy and faint, I spent the next few hours laying down on a bench hoping for this saga to end. Early in the afternoon, the waves started rising and hitting hard against the front of the 100-foot yacht. The vessel was wobbling as the captain initiated a mayday call on his wireless equipment in Greek: "*Mayday, mayday, apo Christiana*"—Christiana was the name of the boat.

1. Frankl, *Search for Meaning*, 89.

Darkness fell, waves and wind grew stronger, all passengers sitting in the open-air deck crammed into one closed lounge to avoid getting wet, and what followed was the worst night of my life. Lying on the floor, I was rolling in my own vomit under people's legs from side to side with each wave, while screams for mercy were shouted with every inclination. Then my parents along with a handful of Christians started singing the hymn: "All to Jesus I surrender all . . ." I believed my life was over that night. So did other passengers whom I overheard talking about a movie with a similar scenario that ended with all the passengers perishing at sea.

It was late into the night when the captain finally gave up the attempt to reach Cyprus and turned the boat around back toward Lebanese shores. However, the waves had already caused severe damage to the front of the yacht and strong winds pushed it northbound. By early morning, we had reached the northern side of the Lebanese shoreline near Tripoli's port, but the city was under attack from the coalition forces coming into Lebanon from Syria who started shooting warning shots at the vessel. The captain quickly steered the boat north until we docked in the port of Tartus, a city on the Mediterranean coast of Syria. The officials kept us on board until they checked the manifest. By then, my frail dehydrated body could not take it any longer. I fainted in my parent's arms while some adults tried to revive me with fresh water and biscuits.

After 30+ hours lost at sea, we were allowed to disembark the boat and given the choice to continue our trip to Cyprus after repairing the yacht's bow, or choose an alternative route. My father's cousins lived in Latakia, so we decided to head to their home, exhausted and traumatized, yet happy to have survived the failed trip. The next few days were spent washing and drying our sea-water trenched luggage before arranging a flight a week later from Damascus airport to Larnaca. We then settled in a small apartment in the inland capital city of Nicosia. Nowadays, every time I hear or read a story about a refugee boat lost in the Mediterranean Sea, I can somehow relate to their dilemma.

So why am I sharing this childhood story, which most children would probably want to forget? A few months later in Nicosia, our teenage neighbor was exiting the apartment building; my curious sister and I asked where he was heading, and his response was to the movie theater. We begged him to take us with him, and after convincing Mom, we accompanied him to the movie theater. Aged 12 and 10 respectively, my sister and I watched the 1975 JAWS movie! I loved swimming; the swimming pool next to our apartment in Nicosia was my daily activity, but watching that movie at that age shook me to the core. Between the boat trip and the Jaws movie, you would think that the sight of a sea would be traumatizing . . .

On the contrary. I love the sea, ocean, lake . . . I try to swim daily about one kilometer into deep waters, especially when I am in Cyprus (although I avoided some of the beaches in Australia!). And I am a regular snorkeler and a PADI Open Water Diver who has enjoyed some of the best dives in the world, including the Red Sea reef. I often wondered where did this resilience come from? How did I unconsciously build a wall to overcome my fear of almost losing my life on a boat trip and getting scared out of my wits from a graphically-violent movie?

Resilience is a common word used today to describe effective or potential leadership skills. "*He is resilient . . . Her resilience is amazing . . . Our organization's resiliency is unmatched . . .*" are examples of how often we use this word, particularly after the recovery measures following the CO-VID-19 pandemic and other crises. We often attach another word to it to identify the area of expertise, such as *human, emotional, cognitive, physical, organizational,* and *corporate resilience.*

Resilience is best defined by Oxford Dictionary as the capacity to recover from challenges. The American Psychology Association (APA) defined resilience as "the process of adapting well in the face of adversity, trauma, tragedy, threats, or significant sources of stress."[2] It involves two elements of human behavior: bouncing back (recovery) and personal growth (learning). Resilience is also coupled with the concept of change management, as change and flexibility are prerequisites for building a resilient individual, team, and organization.

The word "resilience" is derived from the Latin verb *resilire*, meaning to jump, leap, spring back, or recoil.[3] It entails the ability to bend, stretch, and bounce—only to return to its original shape. An appropriate scientific and technical description of resilience would be "elasticity"—the ability to bend or absorb a shock, yet return to its original form, shape, or structure.[4] In this chapter, I would argue that resilience should not only enact us to return to our original format, but should also shape us to become a better version of that original template, similar to many people's Christian transformation testimonies. It is an opportunity to enhance ourselves to become a better and stronger form of ourselves.

2. APA, *Building your Resilience.*

3. Morwood, *Oxford Latin Dictionary.*

4. Ferraro, *Resilience in Coming Back,* 98–101.

No one is born resilient; it is a skill that we need to acquire over time. It requires work and dedication.[5] While reading the opening story of this chapter with my sister to cross-check the facts (she is only 32 months older than me), we relived the details of those incidents as if we went through them only a few days ago. However, when I mentioned my continued love of swimming and diving in the open seas, she did not reciprocate. In fact, she shared that she still feels traumatized from the memory every time she is exposed to open water or boat trips. This raises the question as to our human responses to crises, the skills required to bounce back, and the ability to move forward. Resilience is not unleashed; it is built.[6] How do we build that resilience wall that allows us to overcome adversities?

There are two more misconceptions about resilience worth mentioning: It is neither a *blanket* nor an added ability for *resistance*.[7] Resilience does not serve as a bullet-proof cover that safeguards individuals, teams, or organizations during hardships. Even bullet-proof vests have weak spots that may cause injury under a direct line of fire. Nor is it a heightened level of resistance that can withhold storms and winds until something breaks. While the concepts of "endurance" and "toughness" resonate well with some of the proposed ideas, resilience's flexibility should not break but rather return with an enhanced nature, just as gold is purified by fire. To *build the resilience wall* (the title of this chapter) is about a protective or a resisting wall; it is a brick-by-brick built wall while the leader is sitting on top of it, thereby enabling the leader to observe the waves and turmoil of the crisis from a bird's-eye view, make sense of the warning signals, and able to evaluate the opportunities arising from the crisis.

In this chapter, we will examine some of the sources of resilience and how it can be accrued through life's experiences and reactions to challenges. We will be looking at the *recovery* aspect of the term, particularly in a crisis' final stages as noted in chapter 2. However, we will also be addressing the *learning* perspectives as a platform for exploring new opportunities, as will be explored in chapter 4. While resilience includes a vast array of disciplines varying from emotional, physical, personal, group, organizational, or cognitive resilience, the focus of this book is on the ability to navigate *leadership . . . in crisis.*

5. Ferraro, *Resilience in Coming Back*, 98.
6. Ferraro, *Resilience in Coming Back*, 99.
7. Ferraro, *Resilience in Coming Back*, 98–101.

Sources of resilience

Let's start with the end in mind. The ultimate source of resilience is our inner selves—call it your faith, values, belief system, norms, upbringing . . . We need to search deep into our being to discover that hidden *well* of fresh resources that would quench our resilience *wall*. This is easier said than done! Following are a few proposed sources of resilience:

1. Hope

"Hope is a choice, not a feeling."[8] The late Terry Law, founder and president of World Compassion wrote in his book *The Hope Habit* that we have a choice to choose hope. *Choosing hope is our choice . . . and as Christians, we have no choice but to choose hope!* Viktor Frankl adds: "*Between stimulus and response there is a space. In that space is our power to choose our response. In our response lies our growth and our freedom.*"[9] In any crisis, we have that window to choose hope rather than despair by setting clear aspirational goals despite the challenges.[10] During our failed boat trip to Cyprus, the hopeful goal that I was reiterating in my mind was how to become a good swimmer when all this ended, so that a repeated similar situation would not cause the same level of anxiety.

2. Self-efficacy (confidence)

No doubt, there is a direct correlation between self-confidence and resilience. Building on past experiences (which we did not have on the boat trip, as it was our first ever international voyage), one could focus on past successes, relinquish control of the factors outside their control, and try to role model replicating situations. Dimino and colleagues advised frontline nurses to develop self-efficacy through (1) *Mastery Experience*—Personally accomplishing a challenging task; (2) *Social Modelling*—Learning by observing others accomplish a task; (3) *Social Persuasion*—Respected peer or mentor convinces individual that they have what it takes; and (4) *Psychological Responses*—Awareness of emotions and reframing experiences

---

8. Law and Gilbert, *The Hope Habit*, 16.
9. Frankl, *Frankl Quotes*.
10. Dimino et al., *Frontline Heroes*, 593.

in a positive way.[11] The last point is crucial, as the more we share about our crisis experiences, despite their failures, the more we are apt to learn from them. The emotional response between my sister and myself to our boat trip was quite different; my response was that of challenging the experience positively, whereas her response was more passive.

3. Optimism

We have already covered Dr. D'Souza's realistic-optimist outlook in the previous chapter. It is important to add that optimism entails thinking about the future in a positive way. Contrary to our beliefs, optimism can be developed through focusing on the positive aspects, sharing past experiences and their positive outcomes, and looking forward to future opportunities.[12] A colleague recently shared this quote from French General Napoleon Bonaparte: "A leader is a dealer in hope." *Leadership . . . in crisis* must always foster an optimistic future based on past experiences and future opportunities. As mentioned in the introduction, the appropriate question to ask upon the onset of a crisis is not *"When will all this end?"* but rather *"How will all this end?* The "how" entails an opportunity to make something positive out of a seemingly negative situation.

4. Protective factors

In any crisis, we must count on others to extend a helping hand. The "in-group" noted in the introduction should serve as a protecting factor. A leader needs to reach out for help in times of crisis. Knowing that there is a support base for leaders provides the necessary resilience as a source for recovery. My parents' attempts, although futile, to provide some supportive factors within the rough sea waves was one way that most parents practice under such circumstances. We often tell our children *"It's going to be alright"* without really knowing that it will be alright. On a leadership level, protective factors include having a support group, a well-balanced work life, initiating stimulation and growth, making sure we remain within our boundaries, and being able to express emotions.[13] Other protective factors

11. Dimino et al., *Frontline Heroes,* 594.

12. Dimino et al., *Frontline Heroes,* 594–95.

13. LeMoine et al., *Promoting Professional Resilience,* 55–56.

include strong relationships, positive thinking, living a healthy lifestyle, and maintaining a joyful and humorous attitude.

5. Mindfulness

Mindfulness is *"an ability to be fully present, taking in what's going on in a way that is non-judgmental and accepting. It is about being fully aware of one's emotional experiences in order to put distance between the stressors in one's life and how one responds to those stressors."*[14] I recall every moment of that boat trip down to the details, and although I was only nine-years-old and 32 months younger than my sister who could not recall all the details of the trip, my mind was able to capture every moment vividly. I was taking everything in. Many people are living in the past; others are in the future. Living in the present and absorbing all warning signs objectively builds the resilience wall. It allows us to be mindful of the situation and handle stressful conditions calmly, accurately, and effectively. *Leadership . . . in crisis* needs to be mindful of the momenta of the crisis as leaders seek to enhance their resilience wall.

6. Self-care

Time to take care of yourself. It is not possible to lead in a crisis situation when you are physically and emotionally drained. Hence the concept of self-compassion has proved to improve resilience levels.[15] I am a strong advocate of the time management matrix that Steven Covey introduced in his best-selling book: *The 7 Habits of Highly Effective People.*[16] When leaders function in the *Urgent/Important* quadrant for prolonged periods, they are bound to break. Any minor hiccup or added calamity would break their backs. Personal growth happens in the *Not-Urgent/Important* time quadrant. Having served on an educational institute's Board of Trustees several years ago, I was once asked if we could meet on some Thursday afternoon, and my immediate response was negative. A colleague sitting next to me whispered "Why? Are you traveling?" and was shocked by my response that Thursday afternoons were booked for tennis! Self-care enables both personal and professional wellbeing. Daily exercise, balanced routines,

---

14. LeMoine et al., *Promoting Professional Resilience*, 56.

15. LeMoine et al., *Promoting Professional Resilience*, 56.

16. Covey, *Highly Effective People*, 151.

social and personal relationships are a few examples of effective self-care. These will only become evident when the leader is facing a certain crisis.

7. Reflective practices

There is always the opportunity to reflect on past experiences. What worked and what didn't work. The experience of the kidnapped colleagues from Syria in the previous chapter ended with a debriefing session between key leaders as to what we could have done differently. These reflections are windows of personal and professional growth. Learning from past mistakes is crucial. We do not always get the opportunity to reflect, particularly when the crisis was painful and we really want to forget it rather than ponder on it. Continuous self-learning and self-managed learning are essential for building the resilience wall. Slowing down and appraising previous similar scenarios has important implications on future decisions.[17] These practices also serve to imrove mindfulness and self-care.

Having looked at these seven possible sources to enhance our resilience wall, let us now examine some of the practical tools that sustain that wall.

Practicing resilience

In the following section, I will attempt to provide some tips on how leaders can adopt the practice of resilience as a way of life. It is not a matter of consciously deciding, *"Today, I want to practice resilience!"* It is more likely an unconscious pattern that *leadership . . . in crisis* adhere to in order to continue building the resilience wall. Such patterns are noticeable when leaders are energized, or even thrive, through crises. We will examine the *why, when,* and *how* of practicing resilience to put things in perspective.

Why should leaders practice resilience?

Some leaders may settle for a pacifist attitude, a laissez-faire style, mainly known as "hands-off, let it ride" or non-leadership.[18] Citing that every crisis has its own specificities and circumstances, they argue that it is best to cross

17. LeMoine et al., *Promoting Professional Resilience,* 56.
18. Northouse, *Leadership Concepts,* 196–97.

that bridge [of the next crisis] when they get to it. They even believe that the set of skills gained through one crisis is useless and irrelevant when facing the next. They never understand the *why* behind practicing resilience, which is the capacity to adapt and restore stability in crisis situations.[19] Unfortunately, such leaders lose out on learning opportunities and waste valuable lessons.

Conversely, practicing resilience offers hope for the future and strength to tackle the next crisis. Victor Frankl who wrote about his experiences in a WWII concentration camp in his book *Man's Search for Meaning* argued that any prisoner who lost faith in the future was destined to fail.[20] He noted a series of mental and physical deteriorations following the loss of faith in the future, ultimately leading to early death. For those of us who have been in similar conditions when it was easy to lose hope and get side-tracked, the rebuilding process was longer and more tedious. Any small crisis would crumble established leaders if they were non-resilient practitioners.

Looking back at our [and other] generations that lived in wars and uncertainties for decades, one could identify two types of people that were shaped by such adversaries. Those who practiced their resilience, learned valuable lessons mostly the hard way, and moved on; and those who still lingered in the past. A handful of my high school classmates have very successful global tenures simply because they enhanced their resilience while the rest remained in the same parking spot of the past afraid to take the next step in life, even decades later. Frankl described the latter group as those prisoners who did not even have the purpose to get out of bed in the morning, giving up even before the crisis began.[21] It is vital that we embrace the practice of resilience as a lifelong pattern of existence.

When should leaders practice resilience?

All the time. Some of the major leadership failures in history occurred when leaders thought they were unbeatable and did not require additional formation or attention to warning signals. How many times have we heard leaders explain to their stakeholders that *"we did not see this coming"*? This is the usual excuse for not abiding by the continuous journey of practicing resilience. As I write this paragraph, the world is looking at Kabul airport,

19. Luu, *Worker Resilience*, 1594.

20. Frankl, *Search for Meaning*, 82.

21. Frankl, *Search for Meaning*, 82.

Afghanistan, where thousands of foreign workers and their Afghan aids are trying to flee the country by the end of August 2021. The scene is horrific, as parents give up their babies to be put on the next flight out of Kabul, and *. . . no one saw it coming?*

Research indicates that the next decade will include multiple crises, hence endorsing the need for the continuous practice of resilience.[22] Some leaders may think they have reached the resilience finish line and should not need additional bricks to continue building their wall. This contradicts the mere definition of crisis—an unexpected, disruptive event or series of events that could alter the planned course of action. The continual practice of resilience does not protect us from the next unexpected disruption, but rather enables us to maneuver through it based on the bank of resilient tools leaders have accumulated throughout their years of experience. Back to the Afghan news, various leaders were making public appearances to either blame one another or distribute responsibility rather than address the lack of resilient and endurance practices that led to yet another humanitarian crisis.

People usually feel more confident and comforted when they interact in a positive manner with their leaders during crises. The transmitting of reassuring messages while maintaining objective optimism is necessary. For example, currently in Lebanon (and in many developing countries) a lot of young talented people are leaving to pursue better opportunities abroad, in another brain drain wave faced by this tiny country and similar nations. When I encounter young adults who are feeling left behind, I usually encourage them to stay focused and hopeful despite the multiple crises they are facing. I usually use these three arguments:

1. *Every crisis has an end.* Every single crisis in human history had a lifespan. None were permanent, although some crisis consequences lasted much longer than the crisis itself. When the crisis is over, it opens an opportunity for growth and development, thereby offering its "survivors" a unique occasion to accompany the recovery plans.

2. *Every crisis offers new learning opportunities.* I usually share my own experiences having been through similar crises in the past and the similarities between past and present crises, and how I used them to learn valuable lessons. I make it a point to emphasize that the crisis

22. LeMoine et al., *Promoting Professional Resilience*, 53.

placed me in a distinctive position, offering new resilience tools that were acquired, sometimes without noticing, unlike those who were leaving to evade the crisis.

3. *We emerge stronger after the crisis.* While the brain drain is unfortunate and sad, those qualified young people who remain behind will become fewer yet more sought after due to their competitive edge and earned resilience. The acquired tools and fewer skilled peers in the market offers new competitive positionings. As mentioned in the chapter's opening mantra, *that which does not kill us makes us stronger.*

In fact, those who returned from abroad after the wave of crisis was over could not make it during the growth period, because they lacked the resilience tools developed by those who stayed behind. They looked back and saw the country booming again, and wanted to give it another shot, but failed. So, the simple answer to *when should leaders practice resilience* is ALWAYS.

How should leaders practice resilience?

Although it is pretentious to assume that there is a *how* or several of them to practice resilience, I would offer a few humble tips based on my experiences and latest research. The first step is to dedicate time in the post-crisis phase to capture the distinctive lessons learned, regardless of their harshness, during the previous crisis. The wall of resilience is built in the window offered *after* a certain crisis has surpassed and *before* the next crisis hits. This window, also known in Crisis Management as the *preparedness* segment, is how leaders practice resilience.[23] It offers an opportunity for enhancement, which many leaders, unfortunately, ignore and actually lay back and relax after a crisis rather than prepare.

The second step is to accept the changes enforced by the crisis. Following a certain crisis, many leaders exert a lot of energy to return things to the way they were. This is a waste of time, effort, and energy. Recorded experiences indicate that crises result in multiple changes—changes to the way we do things, relationships, structures, interactions . . .—and through practicing resilience, leaders are better able to cope and adapt to the new realities. For example, the impact of the COVID-19 pandemic changed and will change human and business interaction in the near future. Resilient

23. Ferraro, *Resilience in Coming Back*, 101–5.

leaders will understand that going back to the "old normal" is no longer an option; they need to learn the lessons offered by the "new normal" in order to better cope with the "next normal." That is how leaders practice resilience.

Practicing resilience requires time for reflection, quality contemplation, and awareness.[24] This can only be accomplished after the winds and waves of the crisis have subdued. In that space lies our ability to learn and adapt new resilience tools. Taking a deep breath to absorb all aspects of the crisis, the changes dictated by it, and a clear vision of what to do next enhances the practice of resilience.

Nancy Koehn wrote a book in 2017 entitled: *Forged in Crisis: The Power of Courageous Leadership in Turbulent Times.* Having suffered from three personal crises within a period of three years (loss of her father, bitter divorce, and breast cancer), she indulged in a journey through history to identify how some leaders practiced resilience to overcome their adversaries. She explained in one of her book interviews how her selected leadership models were facing very low chances for success, coupled with fear and uncertainty, yet each leader managed to find the strength and resilience to overcome the challenges.[25] *How?* Each one followed a different path, but they all had to accept their failures, straighten their path, and overcome every obstacle they faced.

The final step is to deal with the brutal realities that emerge during crises. This could be anything from a failed financial or IT structure to low staff morale. Remember: Leaders are as strong as the weakest team member. I call this the *confrontation aftermath* that every leader must address to enable new learning and opportunities, which will be addressed in the last two chapters.

Koehn invited every leader to embrace the following three practices: Demonstrate resolve, emphasize role and mission, and focus on the opportunity for learning.[26] If you realize that some of your team members or the organizational structure have repeatedly failed to bounce back to the required level, this is the time to confront and implement new processes. Do not wait until the next crisis approaches.

24. Ferraro, *Resilience in Coming Back*, 105.

25. Gerdeman, *Leadership under Fire.*

26. Koehn, *Forged in Crisis*, 8.

Building the wall

In the summer of 1980, our family took a long vacation and visited the United States. It was our first trip to the USA, and we wanted to do almost everything—as tourists—in that big nation. Hosted by our extended family members, we made a trip to Universal Studios in California. I was 13-years-old then, and taking everything in . . . until our guided tour in the open-side sightseeing bus was about to get close to a lake with some explosions, sound effects, and a fake JAWS shark attacking the right side of the bus. As I monitored the bus ahead of us, I slowly made my way to the left seat, exchanging seats with one of my cousins under the pretense that I wanted to sit in the shade. No one noticed anything, and we passed that section with the usual giggles and awe.

Obviously, my resilience wall resulting from the boat trip and the Jaws movie crises was not quite ready at 13. Although I was definitely sure that both the movie and the short reliving of the scene at Universal Studios were completely fictitious, I was still not ready to relive that crisis even for a few seconds. Building the resilience wall takes time, effort, sacrifice, willingness, endurance, toughness, vulnerability, facing our fears . . . and the job is never over. Every brick that we use to erect that wall comes at a cost. The purpose of the wall is to allow leaders to see clearly what is happening around them and how to maneuver or carve a path in a minefield. The wall offers, to a certain extent, a bird's-eye view of the crisis maze. My only tactic at 13 was to switch seats with a cousin to avoid recalling those traumatizing moments of my childhood. And it worked.

In this last section, I will offer two different research concepts that could contribute to your own wall-building efforts. The first one is by the Center for Creative Leadership on the lessons learned from a crisis, which I believe can serve as your building blocks. The second are some soft skills offered by Koehn based on her analysis of historically-acknowledged crisis leaders.

The Center for Creative Leadership offered four lessons, or building blocks, learned from crisis.[27] They are:

27. Center for Creative Leadership, *Lessons Learned*, 4–5.

1. Compassion and sensitivity

A crisis can turn you into a harsh, defensive leader, or a soft, humbled one. The experience of hardship should make you compassionate and sensitive toward others who are experiencing a similar crisis. For example, our failed boat trip to Cyprus has raised my understanding, concern, and empathy toward migrants who risk their lives trying to cross the dangerous Mediterranean Sea from North Africa to the safe shores of mainland Europe. While I know that many people do not share this sentiment and can be aggressive and defensive toward illegal migrants risking their lives on a boat trip, I personally associate with their adversity. Attending an international conference on the Island of Malta in 2012, the conference participants were asked to sign up for various activities one afternoon. I, along with a handful of participants, chose to visit the holding place of migrants who were trying [but failed] to cross the Mediterranean. I was eager to listen to their stories and hear about their ambitions because of my shared experience.

2. Self-knowledge and perspective

A crisis can test your core abilities and shake your beliefs and values. A leader could either take advantage of the more vulnerable components of the crisis or uphold what is right and just. I have witnessed many leaders take advantage of a crisis to better position themselves. They manipulated and withheld resources for their own benefit. Authentic resilient leaders, particularly Christian leaders, should never forsake their values and belief systems, should always acknowledge their limitations and emphasize their skill-set to build that wall. A crisis also offers an opportunity to put things in perspective and unleash your self-awareness. For example, I have had issues with some of my friends who immigrated to the USA, Canada, Australia, or Europe, yet are very vocal against accepting new immigrants—now that they are citizens of their new homelands. There is a lack of perspective, self-awareness, and empathy when someone enters the door and wants to shut it to keep the comparable others out.

3. Limits of control

One of the most powerful building blocks is the understanding of what a leader can control during a crisis, and what is beyond her/his control.

While I am a strong advocate for the concept of self-fulfilling prophecy (SFP), I always remind my mentees that there are certain things that are outside the leader's control and should be relinquished. Otherwise, their futile attempts to control the uncontrollable factors in a crisis could become a destructive rather than a constructive force in building their resilience wall. Understanding some of the factors that cannot be controlled releases energy and stamina that could be used to manage the factors that are controllable. Perseverance can yield results only in matters that are manageable. For example, our youngest son who was living in Dublin, Ireland, during the pandemic, wanted to maintain his annual travel plans despite the COVID-19 lockdowns and shutdowns. He was continuously disappointed and frustrated with every new imposed travel ban and restrictions, canceled flights, and halted itinerary. A lot of energy was wasted trying to bypass these uncontrollable factors, including spending 14 days in a third country to be able to travel to the USA due to temporary travel bans between the US and Europe. Now that he is vaccinated, many of these uncontrollable crisis factors are more manageable.

4. Flexibility

Another important building chunk is our ability to be flexible during a crisis. This refers to our capacity to change and accept the changes as the new norm. Change is good; there is no change that does not carry some new opportunities. Albert Einstein is quoted saying: *"The measure of intelligence is the ability to change,"* thereby associating our ability to accept change with our intelligence. A leader's aptitude to embrace change, build on it, and look back on a crisis with positive reminiscences is crucial for erecting our resilience wall. For example, I used to travel internationally 2-3 times per month. In fact, I turned down two trips in the first two months of 2020—one to the USA and another to Lahore, Pakistan—because of my heavy travel itinerary scheduled for that year. Then in March 2020, total lockdowns and travel bans were enforced. I found myself sitting at home with very unfamiliar work arrangements, yet can share at least two positive change agents that I embraced. Physically, with the gym closed, I decided to jog or alternately walk daily for almost 5 miles (8 kilometers) regardless of weather conditions, followed up with a daily routine of resistance training to maintain the muscle mass. When the lockdown was eased off, I had lost almost 30 pounds (14 kilograms) and have been able to maintain this new lifestyle ever since. Cognitively, I managed to switch all my training materials to online and virtual learning management systems, and implemented at least five training modules and workshops with 85+ participants from around the globe (including my colleagues from Lahore!). Now I look back at the lockdown crisis as a changed leader with a positive attitude despite the negatives associated with this pandemic.

Koehn offers additional soft skills that could reinforce the building process.[28] Interestingly, Koehn attributes building resilience through continuous interaction with those around us. These include:

1. Acknowledge people's fears and encourage resolve

Koehn quotes from US President Roosevelt's 1933 inaugural speech during the Great Depression: "The only thing we have to fear is . . . fear itself."[29] Most people fear "fear." A resilient leader should address these fears, talk about them in the open, and work around them. It is a pre-emptive action to place "fear" in its rightful place and move forward, reminding people of what really matters rather than what cripples them.

2. Give people a role and purpose

Get people busy with activities that matter. Focusing on the mission of the organization will leave little room for fake news, rumors, and pessimistic outlooks. This is what Jesus Christ did with his disciples, as will be seen in chapter 10. I always remind people that every crisis has an end, and invite them to think about where they will be when it ends. Some choose to say "Away from all this," while others are challenged to respond "on top of things." Helping others may shift the focus from your own needs to those of others.

3. Emphasize experimentation and learning

The chaotic conditions accompanying any crisis may also be an opportunity to explore options that would never be considered under normal

---

28. Koehn, *Forged in Crisis*, 2–8.
29. Koehn, *Forged in Crisis*, 2.

circumstances. This is an important factor in building the wall, as the best ideas have always come through when the status quo is no longer the norm. Allow space for errors as a means for learning and building. Keep asking yourself and those around you: *"What are we learning from this?"*

4. Tend to energy and emotion

I have always felt that a crisis situation energizes me. This may not be the case with other individuals who indulge in an endless analysis of the outcome of the crisis. I recall a few years ago when I was sharing with our senior leadership team about a serious issue with the management of a neighboring country which I am responsible for the team. One of the members smiled and said: "I look forward to seeing how you will resolve this crisis." This was a clear message that my tenure reflects a personality that thrives during crisis . . . and so should you.

In this chapter, we contemplated seven sources of resilience, the *why, when,* and *how* of resilience, and several tools for building and maintaining our resilience wall. While many leaders, mainly in the ministry, may feel that resilience is unnecessary as they prefer to depend on faith practices, such as prayers, the response is that we need both. Jesus Christ built an incredible resilient wall yet prayed continuously, and so should we. In the next chapter, we will discover how our resilience wall could serve as a jumping pad for discovering exceptional opportunities during a crisis.

Recommended action points:

- Choose *hope* as the primary platform for your resilience wall.
- Tend to colleagues who are stuck in a crisis by acknowledging their unique learning opportunities and potential to emerge stronger.
- Differentiate between the controllable and uncontrollable factors in any crisis.

Chapter IV

Understand the Spiral Effect
of Discovering Opportunities

When written in Chinese, the word 'crisis' is composed of two characters.
One represents danger and the other represents opportunity.

(JOHN F. KENNEDY)[1]

IN THE MID-EIGHTIES OF the previous century, I had started my college studies in Cyprus and wanted to transfer to a good university in the USA. The tiny college in Cyprus had suddenly grown in size due to another influx of students coming from the Middle East to escape ongoing regional crises, and I was amongst those students. While the higher education level at the college was acceptable, I wanted a more challenging and rigorous experience, thereby started exploring my options. The choices were limited, as the college had a handful of credit-transfer agreements, mainly with universities on the East Coast.

Eventually, I landed at JFK airport in New York and took a shuttle to C.W. Post Campus of Long Island University, situated right in the middle of the so-called island. The shuttle dropped me at a large gate with all my belongings fitted into two heavy suitcases. With no one in sight, I carried the bags to the closest building—a dorm—and asked a total stranger if he could keep an eye on my luggage, as I made my way to the residence coordination building to find out where my new home for the next year would

1. Kennedy, *Remarks of Senator Kennedy.*

be. Fortunately, my room was in that first-sited building; unfortunately, I was registered as a freshman and not a transfer junior [and almost a senior] student, and that dorm was exclusively for freshmen.

My two roommates were from Greece, which was a nice surprise, as I was coming from Greek-speaking Cyprus with cultural similarities. But the wild atmosphere of that residence hall was unbearable. Loud parties, young freshmen excitedly starting their first semester, crowded hallways, and ongoing festivities infiltrated my otherwise quiet Cyprus life into the early hours of the morning. As a light sleeper, I could not get any proper sleep before 5-6 AM every day, only to get up and head to my courses by 8 o'clock in the morning. I tried to switch dorms but it was too late to do so that semester. I also needed to work to support my tuition, yet with sleep deprivation and lack of good food (I hated the cafeteria food), I was always out of energy.

It took me about two weeks to change this seemingly crisis situation around. My roommates and I rearranged our room so that each one could have a small private and quiet corner for studying and sleeping. I would play music on my Walkman headset (today's equivalent of an iPod) to lessen the noise pollution and try to get some sleep. We also bought a small fridge. I signed out of cafeteria food and started cooking a rotational menu every week. I found a job working four weeknights per week at the sign-in desk of another quieter residence hall from 1-7 AM. I used the idle night time to study while getting paid, and caught up to sleep in the afternoons and weekends. And I connected with a small local church that needed a volunteer to lead the youth work and help out with worship music over the weekends, which I gladly did in return for spending the weekends on the church campus and away from that freshmen dorm.

This may not sound like an impressive story unless you take the context into consideration. I was in my late teens, having just arrived in a foreign country alone, fleeing from a war-torn homeland with hyperinfla-tion, poor on many standards, entering a new educational system at one of the largest private universities in one of the wealthiest areas in the US, English being my second language, culturally shocked . . . I recall it took me three weeks to send a message back to my parents to inform them that I had arrived safely. In fact, I had accumulated enough resilience in my early childhood and teen years to turn the unfavorable conditions to my benefit. Others—and I know many—would have turned around and headed back to their homelands and lost out on the opportunity. That undergraduate degree received from Long Island University was an opener for greater and better future opportunities and continued education.

In this chapter, we will discuss the need to explore the opportunities available in any crisis, and how these opportunities can serve as a launching pad to introduce new windows and breakthroughs in mostly unfavorable contexts. Through research, experiential findings, and testimonials, there are always ample options as to what could be done in crisis situations and beyond. We will also be addressing the *learning* perspectives as a platform for assessing new opportunities in the midst of a crisis. With a strong resilience backbone, *leadership . . . in crisis* can become a positive platform and spiral catalyst for transformation.

I will commence with a recently published White Paper by the Center for Creative Leadership entitled: *Turning Crisis into Opportunity*.[2] The paper focused mainly on organizational transformation of what will come *after* the crisis, and placed the onus on leadership. During any crisis, leaders are faced with two choices: (1) retreat, or (2) reinvent the future. In simpler words, survive or thrive. The authors offer three strategies that can serve as a spiral effect for discovering opportunities and are summarized under three actions required in hardship situations.[3] These include:

1. *Articulate a bold and flexible vision.* Without vision, people will perish. These biblical words were written when God's people were in a crisis, trying to survive. Opportunities are best found when leaders reiterate their personal or organizational vision while allowing room for realignment. Enlarging the scope of the vision and introducing more holistic approaches could rekindle new opportunities. The required action is to build *Direction:*[4] Reminding yourself and your team on the agreed vision and ultimate goals. In arriving in the USA for my continued higher education, I had to keep reminding myself of the main objective—getting a prime educational experience regardless of the hardships, sleepless nights, unfavorable foods, long working hours, loneliness, and disparity.

2. *Cultivate a culture of innovation.* This is where team efforts are best depicted. The leader's role is to foster and encourage a culture of creativity and innovation, nurturing new avenues to navigate toward a

---

2. Pasmore et al., *Turning Crisis into Opportunity*, 1–18.

3. Pasmore et al., *Turning Crisis into Opportunity*, 9–14.

4. Pasmore et al., *Turning Crisis into Opportunity*, 9–10.

fresh future. This can only be done effectively when the team is co-ordinating and collaborating well, and the flow of communication is smooth. The required action is to strengthen *Alignment:*[5] Focusing all efforts on coordinating activities and achieving synergy. This requires a delicate balance between what you have to do versus what you like to do. In my university story, I put all my efforts into achieving the set goals while sacrificing what I enjoyed doing—at least for a limited time. The secret ingredient to synergy is doing what you have to do despite the hardship conditions and your own comfort.

3. *Lead change with empathy and integrity.* As a change agent, the leader must understand that role and pave the road so that new opportunities may emerge from within hardships. This requires a genuine, honest, and transparent attitude, which is not usually easy to adopt during crisis times. Patience coupled with firmness ensures that the needed changes are understood, essential, and that there is good buy-in from the team. The required action is to inspire *Commitment:*[6] Assuming responsibility for your own—and others'—destination. We tend to blame external—and often unknown—forces for our inability to achieve our goals; but in reality, most of our failures result from our lack of commitment to our vision and inability to embrace change as a needed step to discovering new opportunities. Change is good, regardless if we can realize that "goodness" when we are in the midst of change waves. My ability to change my mindset, way of life, pool of friends, and eventually receive an undergraduate degree from a renowned American university was key. All my efforts and cognitive empathy were committed toward unfolding that opportunity.

With these three strategies and *D-A-C* actions in mind, we can now revert the focus on the spiral effect as a basis for discovering opportunities in the midst of crisis to three main concepts: (1) our knowledge and access to information, (2) our resilient sustainability[7], and (3) our focus on positive meaning in every experience.[8]

---

5. Pasmore et al., *Turning Crisis into Opportunity*, 10–12.
6. Pasmore et al., *Turning Crisis into Opportunity*, 12–13.
7. Winnard et al., *Surviving or Flourishing?*, 303–15.
8. Wong, *Meaning Seeking Model.*

Knowledge-based opportunities

Based on our accumulated resilience and awareness of warning signals, *leadership . . . in crisis* is capable of utilizing knowledge, experience, and access to information to create or discover new opportunities. The question of whether opportunities are *created* or *discovered* continues to puzzle both researchers and practitioners, but there is an overall consensus that it is a perceptual issue (created vs. discovered) and that the balance is about 50:50 in either direction.[9] Regardless of this debate which is outside the scope of this book, knowledge provides the necessary tools for finding the right opportunities after a crisis subdues.

Winnard and colleagues provide a clear matrix on how access to information could foster the birth of new opportunities.[10] The four quadrants based on the accessibility and uncertainty of information stipulate four possible outcomes:

FIGURE 2

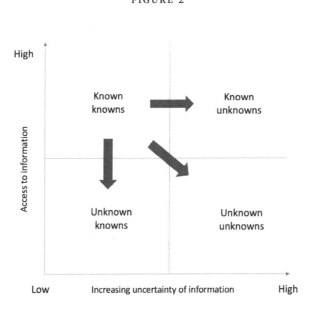

9. Guo and Bielefeld, *Social Entrepreneurship.*

10. Winnard et al., *Resilient Sustainability,* 1599.

Modified from Winnard et al.[11]

- *Low access/low uncertainty—Unknown knowns.* These represent knowledge and information that you or your team do not know that you possess, so they remain untapped or undiscovered. Such was the case with my English language skills when I arrived in the USA. Having spent some of my childhood and teen years interacting with American missionary kids, attending a British Quaker-run school in Lebanon, and British-influenced Cyprus, I had developed strong grammar and communication skills in the English language. The course evaluator at Long Island University was swift to discover this and differentiate me from other foreign students, claiming that my English accent was "neutral" and did not need any enhancement, unlike my other peers who transferred from the same college. I did not know these knowns until that moment.

- *Low access/high uncertainty—Unknown unknowns.* Such data is rarely discoverable, few people can claim knowledge of, are rare and difficult to anticipate. These double *unknowns* are the main reason why so many leaders fail to gain new lessons following a crisis; because of their high improbability, such opportunities remain untapped. I never realized the intensity of my college experience until years later, when I joined the MBA program and started unpacking some of the knowledge hidden within the resilience wall. These "unknowns" were a wealth of resources that simply needed to be unraveled.

- *High access/low uncertainty—Known knowns.* This is our comfort-zone area of knowledge and information we are certain about and are easily accessible. Unfortunately, many leaders function only within this quadrant, take decisions accordingly, and rarely take risks beyond the two *knowns*. I personally find this quadrant a killer of opportunities, and the only way out is to recreate and push its boundaries toward the other three quadrants. By continually accessing new knowledge through life-long learning and eliminating the ambiguities surrounding unconfirmed information, a leader can enlarge these boundaries and unravel new opportunities. How many times have we heard the phrase *"if only I had known this . . ."*? Here lies the opportunity to

11. Winnard et al., *Resilient Sustainability*, 1599.

push beyond this quadrant, slowly and carefully, toward uncertain territories.

- *High access/high uncertainty—Known unknowns.* These represent areas of partial knowledge but not the full picture. You can see and access the tip, but you are not sure what the underlying unknown comprises. It is like trying to figure out where a certain chittering noise is coming from in your home or office, and when you complete the discovery, you are more confident with your findings. Herein lies an area of growth and potential, when leaders are inquisitive to the point of learning new abilities. During my years at Long Island University, I was the only business major student on a 50 percent music scholarship, only because I knew I had the talent and some informal training, yet discovered its full potential when I auditioned as a vocalist and made it all the way to the elite Madrigal Singers. The alternative was to stand firm at the *known unknowns* without learning the capacity of my full potential.

Resilient sustainability

The next step in discovering or creating opportunities in the midst of a crisis is the concept of sustainability, which is usually accumulated through a trade-off between risks and opportunities. Actually, sustainability is the filter between unwanted and desired outcomes.[12] There is a complementary correlation between resilience and sustainability, although we have seen many sustainable organizations fail due to their lack of resilience, and many resilient firms discontinue because of the absence of long-term viability.

In a different research, Winnard and colleagues provide another matrix to compare short- and long-term resilient organizational sustainability.[13] I will transform this analysis into an individualized leadership perspective in times of crisis. The four quadrants are summarized as follows:

---

12. Winnard et al., *Resilient Sustainability*, 1599.

13. Winnard et al., *Surviving or Flourishing?*, 308–9.

FIGURE 3

Modified from Winnard et al.[14]

- *Low short- and long-term leadership resilient sustainability.* This is where leadership is *failing* and opportunities are simply limited to *optimizing* current avenues. When a leader is unable to provide even short-term resilient sustainability, the team or organization will not surpass the crisis—nor explore new opportunities. During a crisis, some leaders choose to lay low, not take any risks, and simply maintain the status quo until the crisis is over. Such leaders often find themselves outside the game, as they did not allow room to discover any type of opportunities arising from the crisis. I have seen this quadrant infiltrate several traditional organizations, where opportunities were limited to optimizing the existing activities without additional learning or opportunity breaks. This is when successful leaders and organizations convert into monuments—a place for people to visit, recall the glorious past, and move on.

14. Winnard et al., *Surviving or flourishing?*, 308.

- *Low short-term and high long-term leadership resilient sustainability.* This leadership model is focused on long-term *impact* while managing *change* in the short-term to achieve the set plans. The risk in this quadrant is to lose focus of important present opportunities and sacrifice them in lieu of visionary impactful sustainability. In such circumstances, leaders are only focusing their efforts on the next five years without paying attention to the here-and-now of the crisis opportunities. While such far-fetched optimism is commended, it is also unrealistic, as future opportunities can only be attained when discovered in the short-term. BlackBerry phones were such a case, where leaders were looking at the long-term impacting solutions of BBM but missing out on the short-term touch screen opportunities.

- *High short-term and low long-term leadership resilient sustainability.* With no long-term foresight, leaders are mainly trying to *survive* in the short-range while opportunities are *disruptive* in nature. The presence of temporary resilient sustainability may offer the necessary tools for endurance along with discovering immediate opportunities, but not sustainable in the long run. I am often asked by my team during a certain crisis why our actions are continuously disrupting rather than stable. The answer is that crises are disruptive, and unless leadership actions are equally unsettling so that people are on their toes and more creative, we tend to fall back to the routine. A drowning person will learn how to swim in seconds compared to months of swim-coaching lessons.

- *High short- and long-term leadership resilient sustainability.* The combination of short- and long-term resilient sustainability is the best quadrant to create and discover opportunities. The leadership perspective is that of *flourishing* coupled with *thriving* prospects at all levels. This is not always easy to maintain, particularly when surrounded by skeptical members. For example, some decisions I have taken during crisis times may appear to the team as not well-calculated within the scheme of things, but when I take the time to explain the long-term sustainable reasoning behind them, there is an immediate "Aha" moment followed by buy-in. This quadrant that best combines short- and long-term strategies and opportunities are bound to yield flourishing, thriving, creative, and visionary outcomes over time.

Positive meaning

The third concept is that of finding a positive meaning in every crisis situation, which is the gateway to discovering or creating opportunities. Viktor Frankl shared these possible opportunities in his concentration camp experience. In his own words:

> *Every day, every hour, offered the opportunity to make a decision, a decision which determined whether you would or would not submit to those powers which threatened to rob you of your very self, your inner freedom; which determined whether or not you would become the plaything of circumstance, renouncing freedom and dignity to become molded into the form of the typical inmate.*[15]

The challenge is how to look for a positive meaningful opportunity in the midst of a disaster. It goes back to our resilience wall—how we built it, how strong it is, and how high over the circumstances it towers. I still recall the comments of my colleague when we were facing a crisis situation, when he said: *"I am looking forward to how you would resolve this crisis."* He saw the positivity beyond my own limitations. Meaningful opportunities are always available; we simply do not see them. The more meaningful the opportunity is, the higher the success criteria. Without sinking into their philosophical values, Wong[16] presented yet another matrix to evaluate the success criteria of opportunities with four possible outcomes as follows:

15. Frankl, *Search for Meaning,* 75.
16. Wong, *Meaning Seeking Model,* 14.

FIGURE 4

Meaningfulness

Sacrificial
Opportunities

Ideal
Opportunities

Failure ———————————————————— Success

Wasted
Opportunities

Shallow
Opportunities

Emptiness

Modified from Wong[17]

- *Failure-Emptiness: Wasted Opportunities.* This is the most unfavorable situation any leader could confront. Successive failures coupled with a meaningless life purpose. This vicious circle is a downward spiral, as more failures tend to add to the empty hole of life, which tends to lead to more failures. An unfortunate situation that Frankl witnessed amongst many other prisoners of the concentration camp. This reminds me of bankruptcy situations where leaders lose focus on possible ways out or opportunities, and are sucked up by the whirlwind of circumstances. The best strategy leaders could adopt in this quadrant is to look for tiny opportunities and little wins that could stop the spiral downfall. One win at a time will build the success deposits and give some positive meaning to life.

- *Failure-Meaningfulness: Sacrificial Opportunities.* These tend to be good-hearted leaders with good intentions, yet their quest for successful opportunities lack the pragmatism required for their success. They sacrifice so much but keep on failing, ultimately losing even the

17. Wong, *Meaning Seeking Model*, 14-15.

meaningfulness of their opportunities. Many warlords who emerged during a crisis fall into this category. They are usually well-meaning, but fail to create successful opportunities. As a 16-year-old, I remember having this late-night conversation with an older teen before I left Lebanon for Cyprus to start my college years. He was insisting that we need to stay in Lebanon and carry arms for the "cause," while my argument was that we could be of better help with our intellectual abilities. That same year, Ghassan lost his life sacrificially for the "cause" and was forgotten. To shift toward a more successful quadrant, a leader needs to adopt practical opportunities over idealism.

- *Success-Emptiness: Shallow Opportunities.* There are a few fortunate leaders out there that are successful despite their emptiness. We see them daily, even among movie and rock stars who are extremely successful yet shock us one day with news of their suicide death, apparently stemming from their emptiness. This is by far the most difficult quadrant to be in, as the gratification of succeeding through shallow opportunities tend to num our feelings of purposelessness, and prolong the inevitable reality until it strikes . . . hard. Many successful but empty leaders shift toward philanthropy in pursuit of meaningfulness, and some find this positive significance and move toward the last quadrant. The real question to ask is: *What gets you out of bed every morning?* Is it your temporary success or your meaningful life?

- *Success-Meaningfulness: Ideal Opportunities.* The combination of successful meaningful opportunities is what has changed and continues to change the world. Leadership models, such as Mother Teresa and Nelson Mandela, are examples of people who had experienced all three quadrants mentioned above, yet managed to thrive with ideal opportunities that have, indeed, changed the world. In the movie *Invictus,* Mandela is quoted saying, *"Forgiveness liberates the soul. It removes fear. That is why it is such a powerful weapon."*[18] Such profound thinking from a person who was imprisoned for 27 years could only lead to successful opportunities and ignite a meaningful leadership journey. From a poor Albanian nun to an awarded Nobel Peace Prize and sainthood in the Catholic Church, Mother Teresa was able to shine in this quadrant in her ministry to leprosy and other rejects. Her legacy included unprecedented opportunities.

18. Mandela, *Invictus Quotes.*

Learning dimensions of resilience

Having looked at these three matrices on knowledge, sustainability, and positive meaning as opportunity platforms amidst crises, we will now shift focus toward the crisis-learning aspect of resilience. Research experts on resilience tend to agree that learning is vital to thrive during a crisis.[19] And learning is closely associated with our ability to change, adapt, and move on, which will be covered in chapters 7 and 8 under the concept of agility. How we respond to a crisis determines our learning outcome; it could be a creative solution to the current system, or an innovation to reinvent the future.[20] Resistance to change, on the other hand, can hinder the learning process.

To conclude this chapter, I will revert back to the Center for Creative Leadership White Paper[21] who offered six lessons that *leadership . . . in crisis* can learn in building their resilience wall and fostering opportunities.

1. *Do not let the crisis overwhelm you.* A crisis can absorb a leader and even deplete her/his resilience resources. This is the case with any sudden change in your routine life—starting university, having a newborn, starting a new job, moving to a new country . . . Make sure there is time for YOU, to rest, recover, and replenish. I recall commencing my doctoral studies while maintaining a fulltime job, having three dependent children and parents on my hands, juggling travels with personal and professional demands, and being required to find 30–40 hours per week for this doctoral program. The first month, I could not contemplate the idea of going to the gym or out for a jog. Then it hit me. If this was going to continue for the next four years, then I needed to adapt, and quickly. As Steven Covey wisely advised in his time management matrix: *Do not prioritize your schedule; schedule your priorities.*[22] This will allow you room for learning important lessons when least expected.

2. *Confront your failures and mistakes.* How can we possibly learn if we don't try and fail? In some cultures, it is a shame to fail or make mistakes. In others, it is ok to struggle or fail, multiple times, to the point

19. Strategic Direction, *Blending resilience and sustainability.*
20. Hu, *A Crisis-Opportunity Perspective,* 277.
21. Center for Creative Leadership, *Lessons Learned,* 5–6.
22. Covey, *Highly Effective People,* 81.

where success becomes meaningless and valueless. Somewhere in the middle lies our ability to learn, grow, and explore new opportunities. When we use the phrase: *"I am sharing this from my own experiences,"* those "experiences" include the good and the bad ones. The good ones are great lessons to adopt, and the bad ones are also great lessons to avoid! In one of our recent well-being team activities, all members were asked the same question: *What is stopping you from achieving your full potential?* Several honest participants responded: "fear of failure." The biggest dilemma in life is not a failure or mistake; it is parking your life where you failed and missing out on many future opportunities.

3. *Do not be defensive.* It is typical that during a crisis, people tend to blame external circumstances for their shortcomings instead of focusing on how to solve some issues. When a leader adopts a defensive attitude, s/he is blocking any opportunity to learn new skills that add stature to the resilience wall. Instead of defensiveness, choose inquisitiveness. An inquisitive crisis leader is someone who accepts her/his shortcomings, explores ways to improve them, and does not blame others for the surrounding problems. Unfortunately, most of the leadership models, including political leaders who are on the stage today, are defensive. They cannot express themselves without an apologetic attitude. And if there is an outlier who comes out in the open to admit a limitation, s/he will be scrutinized. In a crisis situation, blaming others is a weakness while accepting the blame is an opportunity for learning new lessons. Choose wisely.

4. *Be inquisitive.* As noted above, ask questions, seek counsel, and espouse humility. No one expects *leadership . . . in crisis* to know everything about everyone all the time. In fact, a pretentious leader will not last long in a crisis situation. People will call their bluff, and unfulfilled promises will backfire. I have been through multiple crises to know better than to assume I know everything. Expressing some vulnerability is human. Always ask questions to understand the context before offering advice. And seek a learning opportunity. I recall my first trip to China in 2013, a very intriguing eye-opening experience. While other members of the visiting delegation were defensive, my inquisitiveness was entertained. The one-child policy was particularly fascinating, especially when seeing on the streets one child surrounded by six adults (two grandparents from each side, and parents). Having

earned his respect, I posed the question to our guide: *"If you had the choice, how many children would you have?"* The answer was a lesson. *"Just one, as we cannot provide high-quality living and education to more than one."* Assumptions are corrected through inquiry.

5. *Build bridges.* While many leaders may consider crisis times as phases to focus vertically and internally, it is also a time to connect horizontally and externally. Crises bring humanity together. Rather than cuddling in your own comfort zone, it is time to open up, be relational, and share experiences. Learning opportunities are best depicted when shared with others. A few months ago, I called one of our contractors to discuss their billing hike. The owner-manager tried hard to explain the billing increase in their invoicing during the crisis. I responded with a couple of strategies that he could use without the need to increase the value of the invoice. His response was: *"I wish we had this conversation one year ago!"* People are keen on building bridges, connecting, seeking new opportunities, and learning together. No one wants to be alone in a crisis situation. In fact, we learn from one another, what worked and what didn't work.

6. *Reflect on lessons learned.* A crisis situation may be hectic and tense, but there is always an opportunity to evaluate and derive the important lessons learned from a certain situation. As mentioned earlier, experience is the real teacher, regardless if this experience had a positive or negative outcome. The lessons learned are key openers for future opportunities. I have heard many leaders exclaim that they do not want to repeat their "bad" experience after a crisis, such as the COVID-19 pandemic lockdown. I look back at the lockdown as a positive learning lesson that taught me to exercise daily, stick to an intermittent fasting diet, communicate daily with those that matter, conduct online workshops in three languages, and limit my screen time. Even writing this book was part of the lessons learned! Therefore, do not underestimate the significance of the opportunities available through learning experiences in crisis situations.

To conclude, in this chapter we looked at three strategies and actions to turn any crisis into a bundle of opportunities. We also explored three matrices that emphasized learning opportunities, mainly the quadrants relating to *High access/high uncertainty: the Known unknowns; High short- and long-term leadership resilient sustainability;* and *Success-Meaningfulness:*

Ideal Opportunities, and how these quadrants should be expanded to lessen the impact of their rivalry quadrants. And we summed up six lessons that leaders could learn in their resilience journey. Remember Viktor Frankl's words: *"What you have experienced, no power on earth can take from you."*[23]

Recommended action points:

- Adopt a clear vision that builds *Direction, Alignment,* and *Commitment* during a crisis.
- Aim for short- and long-term resilient sustainability that offers *flourishing* and *thriving* opportunities.
- Seek genuine learning dimensions resulting from a crisis.

23. Frankl, *Search for Meaning,* 90.

Chapter V

Achieve the Endurance of Marathoners

In the race for success, speed is less important than stamina.

(B.C. FORBES)[1]

I AM NOT A runner. As a teenager attending the British-Quaker school overlooking the hills of Beirut, my favorite Physical Education (PE) session was the cross-country run. It was a time to leave studies behind, school campus, friends, routine, reality . . . and simply follow the PE teacher into the woods for a free run. I did not mind the weather, as rain showers were always a refreshing ingredient. But it seemed that every time our PE teacher did not have something programmed for that session, we ended up in a cross-country run, roughly about once a month.

Although I enjoyed these runs in my early teen years, it was never a planned activity or a way of life. The runs freed me from the surrounding circumstances and allowed my imagination to take over as we trotted through the hilly woods around our campus. Little did I know that these wild unorganized runs would create an inside craving for sporadic running. Having a slim body with little weight to carry, running became an unintentional daily activity. I would run to the tennis court, the basketball court, to my friend's home, and to almost any walking-distance destination that did not mind this teenager arriving all sweaty and panting.

1. Forbes, *Quotes.*

This continued into my young adult years. I would never turn down an invitation to run, although it was rarely a systematically organized run. After getting married and parenting children, "running" became part of my gym time, trying to balance a personal-professional healthy lifestyle. Running on the treadmill in our country club was not the same, but it was convenient and manageable. When I traveled, I would ask the hotel reception for running trails, about 5 miles (8 kilometers) trails that would help me discover the surrounding area. Of the 60+ countries that I have visited so far, I have probably jogged in more than 200 cities on all five continents, ranging from running on the frozen Baltic Sea off the coast of the Gulf of Finland in Helsinki to the high cliffs of Anglesea in Victoria, Australia, on the Surf Coast Shire.

I was often asked about my running strategies. My answer was simple and unsophisticated: *"I run like Forrest Gump."* In that beautiful movie that combines all aspects and contrasts of recent American history and culture was the mantra *"Run, Forrest, run!"*—run from being bullied, run for the football team, run to save the wounded comrades during the Vietnam war, run across the country, run to meet Jenny, the love of your life . . . Seemingly irrational running, but in reality, very purposeful in each scene. The words of Tom Hanks impersonating Forrest Gump in his coast-to-coast running spree explains it best:

> *"That day, for no particular reason, I decided to go for a little run"*
> *Forrest tells a stranger on the bus stop bench. "I ran to the end of the road. When I got there, I thought I might run to the end of town. When I got there, I thought maybe I'd just run across Greenbow County. I figured since I run this far, maybe I'd just run across the great state of Alabama. That's what I did."*[2]

And that was my running style . . . just around the block, maybe to the end of the street, just to that bridge, crossing over the river, circle back on the other side of the river . . . Maybe the only strategy that I would admit to is that, after running about 30 minutes in one direction, I would need to retrace my path and arrive back to the starting point to avoid having to take a taxi back to my venue!

Then came the first ever Beirut International Marathon in Lebanon, November 2003. This was the first marathon organized in my home city, and I was not going to miss it. My running patterns had never exceeded 20-25 percent of the marathon distance, but I was determined to participate

2. Topel, *Forrest Gump Run.*

for nostalgic and national-pride reasons. I signed up for the 42.195 kilometers (26 miles) run, read some online tips on how to prepare myself for the race, and trained weekly for this seemingly easy task. In the months leading up to the race date, I was never able to run more than 30 percent of the total distance in one go, but nothing was going to stop me from partaking in this event.

The marathon organizers shared the race course about one week before the event. The map was to run around Beirut city twice using the same track until the distance was completed. So, my first target was to finish the first lap before those professional athletes, mainly from African nations, surpassed me to finish the race. In other words, I wanted to complete the first 13 miles (21 kilometers) before they finished the entire distance. The second target was to finish the marathon no matter what. Marathon organizers usually set a maximum time to complete the run; in Beirut's case, it was 8 hours. Doable, unless you have an injury along the way, or need to eat, drink, use the toilet, etc. in the next 8 hours.

Some of the important running tips I received were: (1) start slow, then gain speed along the way so that you end the race faster than the starting pace, (2) run at your own pace and do not couple up with any other runner as the two paces may differ, and (3) hydrate at every possible pitstop, even if you are not thirsty.

What was missing was an incentive, a drive, to help me complete the marathon no matter what. I decided to run for a cause: *Running for Bibles*. I wrote to all my friends and family around the globe asking them to sponsor each mile for the said cause. I raised about 6,000 dollars and now all I needed to do was to reach the finish line of the marathon. The *cause* provided the necessary motivation, stamina, and drive to compensate for my inadequate training.

That early morning, a colleague dropped me at the starting line, and in full confidence, I asked him to meet me at the finish line in four hours. I started the run with a slow pace, eventually surpassing many enthusiastic, yet tired, runners, while a handful of runners were gaining on me. I stopped to drink at every water pitstop, and made sure I deposited the plastic container in the garbage bins, unlike many other runners who were littering the streets. I completed the first lap in less than two hours, hence not being surpassed by the elite runners. Then I fumbled through the second lap. Slowly and consistently, I reached the last 10 kilometers of the run, now every bone and muscle hurting, and almost out of energy. By the last five kilometers, I was running at a slower pace than the starting pace, which was not a good sign. Hundreds of runners surpassed me in those final few miles just because they stuck to the first tip mentioned above, finishing the run at a faster pace than the starting one.

A little more than four hours from the start, I crossed the finish line. I had never stretched my body's tolerance to this level. It took me a few days to recover, and then I was ready to do it again in 2004, this time inspiring more than 80 people to run with me for the same cause. Having learned from the experience of the first marathon, I was able to finish the run with an improved 30 minutes time.

Although the opening story may not be impressive to those involved in ultra-marathon runs, such as Dean Karnazes[3] who would make my story seem insignificant, there are valuable leadership lessons acquired from this experience. First, you have no idea what kind of tolerance and endurance you comprise unless tested to its full extent. Second, with the proper cause and drive, your stamina can multiply your energy levels. And finally, as per the chapter's opening epigraph, speed is not as important as finishing the task.

Most athletic and fitness themes focus on three areas: *Strength, cardio,* and *stretching.* In *leadership . . . in crisis, strength* and body-building resemble *resilience,* the ability to build enough muscle mass to over-power (and over-tower) the waves of crisis. The *cardiovascular* exercises associate with *stamina,* which is a journey in endurance, perseverance, and tolerance. And *stretching* and flexibility are about *agility,* the capacity to maneuver and flex during crises, which will be covered in chapters 7 and 8.

In this chapter, we will be addressing the concept of long-term endurance, perseverance, and high tolerance, all under the theme of crisis-leadership stamina. Stamina is all about taming your body, mind, decisions, and upholding the consequences. But it does not come without perseverance, patience, and performance (hard work). From the world of sports, we will address the principles that I followed in running my first-ever marathon, and transform them into tools essential for *leadership . . . in crisis.*

But first, there is no denial that stamina must be associated with motivation. Finding the right motivational reason is the key behind a driving force to accomplish a goal. Derived from the Latin word movere, that is, movement or to move,[4] motivation is defined as the "energizing force that

---

3. Karnazes, *Utlramarathon Man,* 3–13.

4. Johnson, *Getting and Staying Involved,* 5.

steers people toward desired end states."[5] According to Bernard and colleagues, motivation is a "purposeful behavior that is ultimately directed toward the fundamental goal of inclusive fitness."[6] It is a driving force that feeds our stamina levels.

You can count on your endurance if your motivation levels are corresponding to your driving forces. Based on my doctoral research on motivation, once a cause is aligned to your values and mission, there is no limit to the "energizing force" that can produce extra effort.[7] Concepts such as *mission-driven* and *mission as incentive*[8] generate the added push required to complete a task, thereby combining extrinsic and intrinsic drivers to achieve the necessary synergy. It is important to adopt an extrinsic factor, such as a worthy cause to support (as in my case, *Running for Bibles*), in order to enhance the intrinsic drivers that we all possess. I usually label intrinsic motivators as a *sleeping giant inside each one of us* that can be awakened through the right extrinsic elements.

I will address five key strategies required for enhancing endurance levels, finishing the task, and overcoming the crisis. These are:

1. Discover your motivational cause

In his book entitled *Drive*, Daniel Pink attributes three chapters to talk about *Autonomy, Mastery,* and *Purpose* as elements of motivation.[9] *Autonomy* gives you the choice rather than independence. Many of us have witnessed this tension with our teenage sons and daughters, where they want to become independent (most of the time prematurely) whereas parents want them to develop their autonomy: taking responsibility for their own lives, decision, consequences, choices . . . To discover the true motivational cause behind endurance, there should be room for freedom to choose from alternative routes or plans of action, although the end result is mutually exclusive.

At least four of the six motivational theories that are highlighted in my own research attribute motivation at work to *Autonomy*.[10] These theories

5. Borgida and Mobilio, *Social Motivation*, 347.

6. Bernard, *Individual Differences in Motivation*, 129.

7. Bassous, *Factors that Affect*, 364–65.

8. Bassous, *Factors that Affect*, 376.

9. Pink, *Drive*, Chapters 4–6.

10. Bassous, *Factors that Affect*, 359–61.

include Maslow's[11] *self-esteem* and *actualization* needs, Herzberg's[12] *job enrichment* theory, McGregor's[13] *Theory Y* approach, and Hackman and Oldham's[14] *achievement* characteristics. Attributing autonomy is the first step in discovering a person's own motivational drivers and seeking to achieve them. Pink highlights four aspects of *Autonomy*: Task, time, technique, and team (4T's).[15] Once a person acknowledges the significance of the task and has the autonomy to achieve it, there is no turning back.

Our eldest son, George, is probably one of the most "staminized" people out there, working nonstop for one of the largest financial institutions in the world, based in their headquarters in NYC. During his childhood, George's athletic stamina was lagging, so we signed him up for several races, including the Beirut Marathon 10K Fun Run, and it did a phenomenal job in boosting his endurance levels. I recall a funny story when George was still in his early teens and we signed him up for a cross-country run at his school. He had just finished running the first of two laps, and as a proud father I ran along his side coaching him with statistics . . . "*there are three runners ahead of you . . . slow down on the uphill . . . accelerate on the downhill . . .*" His gasping response came back, those words I will never forget: "*Don't worry dad . . . I have a plan.*"

Given the necessary autonomy but a clear cause to accomplish, people should be free to task their plans that achieve the goal. I do not recall if George's plan worked or not, but I surely commend his autonomy to select his own task, time to implement it, his own technique, and if necessary, choose the right team to attain the cause. One last thought on *Autonomy*. It should never discourage accountability.[16] My son did not feel diminished that I was trying to prompt him with sports statistics; he acknowledged that he was accountable to himself and no one else. Discovering your own motivational cause is a personal journey of discovery, and no one else should make that journey on your behalf.

Pink's following chapter is about *Mastery*. I call it a process of aligning your extrinsic and intrinsic values. One of the main demotivators is when a leader asks someone to accomplish something that they do not possess

11. Maslow, *Understanding Human Behavior*.

12. Herzberg, *Nature of Man*.

13. McGregor, *The Human Side*.

14. Hackman and Oldham, *Work Redesign*.

15. Pink, *Drive*, Chap. 4.

16. Pink, *Drive*, Chap. 4.

the set of skills to attain. It simply adds to their frustration and failure levels. Likewise, an assigned task that is below the mastery level could lead to boredom and lack of enthusiasm to attain the goal. Had I chosen to run the Beirut Marathon 10K Fun Run rather than the full marathon in 2003, I would have never discovered my real capacity and endurance, simply because the 10K Fun Run would have been within my comfort zone.

Pink highlights three aspects of *Mastery*: Mindset, pain, and asymptote.[17] The first two are quite obvious in building stamina levels, but what is an asymptote? For geometry lovers, it is the relationship between a straight line and curve that tries to approach the straight line, but never intersects it. In simpler terms, it is a lifetime quest to reach the goal but never traverse it. In the Christian faith, we talk about Christ-like behavior, but know that we can never, as frail humans, achieve His transcendent behavior, although people spend a lifetime trying to pursue it. Such motivational factors are crucial for stamina levels.

The final one is *Purpose,* probably the most important aspect of finding the right cause. It poses questions pertaining to the goals behind the cause, articulating the right words, and adhering to a set of policies.[18] In my own research on motivation, I discovered that mission and purpose were closely associated. The only cause worthy of your motivational endurance is the one embedded in your value system, the one you have been brought up with, a passionate and transcendent one. Finding that purpose is finding the keys that unleash the source of endurance and tolerance.

For me in 2003, it was *Running for Bibles* that prompted my endurance to finish the marathon in a little over four hours. Choosing the "cause" was my own choice, a cause embedded in my value system since childhood, as a Gideon businessperson later in life, and at my current vocation with the Bible Society. The "cause" provided me with the autonomy to pursue its acclamation using my own route, increased my mastery over my body's tolerance levels (and for those runners out there, mastery over the mind is as relevant), and it was purposeful.

Now moving on to the next strategy . . .

17. Pink, *Drive*, Chap. 5.
18. Pink, *Drive*, Chap. 6.

2. Start slow, then accelerate

There is a well-known children's fable (I think known in most cultures)—where a turtle challenges a rabbit to a race.[19] The rabbit takes off quickly at the start line and disappears while the turtle slowly moves forward. Thinking that the competition was over, the rabbit starts losing focus, wasting time, taking a nap . . . and then resumes the race to the finish line, only to find the slow steady-moving turtle had already crossed the finish line and won the challenge.

This story is a good indication of how to practice endurance and stamina rather than depend on speed. Although the latter is an important ingredient in any challenge or crisis, one should never start at a faster pace than the finishing pace. That was my mistake during the 2003 marathon, which I learned from and adapted in 2004, hence improving my time by about 30 minutes. Starting slow is always a problem, as the adrenaline and excitement levels may stimulate any athlete to ignore this strategy. Don't get carried away. Basketball superstar Kareem Abdul-Jabbar acknowledges that "*Your mind is what makes everything work.*"[20] This is the classic mind-over-body struggle.

To start slow and build endurance that can sustain *leadership . . . in crisis,* medical doctor Mary McCarthy[21] offered some tips on how to maintain stamina during a crisis, specifically during the COVID-19 pandemic. Her first tip was to train our minds and enhance our mental toughness, which "*involves an unshakable self-belief, resilience, motivation, focus, and ability to perform under pressure and manage physical and emotional pain.*"[22] This advice resonates with what was already mentioned in the first strategy regarding the motivational cause, and builds up the necessary speed and ability to deal with the pain.

The last 10K of the 2003 marathon run were excruciating. Every bone and muscle in my body was aching. I recall asking paramedics to spray Deep Heat on my joints to numb the pain, but in the last 5K, I jokingly asked the last pitstop paramedic to spray my entire body, including my head, to stop the mental and physical pain. But it was amazing how the pain disappeared the moment you spot the finish line. Suddenly, unfamiliar

19. Moral Stories, *Rabbit and the Turtle.*
20. McCarthy, "*I didn't train for this,*" 10.
21. McCarthy, "*I didn't train for this*" 10–13.
22. McCarthy, "*I didn't train for this,*" 10.

stamina is injected into your body and you start running—even sprinting—to cross that finish line.

You have probably heard the term "quit while you are on top." Many athletes abide by this strategy. They retire when they are ahead of the game, starting slow, accelerating along the way, and stopping when they have reached the climax of their performance. Such endurance building is remarkable, particularly when you know when to stop. Mentally, it requires maturity and ego suppression to let go of success, recognition, fame, and a string of winning streaks, but it is the right strategy once compared with a slowing-down paced athlete who keeps getting humiliated by a much younger competitor in each event.

Starting slow and then accelerating requires persistence to cross the finish line toward the post-crisis phase with minimum damage. If our muscles hurt, or if the crisis conditions take their toll, one should ignore the pain and persist onwards.[23] Persisting in times of crisis, as in running a marathon, requires proper planning and implementation, deliberation, and decisions. It is not easy. You start slow to make sure that every step is concrete and secure, and once the confidence is built, you can accelerate the speed.

McCarthy continues her argument of mind over body by inviting athletes to think positively throughout the crisis, visualize the track and finish line, plan the hurdles along the way, and manage the pressure.[24] *Think positively*. How is that possible when you are already tired from the first 5K and still have 37K to go? Interestingly, the human body is a slow-moving machinery that starts running smoothly after it warms up, so give it time. *Visualizing*[25] the race track from a bird's-eye view provides perspective, both in a race and in a crisis using your resilience wall. *Expect setbacks*,[26] as not every planned activity will be implemented and is subject to changes. *Managing pressure*[27] is part of any crisis, but as leaders accumulate higher endurance levels, they can persevere even in difficult circumstances.

One of the best rewards a marathon runner experiences is when s/he is passing exhausted fellow runners along the race track, but one of the

---

23. Thürmer at al., *Times of Crisis*, 2165.

24. McCarthy, *"I didn't train for this,"* 10–11.

25. McCarthy, *"I didn't train for this,"* 11.

26. McCarthy, *"I didn't train for this,"* 11.

27. McCarthy, *"I didn't train for this,"* 11–12.

worst feelings is when s/he is surpassed by others. So, start slow, then accelerate, but do so at your own pace.

3. Find your own pace

Determining your own pace to maintain and not deplete endurance levels is crucial. Ultra-marathoner Dean Karnazes, in his chapter on *The Ultra-Endurance World* began with this opening statement: "*Just as the boundaries of technology are being pushed at an accelerated rate, so, too, are the frontiers of human endurance.*"[28] To stretch boundaries to their extent, a runner—and a leader—must regulate the pace to ensure that the resources are sustainable during a race—or a crisis—to reach the set destination. Each person, team, organization, and entity must find its own pace during a crisis and preserve its energy level and resources throughout the crisis phases.

From my running experience (and I know that many readers who are also runners can relate to this), I have gotten accustomed to a certain running rhythm after the first 2-3 miles when my breathing becomes systematic, my lungs are inhaling and exhaling the right amount of oxygen, I am not panting, my legs are trotting in an orderly fashion, and my mind is wandering off with positive thoughts and creative ideas. At that pace, the brain is no longer counting every painful step taken nor worrying about the remaining distance; rather, a feeling that you are an efficient locomotive takes over—at least for a while. It is like transforming your body into a human-machine.[29]

I would call this systematic pace the *hybrid pace*. Similar to a hybrid car when it reaches a certain speed and leveled elevation where energy, resources, and speed are complementary. Achieving that *hybrid pace* requires knowing your bodily [and organizational] capacity, the time frame in which a runner [or team] could glide in that mode, and how to keep replenishing resources to maintain the perseverance. Karnazes referred to ultra-marathon runners (those who run 100+ miles or so mainly on an auto-pilot *hybrid pace*) as having a unique level of commitment, determination, and can endure high physical and emotional pressure.[30] Pacing yourself through your commitment to the cause, determination to reach

---

28. Karnazes, *Utlramarathon Man*, 207.

29. Karnazes, *Utlramarathon Man*, 207–8.

30. Karnazes, *Utlramarathon Man*, 208.

the destination safely, and maintaining optimal endurance levels are key strategies for enhancing stamina during crises.

On the other hand, *pace-setting* is considered to be a leadership style that many leaders, including myself, tend to adopt. This behavioral concept was introduced by several leadership researchers who argued that leaders model the way forward, the speed at which to achieve the destination, and the shared vision.[31] But such behaviors may also be frustrating and demeaning, as not all team members possess the same stamina to maintain the pace. While one person may be satisfied with the pace, a cohort may be struggling, while another may have the potential to go at an even faster pace.

There is a story mentioned in Dave Kraft's book entitled *Leaders who Last* about a hunter who was traveling with a group of people in Africa, pushing them daily to cover a good distance.[32] One dawn during the journey, he started off again but no one joined him. Angered and frustrated, he asked the ungrateful group why they were not moving. One of them answered: *"We are waiting for our souls to catch up to our bodies!"*[33] *Pacesetting* is not always an effective strategy and may backfire.

Having endurance and stamina is a great gift, but you should always respect your body and listen to the signals your mind is sending out, especially when you are running at a faster pace than your own. A marathoner's endurance is an excellent resource in any organization that thrives on highly motivated and hardworking individuals that are driven to achieve personal and organizational goals. However, that should never be confused with workaholism which may result in burnout and chronic depression. I have seen it happen in many organizations, and worse, I have seen it happen in many Christian ministries and missions, which I labeled in the introduction as "ministriholic" or "missionholic" individuals.

Find your own pace. *Pacing* yourself is key for maintaining stamina levels that outlive a crisis. *Pacing* provided Nelson Mandela with the necessary endurance to tolerate wrongful imprisonment for 27 years and then be released to lead South Africa's divided people who witnessed firsthand that *"this man was showing that he could forgive, totally . . ."*[34] *Pacing* gave Tanzania's injured runner, John Stephen Akhwari, the ability to finish the 1968

31. Kouzes and Posner, *Leadership.*
32. Kraft, *Leaders who Last,* 71.
33. Kraft, *Leaders who Last,* 71.
34. Carlin, *Invictus,* 222.

Mexico City Olympics marathon one hour after the winner, saying *"My country did not send me 5,000 miles to start the race . . . they sent me 5,000 miles to finish the race."*[35] Pacing at the mere human race pace, Jesus Christ was able to absorb our inadequacies, love us beyond human understanding, guide us through our life crises, and declare on the cross, *"It is finished."*[36]

4. Replenish your energy levels continuously

I remember this strategy very well from running the first marathon. The race was starting at 7 AM, and there I was eating pasta at 5 AM, as I was told that carbohydrates would provide long-term energy for the approximate 4000-calories depleting event. When the race started, I drank water at every pitstop, even though there was no need to quench my thirst at the start of the run. But after crossing about half the distance, the human body would be dehydrated and require liquids at a quicker rate than the start, so having some reserve was necessary. Close to the end of the marathon, some runners would be having "mirages" of water pitstops due to the low energy levels.

Another tactic is to avoid high-sugary snacks during the run. As in marathons all over the world, many organizations and even well-meaning spectators offer amateur runners [like myself] a little snack, and many tired and hungry runners would kill for a bar of chocolate. That is the worst type of resource replenishment, as the artificial sugar would offer only a temporary spike in energy to be followed by a dramatic drop in the body's blood sugar level. The alternative is to replenish with naturally sweet supplements, such as bananas, dates, or apples. Fruits in general contain more nutrients than just sugar, such as fibers, vitamins, and minerals[37]—all excellent replenishing ingredients for continued performance.

One last piece of advice is to never go for an energy drink. These boosting artificial drinks are detrimental to endurance and stamina levels. They only offer very short-term quenching but have an addictive kickback of wanting more when their effect evaporates. Instead, replace such drinks with natural fruit juices or simply with water. In organizational settings, carbohydrates resemble sustainable resources, such as long-term reserves and secure investments; quenching thirst with water are our daily

---

35. Olympics, *Superhuman Spirit.*
36. John 19:20 (NIV).
37. Kadey, *Healthiest Fruits.*

supplements and income flows; fruits could be our short-term savings and assets. Whereas artificially sweet snacks and energy drinks are like high-interest shark loans that quickly turn against you and deplete resources at a faster rate.

Replenishing energy levels and resources is crucial for *leadership . . . in crisis*. Although crisis leaders understand that every crisis has an end, the onus to function and endure the challenges throughout the crisis phases and beyond lies on their shoulders. The reality is that resources are limited, particularly during crisis times, and replenishment requires preemptive planning, decision-making, and implementation to ensure sustainability.

Thürmer and colleagues offer three important strategies to adopt when managing a crisis: *deliberate*, *decide*, and *persist*.[38] There is always a trade-off in making short- and long-term decisions on the use of resources during a crisis—staff, finances, supplies, etc. That is why it is important to involve your team or main stakeholders in decisions pertaining to personal and organizational energy levels. For example, at the beginning of the COVID-19 pandemic lockdown in early 2020, very few organizations took preemptive measures on the use of their resources. Instead, they continued depleting their reserves by operating business-as-usual until it was too late, and many required bailouts to survive.

Deliberating effectively in times of crisis requires gathering all the relevant information before making a decision.[39] This is not always possible, as some decisions need to be taken urgently. Seek counsel from the team members or other experienced people, even for urgent decisions that may affect endurance levels. I recall getting the best advice for preserving my energy levels during the 2003 marathon from a slightly older experienced lady, who had previously run other marathons in different cities. Her advice was invaluable for maintaining some energy levels to the end.

Deciding for the best outcome in times of crisis ensures the proper balance between scarce resources and the overall good of the person, team, or organization.[40] The trade-off has to be weighed carefully and communicated transparently. There is always a tendency for stakeholders to question a leader's decision on resource allocations during crisis times. This is normal due to high levels of uncertainty and should not reflect mistrust. Ensuring

38. Thürmer at al., *Times of Crisis*, 2157.
39. Thürmer at al., *Times of Crisis*, 2157–60.
40. Thürmer at al., *Times of Crisis*, 2160.

that decisions are balanced and resources are safekept for additional unknowns is wiser than being carried away by short-term wins.

Having participated almost every year in the Beirut Marathon since the first one in 2003, I witnessed every single time those enthusiastic amateur runners who took off at full speed at the start of the race, only to find them breathless on the sidewalk a few miles down the track. I would start the race at a very slow pace, even a walking pace due to the high traffic of runners, and slowly accelerate based on my endurance level. Deciding on the best outcome of the overall race is more important than feeling you are ahead for a few miles and then dropping out of the competition due to lack of energy.

Persisting in times of crisis regardless of external pressures and personal discomfort is key.[41] Persevering and keeping the end in mind is one aspect of balancing resource levels. Try to create a mental image of what the future would look like if you had maneuvered your way through a crisis and are now looking back at the bumpy ride with a smile. In my first marathon experience, and during the second lap of Beirut city, there was a downhill which I gladly embraced and simply let myself go, running down the slope. When I reached the bottom of the hill, every lumbar muscle went into an excruciating spasm. I could hardly walk—forget running. With a few miles still to go, I persistently reignited my energy, walking slowly at first, then faster until I was able to start jogging all the way across the finish line with just enough energy to enjoy my win . . . and finish the task.

5. Finish the task

Once you see the finish line, everything changes. Your energy levels suddenly escalate, your morale, self-esteem, and your mind are dancing with joy. It is incredible how limping and hurt runners suddenly jump energetically and zoom through the finish line, putting behind their hours of agony and mind-war games. This scene reminded me of a similar one, when my wife delivered our eldest son after a few complicated last weeks of pregnancy. The doctors had to perform a C-section, and my wife was brought back from the recovery room groaning with pain. A few minutes later the nurse wheeled in our baby boy and placed him on her chest. Suddenly her pain-filled sounds were replaced with cheerful chitters, having now seen the accomplished mission.

41. Thürmer at al., *Times of Crisis*, 2160–61.

Finishing the task is highly rewarding, as is surviving and thriving through a crisis. But during a marathon or a crisis, there are credible reasons to find excuses to simply quit. The most common reason is the absence or ignorance of the prerequisite condition of building our resilience wall prior to the event. If we are not equipped or trained properly to engage in the task, it may very well end as an unfinished one. This is followed by our motivation—our drive—to accomplish the task through our commitment to a meaningful cause. And finally comes our endurance and stamina levels, maintained through proper strategies and balanced use of our resources. Without these, a leader may find many excuses and cite logical examples to relinquish the task *when the going gets tough.*

Although Pink's book on *Drive* is geared toward workplace motivation, he offered some advice for staying motivated in a fitness program, which I believe are relevant for leaders seeking to complete the task.[42] These four tips include:

1. *Set your own goals:* If you can run a full marathon, then that's great. If not, there are other options, such as half-a-marathon, 10K Fun Run, and even a 5K run. The basic idea is to undertake a task that is within your resilience, motivation, and endurance bracket. If you aim at something that is double or triple your capacity, you are bound to fail. I had struggled with this decision when in some years, and having run 26 miles before, I would not sign up for the full marathon, knowing that I was not fully prepared to undertake the task and had to settle for half-marathon runs.

2. *Avoid the treadmill:* Although this tip cannot be generalized, I would agree with it to a certain extent. Running in your own place is not the most exciting or motivating activity compared to walking or running outdoors, where you can see the accomplished landmarks, enjoy the scenery, and get fresh air instead of indoor recycled gym air. Now the new treadmills are quite advanced and monitor the runner's progress (and you can watch TV or Netflix at the same time), but it is not the same as being outdoors. It is not the same as running on the frozen Baltic Sea off the coast of the Gulf of Finland in Helsinki, where I had to keep my eyes on the fishing holes in the ice so as not to trip into one!

42. Pink, *Drive*, Part 3.

3. *Keep mastery in mind:* Exercising provides renewable energy; it clears our minds and energizes our stamina. I usually come up with the best ideas when I am running (the idea to write this book is just one example). Similarly, new challenges in life enhance our motivation levels and our feeling of self-worth. Dealing with multiple crises sharpens our minds and our abilities to function creatively under pressure, and come up with innovative solutions to problems. Such mastery is not always available when we function within our comfort zones.

4. *Reward yourself:* Once you have accomplished the task, enjoy the moment and record your victory. Choose a meaningful reward to emphasize the importance of the finished task. Having three boys, I never expected gifts to pour on my lap on Father's Day. But we did put in a Father's Day tradition when my boys were old enough to run a few miles. Every year, we would go for a Father's Day cross-country run of about 12 kilometers (8 miles) around our home area. It was a unique circuit that had a lot of valleys and hills to cover, and passed through several villages. The first few years, I was always coaching the boys similar to a drill sergeant, but that quickly changed as we all grew older and I was the last one in after the run. But still, a very rewarding Father's Day tradition.

To sum up, this chapter addressed the endurance required to lead in crisis situations by adopting some of the strategies that long-distance runners use. Stamina is compared to cardiovascular exercises that provide high-level endurance, tolerance, and energy. The five strategies discussed included *discovering your motivational cause, starting slow then accelerating, finding your own pace, replenishing your energy levels continuously,* and *finishing the task.* Such strategies are applicable to *leadership . . . in crisis* as they provide relevant tools for handling an overwhelming situation with high levels of uncertainty. As Nelson Mandela wisely said: *"It always seems impossible until it's done."*[43]

Recommended action points:

- Find your true motivational cause that offers you *Autonomy, Mastery,* and *Purpose* in a crisis situation.

43. Mandela, *Quotes.*

- Check your resource levels continuously to avoid running out of stamina during a crisis.

- Seek to navigate through a crisis, finish the task, and claim the reward.

Chapter VI

Cultivate Stamina that Works in Crises

The secret of endurance is to remember that your pain is temporary
but your reward will be eternal.

(RICK WARREN)[1]

MY EARLY BUSINESS CAREER was quickly elevating through our Group
of companies, as I was seeking to become the Executive Vice President.
I would jump at any opportunity which my peers would be reluctant to
undertake. Local and international travels and assignments would intrigue
me, although I had just become a parent and needed to be around the family more often.

In 1995, the President and CEO of the Group asked me if I was willing to travel to a conservative country in the Arabian Peninsula to open
a branch for our company with a local partner. Without any hesitation,
I responded positively. I had never traveled to that country and felt that
the entrepreneurial experience would enhance my career. Traveling to a
new country, meeting new people, and learning about its business culture
seemed interesting. I had undertaken a similar assignment earlier that year
by traveling to Accra, Ghana, for the same purpose, and that trip to West
Africa was a great learning experience.

This Arabian Peninsula country had no cash restrictions at its borders,
so I was instructed to carry ten thousand dollars in cash from our cashier to
quickly purchase all the office equipment and get things started. My flight

1. Warren, *Quotes.*

was scheduled for Thursday evening, and I headed to the airport and embarked on the flight as I had done multiple times before. When we landed, I passed through immigration and then toward border customs. Since this was a conservative closed country, border customs officers scrutinized all my belongings, looking for any prohibited or unconventional items.

I was asked about the amount of cash I was carrying, and I confidently replied, knowing that it was fully legitimate in this country. Yet, I was requested to undergo additional screening to check the authenticity of the bills I was carrying. Out of the 100 $100 bills checked through a manual machine, one bill would not pass. The border officer called his colleagues and started contemplating this issue. I remained obliviously calm and unaware of the seriousness of the situation.

Eventually, I was escorted to the head of police at the airport. After a few routine questions, I signed a statement without knowing exactly what it contained. I later learned that the police chief wrote a short report stating that I was attempting to test the security level of the airport borders by putting one counterfeit bill into a bundle. Suddenly, two policemen appeared out of nowhere, asking me to hand over all my belongings, belt, money, phone, and luggage to our local partner, who had now joined me and was panicking to no avail. They escorted me to a transport vehicle as I was being transported to a downtown department that dealt with counterfeit currencies.

It suddenly dawned on me. I was being arrested in a foreign and strange country around midnight, with no family or friends around, no one knowing what was happening to me, and now being escorted to God-knows-where, with no means of communication or ability to negotiate using a common language. A quick image of the 1978 movie "Midnight Express" came to mind, where a young student was imprisoned in a Middle Eastern country and subjected to all kinds of austerities.

This was not happening to me. I just wanted to wake up from this nightmare and see myself behind my fancy office desk, bossing people around, and being served my usual black coffee. This scenario was only a few hours before. Yet now I was in the back of a vehicle on a dark, lonely desert road between the airport and downtown, being escorted by two policemen to an unknown destination. Bizarre ideas started racing through my head. Maybe I should jump out of the vehicle and disappear into the wilderness. Or simply go into a silent mode in objection to my ill-treatment. But I held my ground, reciting a little prayer throughout the road trip until we reached the destination.

Crying desperately to God in the middle of the night on a desolate desert road in a baren strange country was my only life-saving raft, which I held onto earnestly. It was almost dawn on Friday morning when we reached our destination. Since this country's weekend was Friday and Saturday, I knew that I was doomed to spend the "weekend" incarcerated before there would be any hope of explaining my case. I recited my prayer as we disembarked the vehicle.

The two policemen escorted me to the officer on duty. They jokingly handed over the paperwork to him, sarcastically saying that they found ONE "wrong" bill on me. I immediately picked up the signals they were sending, that this situation was not as serious as the airport police had indicated. The officer-in-charge reciprocated with another humorous remark, and suddenly the atmosphere was friendlier. He asked me to recite what had happened, which I gladly did. Up till that point, I did not realize the allegations made against me by the chief of police were serious yet baseless claims.

Thankfully, I was never hand-cuffed throughout the process. Upon the request of the officer-in-charge, I picked up a pen and started writing my statement with my own words, explaining exactly the truthful circumstances. I was now offered tea to relax my tension, and asked who was our local sponsor partner. I had no phone or records on me, but by pure divine intervention, his name and phone number were mentioned in the airport report.

The officer-in-charge picked up the phone and to my surprise, rang and woke up the local partner, asked him to come and collect me, on the condition that I would still need to make a full statement on Sunday morning. A couple of hours later, though sleepless, I was enjoying a cup of coffee with our local partner. Sunday came and I gave my full statement, conducted the business operations I was sent to do, then left the country on Monday evening. To me, that officer-in-charge, although remaining nameless, was an angel sent by God to uphold my righteous case.

This is not the end of the story . . . A few months later, I was asked to make that same trip again. Recurring images of my previous crisis experience were racing through my mind. Any other rational person would have never contemplated the choice twice. Forget it! But I was relentless and went ahead for this second trip, and it was uneventful. I learned that overcoming one crisis does not necessarily mean that the same crisis conditions may repeat, although our minds may cripple us from trying to face it again. Such worries are usually baseless.

This is still not the end of the story . . . A few months later, our local partner called to inform me that the counterfeit department called him to come and collect the "wrong" bill. Apparently, it was an old 1936 print that was not recognizable within the modern counterfeit detecting machines. Since that experience, I have never traveled with cash under any circumstances. I would rather beg for money than carry it!

Panicking or overreacting in a crisis situation is never helpful. While my story may sound absurd to me first, and maybe to you, any wrong or inappropriate outburst or reaction may have diverted the outcome to unwarranted consequences. In any crisis situation, our reaction is probably more detrimental than the crisis itself. Had I decided to take things into my own hands, jump out of the vehicle, or try anything stupid, the results would have been devastating. The ability to withstand a quick unthought-through reaction requires patience, calmness, grit, and . . . stamina that works in a crisis.

This chapter is about acquiring stamina, but not any stamina—one that is effective in a crisis situation. While in the previous chapter we focused on strategies for enhancing endurance, tolerance, and perseverance, this chapter offers insights on attaining a holistic collective well-rounded stamina level that *leadership . . . in crisis* is in dire need of. We will explore tactics that preserve much-needed energy, balance input-output, and gain traction during unstable times.

Before we indulge in these crisis leadership strategies, I want to explore a historical event as a case study. Zapping through the television channels, I came across a World War II movie that I had seen before: *Dunkirk* (2017). Basically, the movie is a sad story about the Allied forces, mainly the British who were losing the war against Germany in mainland Europe in 1940, and were evacuating the old continent back to the English island. The exodus was riddled with ambushes, death, failed attempts, yet some success and heroic stories. At first, it may seem like a huge failure of managing a crisis, but the end result was the evacuation of 300,000 British soldiers across the English Channel.

Reynolds conducted a generational comparative analysis that compared the stamina level of the British people during World War II, particularly the story of *Dunkirk* with the recent tackling of the COVID-19 pandemic.[2] In the *Dunkirk* event, every abled British citizen with a sailing boat took off across the English Channel to save the stuck Allied soldiers on the French seashore of *Dunkirk* as they were being targeted by German

2. Reynolds, *The Dunkirk Delusion*, 34–38.

warplanes. It was a heroic episode of pure and unplanned endurance. But in reality, it was the lowest point of defeat in WWII for the Allied forces, which prompted Britain's newly appointed Prime Minister, Winston Churchill, to warn the House of Commons that *"wars are not won by evacuations."*[3] From that point onwards, victory was imminent.

Stamina levels are no longer the same in this era, which is quite disturbing and should be reinstated. Many younger generations—millennials, Generation Z, Generation Alpha . . .—are not prone or exposed to high levels of stamina. Even older generations, including the Baby Boomers, have gotten accustomed to an easy life, where a crisis is limited to a short-term drop in the stock markets or loss of electric power for a few hours due to a storm. The Greatest Generation of WWII no longer exists. Therefore, I propose that stamina must be restored by adopting the following leadership strategies.

Preserving energy

Stamina is best described as a *"mental and physical ability to sustain an activity for a long period."*[4] Energy, an integral component of stamina, in science is best described in Einstein's famous formula: $E = mc^2$.[5] Simply put, energy is a result of a combination of mass, or quantity, and multiplied speed. In a study of Kumasi Polytechnic in Ghana, the researchers attributed the following new understanding of $E = mc^2$.[6]

- E is the organization's energy, capacity, grit, and sturdiness
- m represents the mass, the people, resources, and competencies
- c is the conductor of the organizational energy, the leadership
- ^{2} represents the leader's influence and effect on the organization.

The authors further explained this transformed scientific formula to indicate that the most effective energy level of any organization is the balance between concern for the people (m) and concern for the task (c^2).[7]

---

3. Reynolds, *The Dunkirk Delusion*, 37.
4. Zamzow, *Build your Stamina*, 60.
5. Wikipedia, *Mass-Energy Equivalence.*
6. Effah et al., *Managerial Leadership and Energy*, 97.
7. Effah et al., *Managerial Leadership and Energy*, 97.

During a crisis, leadership is required to preserve energy by achieving an equilibrium between their people's well-being and the organizational tasks that require actionable implementation. During the many crises witnessed in my life, I have seen many organizational leaders skew this equilibrium. Some would tilt their energy toward their people while ignoring the tasks that required follow-up, thereby missing out on some important deadlines and landmarks. Others would continue to be task-oriented without any consideration for their people's changing needs and concerns during a crisis situation.

Northouse had done extensive work on what he called *Behavioral Leadership*, comparing and contrasting task- versus relationship-oriented leaders.[8] While task-orientation signifies doers, accomplishers, and results-based leaders, relationship-orientation is more about the well-being of the team, their needs, and the work atmosphere. Harmonizing these two orientations, particularly in a crisis phase, is essential to preserve the necessary energy to endure it. *Leadership . . . in crisis* must uphold both. The following matrix adopted from Effah and colleagues best depict this delicate balance:

FIGURE 5

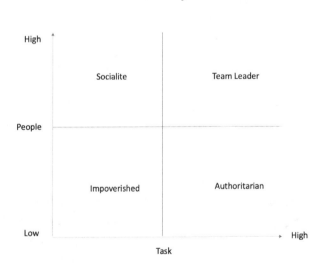

Modified from Effah et al.[9]

8. Northouse, *Leadership Concepts*, Chap. 4.
9. Effah et al., *Managerial Leadership and Energy,* 100.

- *Low task, low people-orientation:* This is a non-leadership quadrant, a *laissez-faire* style of letting things go their own way. The energy levels are already *impoverished* and resources are close to bankruptcy. In a crisis situation, such leadership behavior can only lead to disastrous results, as both energy spectrums—concern for people and for tasks at hand—are already low with an insignificant probability of being increased when a crisis hits. If a leader is managing resources at that level prior to a crisis, it is highly unlikely that s/he will survive the upcoming crisis.

- *Low task, high people-orientation:* When energy levels tilt toward people's needs without any consideration for important and vital task deliverables or deadlines, the organization loses credibility and is bound to fail. Stakeholders expect results even in crisis situations. Simply focusing on relations in the midst of a storm is an unbalanced allocation of much needed resources. Effah and colleagues labeled this quadrant as a *socialite*, just passing crucial time without delivering any results.

- *High task, low people-orientation:* While this quadrant may seem attractive to many, it comes at a price. Energy is dedicated to achieving results, but at the cost of people's well-being. There is no denying that any crisis has a toll on human relations, as they ponder to navigate the many unknowns. A leader who expends all organizational energy merely to fulfill tasks while sacrificing the good intention of well-meaning team members is risking the long-term allegiance of the people. Crises tend to change people's priorities; ignoring these priorities is a peril. An *authoritarian* approach may cause demotivation and turnover, thereby losing additional resources during circular crises.

- *High task, high people-orientation:* Finally, we come to the quadrant where leaders enjoy high task- and people-orientations. This delicate balancing of resources and energy between the two concerns requires mastery. One of our partners, a Christian international NGO leader who is a close friend, was a people person. You would meet him in the hallway and there evaporates the next 90 minutes . . . I even overheard that his team argued as to who would enter his office for an inquiry, which meant a lot of wasted, but personal attention time. In contrast, many leaders treat their team as delivery people: delivery of projects, deadlines, results. Balancing the energies between both pendulums is key for *team leader* success.

In this chapter's opening story, preserving my energy well into the early hours of the morning required balancing my people and task skills. Picking up the sarcastic comments of the escorting policemen to the officer-in-charge prompted me to ride the vibes and in a couple of minutes, turn the seemingly disastrous situation to my advantage. Focusing on the task at hand, first by being released followed by completing the assignment I was sent to do, added to my leadership influence and effect on the task and organization.

Preserving energy to outlive a crisis situation requires the adoption of prerequisites. These cannot be instigated once in a crisis mode, but rather pre-planned as part of the organizational stamina policy. I have chosen three—although there could be many more to add. These include (1) always having access to slack resources that prolong energy levels, (2) utilizing and synergizing all possible resources during a crisis, and (3) diversifying investments and allocations to reduce risks. These apply to organizations, athletes, and any entity aiming at preserving its energy level to reach the crisis finish line.

1. Slack funds:

The concept of slack resources is not always a welcomed one. Some argue that we must use every possible resource; otherwise, it would be labeled as a wasted resource. The biblical parable of the talents—the one who took the talent, dug, and hid it until the master returned—was considered a lazy servant. We must invest most of the organizational resources, but can stamina really operate on fumes without some leeway or access to underlying resources? Most athletic research asserts the fact that extra sleep, rest, and nutrition add to stamina and energy levels.[10] It is all about accumulating enough resources and supplements that come in handy when needed.

Slack funds are those resources you basically forget about, but are available upon the rise of the need. I know so many multi-million-dollar organizations out there who do not enjoy the luxury of any slack funds, as most of their resources are earmarked, similar to a trust fund that can only be used within very limited conditions. One such international NGO

---

10. McCarty, *Stamina and Energy,* 74–78.

working in relief and development has a budget of over $60 million in a tiny country, a fleet of cars worth over $1 million parked outside their premises, yet they could not commit $30,000 for a vital three-year project, as 99.9 percent of their funding is earmarked. Such limitations are not helpful when resources are not used when they are most needed.

2. Synergizing resources:

If slack funds are not readily available, the second important leadership aspect to consider is the ability to synergize existing resources. This requires adopting a mindset that could potentially overcome hurdles and weaknesses.[11] Even if you can access slack funds from different sources, these resources need to be realigned in a synergetic format that can best serve the situation. Some of these resources could be considered depleted or useless, but coupled with other resources, could multiply the impact.

There are many large yet disintegrated organizations out there. They struggle during a crisis simply because their right hand does not know what their left hand owns. Synergizing resources to maintain energy levels resembles a marathon runner drinking water and then pouring it on the head and body to refresh the system inside out. Using any single resource for multiple purposes, or multiple resources for single ones, is justifiable.

3. Diversifying investments:

This is where "grit" is introduced to this chapter. Grit is a long-term investment in a person's—or organization's—portfolio to envisage effective results. It promotes critical thinking in our investments, predicts positive outcomes, and offers practical approaches to preserving energy.[12] The concept of "grit" will be further discussed in this chapter. Similarly, diversifying investment decisions should never be taken under distress, but rather in times of prosperity and calmness; otherwise, it could be devastating and reactive.

Any investment consultant would uphold the principle of diversification. Similarly, preserving energy requires a balanced spread of energy levels amongst various components of the organization. Have you ever

11. Mcelvoy and Hart-Davis, *Charge up on Energy*, 10.

12. Blanco, *Developing Stamina*, 11.

wondered how 100 meters champions, like Jamaica's Usain Bolt, practiced toward their perfection levels? It is not about running 100 meters 100 times a day; rather, it requires a holistic yet gruesome daily exercise drill consisting of gym time, cardiovascular, weights, breathings—and some running! Diversification is key for surviving a crisis and accomplishing the set goals.

Regulating operations (breathing)

This second strategy for maintaining stamina for *leadership . . . in crisis* opts at normalizing operations despite the challenges. Similar to the concept of reaching a hybrid level when running a marathon, leaders, teams, and organizations must seek to stabilize and regulate operations, transforming people and tasks into a synergized well-oiled running machine. This requires wise but sacrificial steps to overcome the pressing demands and preserve the balance; it also assumes that crisis leaders possess high levels of Emotional Intelligence (EQ) to sense people's needs and well-being yet maintain the needed operational rigor.

The Greek philosopher Aristotle defined wellbeing as the overarching goal of all human action.[13] Leaders should never sacrifice their people's wellbeing for any materialistic cause. However, these same leaders are faced with the dilemma of juggling conflicting demands between safeguarding their people's wellbeing and producing much-needed results. Such a juggling act may not always work, as one area may suffer while another flourishes.

Our human breathing process, inhaling and exhaling, is done unconsciously to provide our bodies with enough oxygen while ridding it from unneeded carbon dioxide. Actually, if you do try to consciously monitor and control your own regular breathing patterns, you may end up choking or not providing the proper balance between the two actions: inhaling and exhaling. This is the beauty of a human body, designed by God, that can adapt to various internal and external conditions. When we sleep, our breathing slows down to provide enough oxygen without jerking the body from slumber. When we run or exercise, the breathing accelerates to compensate for much-needed oxygen levels. And when there is an imbalance in this process, we either choke, faint, hyperventilate . . .

Similarly, organizational leaders must provide the exact balance of breathing space to improve stamina in times of crisis. Some resistance

13. Kaur, *Mental Well-Being*, 2.

training may be required to achieve that balance. For example, in a newborn cry, which lasts about two seconds once they take their first breath, only 20 percent is inhaling and 80 percent is exhaling.[14] This is mainly due to the fact that a newborn has been living in a womb for nine months and needs the expiration of that phase. Airflow management is similar to organizational management; sometimes in crisis situations, leaders should allow space for prolonged exhaling. But overall, inputs and outputs should always be compatible.

Back to the opening story . . . regulating my breathing during the accelerated incidents following my arrival at the airport until it reached the climax of being escorted in a police vehicle to an unknown destination in an unfamiliar closed country was a challenge. So many vague thoughts were racing through my mind. The "what if's" scenarios could have drained all my resources instantly, leaving me breathless and choiceless. The choice to stay alert, diligent, and balanced may have saved the day.

To maintain such regulated patterns, I have selected three tactical actions that could assist in maintaining stamina in times of crisis.

1. Continuous communication:

Communication is a two-way channel. It resembles the inhale/exhale relationship of the body, the team, and the organization. One-way communication is ineffective during crises, as recipients would want to address many of their concerns and doubts through proper dialogue. Leaders must possess the necessary interpersonal skills to communicate well with all their stakeholders.[15] It is essential to create a clear, consistent, and continuous communication system that provides input-output data, inclusive-exclusive information, and interior-exterior contexts. For example, at the start of the COVID-19 pandemic lockdown, our team was meeting daily at 9 AM for a well-being activity followed by a debriefing session. Such extensive communication patterns decreased the level of anxiety and room for misunderstandings.

Input-output data provides the crunched numbers and figures required for the decision-making process in a crisis situation. Ensuring a proper balance between the two safeguards the long-term respiration progression of the organization. Inclusive-exclusive information sharing

14. Fleming et al., *Training in Breath Management*, 83.
15. Effah et al., *Managerial Leadership and Energy*, 101.

during crises places all stakeholders on the same level; while past practices excluded sharing of some information with wider audiences, in crises times, it is imperative to spread the information net wide enough to secure support. And analyzing and sharing the factors that are affecting both the interior and exterior contexts provide a better operational understanding of the areas that can prolong the breathing process.

2. Reallocation of tasks:

In some medical instances, a patient is placed on a respiratory system to regulate their breathing. It is unfortunate that humanity has become more accustomed to this new regulatory machine since the COVID-19 pandemic infiltrated the world. Suddenly, a simple respiratory apparatus that was rarely used in the past became a much-needed commodity, and hospitals and medical care units were rated and evaluated based on the availability of their respirators. Many wealthy individuals and communities reallocated tasks to secure the continued availability of respiratory systems to continue balancing the inhale/exhale process. Still, numerous people lost their lives due to a lack of proper inhalation of oxygen into their bodies.

Reallocating tasks is necessary to reinvent new ways to improve the breathing process. There are multiple techniques used by trainers to enhance the breathing process, such as putting your hands on your thighs and breathing in . . . then breathing out lifting your head and shoulders . . .[16] The unconscious breathing patterns mentioned before are no longer viable because of the crisis, consequently requiring reallocation of tasks. In organizational settings, it could mean changing job criteria, adding or lessening responsibilities, single, matrix or multi tasks, or even relieving or relinquishing tasks. The obvious fact that requires grasping is, when breathing becomes more difficult, *leadership . . . in crisis* must step in and reallocate tasks with the aim of improving operational effectiveness.

3. Transcendent goals:

To achieve the desired balance, leaders must always remind themselves of their transcendent goals. *What is the main purpose and meaning of their existence? How should they go about balancing people and task needs within*

16. Mcelvoy and Hart-Davis, *Charge up on Energy*, 10–12.

this existential context? Where is the proposed equilibrium between input and output? Viktor Frankl in his memoirs on finding meaning and purpose in life noted that transcendence is part of self-existence and self-actualization.[17] When that level of self-fulfillment is achieved, life decisions become clearer and stability is reached.

Northouse emphasized that leaders should transcend their own interests to serve others.[18] Those "others" could be multiple stakeholders with conflicting needs and demands. This is where the concept of *grit* earns traction. As defined by Duckworth and colleagues, *grit* is a *"two-factor personality trait consisting of the passion and perseverance for long-term goals and the consistency of interests over time despite failure or adversity, a good predictor of personal performance and success."*[19] Regulating operations over long-term requires continuous learning, growth mindset, and change management within the umbrella of the stated goals. Phrases such as "collateral damage" or "sacrifice for the greater good" is not an option. Neuroscience has proved that grit exists in people who have an open mind.[20] Without compromising transcendent goals, leaders in crisis should seek to thrive in their directives yet be willing to remain in the learner's seat.

In general, there are two types of leaders who are desperately trying to regulate their operations. The first type is fully focused on goals, not allowing any external factors to alternate the course of action. Such leaders become more narrow-minded, extremists, and eventually radicals. They refuse to be questioned about their course of action, create their own reality, and outcast anyone who challenges the status quo. These leaders may eventually reach their goals but with considerable damage along the way.

However, the second type of leadership is focused on transcendent goals but is open to new ways and methods to reach the final destination. During a crisis, leaders who exercise flexibility, change, and innovation tend to reach that goal at a faster pace. By regulating and altering breathing techniques, they are able to increase the function of their diaphragm muscles, thereby allowing lung tissues to expand.[21] Growth and expansion during difficult times is an attempt to swim against the current, challenging undesirable economic conditions, and maintaining the balance.

17. Frankl, *Search for Meaning*, 115.

18. Northouse, *Leadership Concepts*, Chap. 8.

19. Blanco, *Developing Stamina*, 11.

20. Blanco, *Developing Stamina*, 12.

21. Fleming et al., *Training in Breath Management*, 83–84.

Accelerating pace

Once the machine gets going, the science of acceleration kicks in. Acceleration is basically velocity measured over time. In physics, it is defined as the *"rate of change of velocity over time."*[22] Simply put, it would take me one hour to write 100 words in this book, while it may take someone else 30 minutes to do the same. We are looking at the same output, but when time is measured, the former costs double the time of the latter. This is why accelerating the pace wisely and confidently is crucial in gaining ground for building stamina that works in crises.

Newton's Second Law ($F = ma$) derived that *Force (F)* is the result of *mass (m)* interacting with *acceleration (a)*.[23] The larger the mass, the more force is required to accelerate it compared to a smaller mass. Long-distance runners know this formula well. The less weight one carries during a race, the faster their pace, and vice versa. I recall having to rid myself of about 10 pounds (5 kilograms) running the second marathon, thereby improving my overall finish time by about 30 minutes. Hence, one cannot expect to accelerate the pace if the given mass was not aligned with the set level of enforced energy; either more force or a lesser mass is required to maintain the same pace. Accelerating pace requires less weight to carry (smaller mass) or more force to push (extra energy).

Endurance, which is a derivative of stamina, is the level of capability required to sustain a certain activity over a period of time.[24] We have witnessed during the COVID-19 pandemic restrictions and lockdowns some organizations who had the necessary endurance levels to continue with their planned activities over time, and others that needed a bailout plan, or even worse, to close down their operations. Many small and medium-sized enterprises (SMEs) did not possess the necessary enduring resources to nurture their stamina levels, or even attempt to accelerate their pace. Therefore, accelerating the pace during a crisis is not recommended if the person, team, or organization do not possess the necessary endurance energy to cross the finish line.

Back to the chapter's opening story, the negative accelerated pace that took me off-guard required an enduring strategy to overcome the subsequent events and relative consequences that followed. The recovery in my

22. Parisi, *Maximizing Your Athletes' Acceleration,* 16.

23. Parisi, *Maximizing Your Athletes' Acceleration,* 16.

24. Zamzow, *Build your Stamina,* 60.

case was at a faster pace than the actual crisis. This is unusual, as the recovery is normally longer than the intervention. Take for example a medical surgery; the actual surgery may take 30 minutes or so, but the recovery requires days or weeks. But the recovery's pace is accelerated on a daily basis, as the patient gains more energy and moves faster.

On another note, I have noticed from my many years of experience and interactions with emerging leaders that the concept of stamina is contagious, or for a better word, scalable. For example, if I build strong athletic levels of stamina through running long distances, swimming multiple laps, and/or cycling for miles, those learning experiences could be transformed into other areas of personal and professional tracks. From such experiences, one could accelerate stamina levels in life-long learning, building relationships with difficult people or family members, pursuing new and challenging career journeys, growing their own business, or simply never giving up on their marriage. I believe that stamina provides a relentless personality and becomes a learnable skill that can be duplicated in a holistic way.

Here comes the importance of accelerating the pace. The faster you can accomplish a certain feature of your life that requires a clear stamina level, the quicker you can move on to the next stamina-requiring crisis. Attempting to handle them all at once may backfire, as the old Russian proverb advises not to chase two rabbits at the same time, as you will catch none.[25] Same with accelerating the pace in a crisis situation before moving onto the next one.

Most sports depend on acceleration as a key to excellence. Marathon runners know exactly the importance of starting slow, running at their own pace, then accelerating toward the finish line.[26] In organizational settings, persevering through hardships facilitates a culture of credibility, trustworthiness, and accomplishments. People are always seeking leadership personas or organizations that not only survive, but also thrive, during difficult times. While all the surrounding signals may root against these relentless champions, such leading figures remain steadfast and forward-looking in their attempt to finish the task. As one Chinese proverb goes: *"The man who says it cannot be done, should not interrupt a man who is doing it."*[27] The final words of Jesus Christ on the cross, *"It is finished,"* resonate with the same

25. TMH, *Two Rabbits.*

26. MacShane, *Marathon Man*, 1.

27. Proverbicals, *Proverbial Wisdom.*

relentless drive to finish the task despite all the attempts to de-accelerate him away from this mission.

To accelerate the pace as the third and final contributing factor for enhancing stamina that works in a crisis, three additional strategies are discussed.

1. Lead the momentum:

During any crisis situation, people are looking for someone to lead the way. While it is wise to stay behind the curtains (as some leaders tend to do) to reduce the wind resistance in facing crises, the momentum is still yours. My wife, Tassoula, has often monitored my behavior in meetings. She has a Doctorate in Educational Leadership and multiple years of experience in educational psychology. She mentioned to me once that I use something called "Cognitive Economy" in team meetings. I would listen and monitor the collective ideas and proposals, then speak no more than once in the meeting, offering an inclusive solution to the problem being discussed,[28] thereby leading the momentum.

The proper definition of Cognitive Economy is combining *"simplicity and relevance of a categorization scheme or knowledge representation."*[29] In complex times, members need a simple and relevant way forward to adhere to. They are desperate for a leader to step in and declare, confidently, that through an accelerated velocity, there could be a safe shore in the aftermath of the storm. Emergent leaders are an important part of *leadership . . . in crisis.* Such leaders emerge in crisis situations, and although they do not always enjoy assigned leadership positions, they frequently offer a breath of fresh air to their members.[30] During any crisis, the need to lead the momentum is essential, and people will follow the pace set by that emerging leader.

2. Rapid decision-making:

There is no denying that swift decisions are needed in crisis situations. Many models for building stamina are available in the corporate world,

28. Finton, *Cognitive-Economy Assumptions.*
29. Finton, *Cognitive-Economy Assumptions.*
30. Northouse, *Leadership Concepts,* Chap. 1.

including the synonym for *STAMINA*: "*Structured and Time-effective Approach through Methods for an INclusive and Active working life.*"[31] Such models ascertain that, difficult decisions have to be taken, and a trade-off is necessary. The decision-making process can rarely be democratic or consultative, particularly in pressing fast-paced situations.[32] Decisions as to which route to take, what resources to use, and where to allocate primary resources become decisive.

I have made several "unpopular" decisions in crises in the past. Members would feel that such decisions were firm, inconsiderate, and maybe unfair, but in the post-crisis phase, these same members may evaluate if the leader took the appropriate decision or not. I recall in 2006 when we were setting out to distribute humanitarian packages to thousands of refugee families in South Lebanon, I decided to stop the convoy on their journey through uncharted territories and return back to the closest village, thereby not reaching our final destination. It was only hours before we learned that the same route the convoy was about to undertake had vehicle mines planted on the road. There is little room for democratic, consultative, or participative decision-making processes in accelerated paced crises solutions.

3. Fast-tracking processes:

"*In the race of life, it is often those with stamina who prevail while others fall to earth*" stated Mcelvoy and Hart-Davis.[33] The harsh reality is preferential to those who adopt the fast track. The concept of fast-track is a controversial one, offering an eligible sect of people faster access and pace to the finish line. We see this even in marathon races, where elite runners are offered frontlines or preferential starting positions on the race track, thereby excluding them from the vast majority and giving them some sort of competitive advantage over regular runners. But such athletes have years of impeccable records and history, enabling them to bypass amateurs and seekers' consortiums to a preferential position, yet holding them accountable for such privileged positions.

I would not like to be in such a position, where the audience is expecting an accelerated pace simply because of the preferential starting position.

31. Svartengren and Hellman, *Stamina Model*, 2.

32. Northouse, *Leadership Concepts*, Chap. 8.

33. Mcelvoy and Hart-Davis, *Charge up on Energy*, 10.

Newton's Third Law emphasized an equal reaction to every action.[34] If leaders select a fast track to bypass a crisis, they need to be ready to respond to reactions if the action fails. It is better to accelerate the pace using wisely-tested paced steps with the option of fast-tracking the process without sacrificing the process. Creating a good forward program, working out, and managing stress are some tips to accelerate the pace.[35]

In conclusion, this chapter tackled the endurance of stamina that works in crisis situations that leaders need to nurture. Three generic concepts were introduced: Preserving energy, regulating operations, and accelerating speed. Each concept was elaborated to include three tactical strategies: (1) slack funds, synergizing resources, and diversifying investments; (2) continuous communication, reallocation of tasks, and transcendent goals; and (3) lead the momentum, rapid decision-making, and fast-tracking processes. In the next chapter, we will discuss the importance of crisis response for *leadership . . . in crisis.*

Recommended action points:

- Achieve the delicate balance between task deliverables and people relationships during a crisis.
- Commit to a two-way communication plan that transmits operational steadiness despite uncertainties.
- Recognize that stamina is a learnable skill scalable across various aspects of life.

---

34. Parisi, *Maximizing Your Athletes' Acceleration,* 17.
35. Zamzow, *Build your Stamina,* 61.

Chapter VII

Enhance the Timing and Context
of Response

Life is too short to spend your time avoiding failure.

(MICHAEL BLOOMBERG)[1]

AFTER 12 YEARS OF working in the business sector, I was ready to make the move to Christian ministry. The business world was enticing and challenging, but was full of compromises, problems, and back-stabbing. Now the Group of companies was a multinational entity, which required lots of travel and cross-border dealings in countries with different value systems, such as West Africa and Eastern Europe. I was not prepared for such settings that violated my moral compass and value system. In addition, working hours were unhealthy. I would tuck in my toddler boys on Sunday night only to see them again the next Saturday morning, as my working days went late into the night and I could not wake up early enough to see them off to school, which my wife kindly did every morning.

One Saturday morning, as I woke up excitedly to spend the day with my children, I saw my second son, four-year-old Daniel, playing alone with his toys in his room. He looked up at me uninterested in this stranger, and said: "Dad, it has been a while since I saw you . . . I thought you were dead!" That was the last straw. My sons were missing their father at home to the point where he might as well be dead to them. It was that icy-water instant

1. Bloomberg, *Quotes.*

that made me shiver and decide to change my lifestyle. Afterall, what was I investing my life and time in? We usually like to give our workaholic patterns excuses, such as "I am doing this for my children." But in reality, the boys needed a father figure rather than a so-called prosperous future.

It was decided. I sat down with my wife, Tassoula, that weekend and decided that we would both leave the business world (she was working for the same Group of companies) taking a leap of faith; I would join a respectable Christian ministry while she would pursue her higher education. We had built enough equity to secure our future, and now it was time to refocus on impacting lives. I had always been involved in Christian work in my late teens and young adult life as a volunteer, leading children and youth camps, directing choirs, leading worship, and serving on multiple committees, with my wife by my side. But I had to leave it all behind as I advanced in the business world. Now I was ready to return home, like the prodigal son.

It did not take too long before a couple of Christian ministries asked me to join their leadership teams. Orchestrating my exit strategy from the Group, which I was now serving as Executive Vice President, was not easy after 12 years of commitment and involvement. Such a step had reputational and consequential effects on the Group, but I was determined to move on. Talking about my move with the President & CEO was difficult, but he was understanding and respectful of my wishes, although the transition news was still highly confidential. I shared my transition with some key stakeholders, explaining that I was retaining the shares and interest in the Group but moving on with my personal life. All were understanding and supportive. And that day came when I joined the Bible Society as Executive Director.

However, it was only a few months later that the Group, already struggling financially, declared bankruptcy. The President & CEO left the country and never returned. My shares in the company became worthless, and some third parties tried to implicate me in the bankruptcy proceedings, which added anxiety to my life. I questioned God about the timing of this crisis—just when I was about to give up "worldly riches" and commit to the ministry. Why would this happen at a time when I needed security for my family through my investments and was ready to commit to his service?

Some vendors and suppliers tried to include me in the bankruptcy procedures, but I had retained all the necessary signed releases from my responsibilities. Yet, since there was no "President" to go after, the second best was the "Ex-Vice President." I had to appoint lawyers and deal with several legal proceedings for years before it was over. This was not an easy crisis to handle, as I had already moved on to where my heartbeat was stronger. During these few challenging years, I was questioning God about the timing: Why now, why now when I am serving you Lord? And the answer came to me from the Scriptures: *"No one who puts a hand to the plow and looks back is fit for service in the kingdom of God."*[2] Had I maintained my interest and shares in the Group, my heart would have been divided and my allegiance compromised. I was now clinging to one mission, one purpose, one interest, and able to respond to a crisis for the right reasons and with the right focus.

How we respond to a crisis is more crucial than the crisis itself. The President & CEO of the Group of companies decided to leave the country as a crisis response, probably believing that managing the crisis from a distance is more effective. I, on the other hand, although directly impacted by the crisis due to false pretenses, chose to confront them head-on. Often, my wife would say to me that this was unfair as I was being pursued for things that did not relate to me or my decision-making, while the person who should be confronting them left it all behind. In reality, responding to the crisis directly was painful, yet a great learning experience.

In this chapter, we will be discussing the best timing in crisis response, how to respond, and the context. The timing, format, context, and response to any crisis are vital. If the timing is too early, it may backfire, and if it is too late, it may never be an effective response. As noted in the introductory chapter, some leaders choose to jump ahead and lead the initiative during a crisis, which could scorch their efforts due to premature and miscalculated assessments. Leaders rush into so-called bailouts without proper evaluation of the situation, thereby losing much more than the industry average. Other extremes include leaders who wait for the circumstances to change, and when they realize the crisis is here to stay, it may well be overdue. Sometimes it is best to be in second place when a crisis is imminent. Therefore, we will be assessing the leader's response through swiftness, pivoting, and derailment strategies in times of crisis.

Dr. Evans Baiya claimed that in the U.S. alone, close to 100,000 businesses closed down and millions of jobs were lost as a result of the COVID-19 pandemic crisis.[3] He explained that leaders and organizations who were not prepared to handle *VUCA—Volatile, Unexpected, Complex,* and

2. Luke 9:62 (NIV).

3. Baiya, *Agility is Key,* 2.

Ambiguous—events, failed to respond effectively to the crisis. In another comparative study of organizations that thrived during the crisis, Yu and colleagues highlighted companies that were response-ready to explore future capabilities and pivot toward new conquests.[4] Such organizations not only survived the crisis but also flourished, improved their systems, and expanded into new industries.

My own experience with the Group bankruptcy was precisely a combination of *VUCA* events. It was a *volatile* situation, where I had left all these business dealings behind only for them to haunt me. *Unexpected* at any rate, as my shares in the Group should have been a pillow rather than a burden. The crisis was *complex*, including multiple, mostly innocent, stakeholders seeking to lessen their damages. It was *ambiguous*, as there was no clear solution or horizon in sight. However, the responses to each one of the *VUCA* events were proactive and intentional. I remember one of our ex-staff members exclaiming to me how it was possible for me to encompass all the various crises resulting from the bankruptcy, and my response was "one crisis at a time." Looking back, I can now confidently repeat Winston Churchill's comment: *"Never let a good crisis go to waste."*[5] There is always a great learning experience in how we respond to it.

Our response to any crisis is an opportunity. This is where the concept of *agility* comes into the scene. As mentioned in the introduction of chapter 5, *leadership . . . in crisis* requires *strength* and body-building (*resilience*), *cardiovascular* exercises that enhance endurance, perseverance, and tolerance (*stamina*), and stretching and *flexibility* (*agility*), which is the skill to maneuver and bend during crises. *Agility* is the capacity to prosper by responding to changes, challenges, and opportunities with effective solutions.[6] It is the ability to adjust and change plans to address new situations and circumstances.[7] Concepts such as adaptability, responsiveness, modernism, dynamism, and progressiveness interplay within the realm of agility.

In order to tackle the most appropriate and effective timing, format, context, and response to a crisis, we will explore three interrelated approaches. The first is the strategic swiftness that enables responders to quickly and promptly adapt to changing environments. The second is the

---

4. Yu et al., *Surviving a Crisis*, 4.

5. Stubbs, *Agility*, 3.

6. Financial Times, *Brand Agility*, 1.

7. Reibstein and Bedi, *The Agile Nation*, 2.

power of the pivot, or hinge, that allows room to shift gears and directions. And the third is the ability to derail from the set track and change course toward new uncharted territories. Let us examine these three approaches in detail.

Strategic Swiftness (SS)

Strategic swiftness (SS) or strategic agility is best described as the ability to modify or reinvent strategic directions due to environmental changes.[8] Such changes could be internal or external to the person, team, or organization, affecting the planned activities and outcomes. This is exactly what the Group of companies failed to do, which led to bankruptcy measures. For example, the landscape of Eastern European markets in the early nineties following the fall of the Berlin Wall (and eventually communism), where the Group established several companies, was quickly shifting from a naïvely socialistic and bureaucratic system toward a competitive free-market one. Competition became fierce and many local businesspeople were pushing earlier market entrants out of their countries. The Group's inability to find new local partners, merge, and/or sellout in time made all other options redundant.

One of the key criteria for strategic swiftness is creativity and innovation.[9] Otherwise, how can a leader, team, or organization redirect or reinvent themselves without the power of ingenuity? I read about an excellent example of SS during the COVID-19 pandemic lockdown. The title of the story is: *Pizza maker in Chicago uses oven to 'toss' face shields for front-line medical workers.*[10] From selling pizzas to dine-in customers, this pizzeria shifted the supply chain of their number one product—pizza—to produce 5,000 face shields per week for front-line health workers using mostly their existing assets and operational tools.[11] Of course, the changing environment was caused by the pandemic, but when lockdowns were lifted, this pizzeria had two thriving businesses to handle, not one.

While the above case required extreme innovation and creativity, there are more examples that fall within a moderate strategic shift recorded during the lockdowns. To illustrate, successful agile restaurants and small

8. Elali, *Strategic Agility,* 2.
9. Elali, *Strategic Agility,* 2.
10. YouTube, *Front-Line Medical Workers.*
11. Baiya, *Agility is Key,* 3.

businesses had to shift to online, takeout, or curbside services to cope with the new restrictions but stay in business. Educational institutions were forced to shift to work-from-home, online courses, and virtual platforms. Even organizations that were exempted from COVID-19 restrictions, such as healthcare service providers, had to find new avenues and workflows to respect physical distancing, staggered work shifts, and reduced human contact.[12] This required *leadership . . . in crisis* to take in as much information as possibly available during changing environments, make decisions accordingly, and implement innovative changes necessary for survival and even for growth.[13]

SS has also been described as a competitive ability, an aptitude for adaptability, tackling risks, and grabbing opportunities.[14] But how does it come about and how/when can leaders earn or enhance SS? Researchers have identified at least three determinants necessary for strategic swiftness/ agility. These are:

FIGURE 6

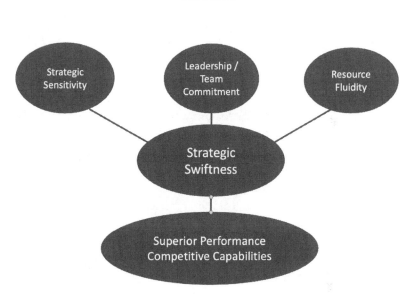

12. Lassiter, *Power of the Pivot*, 2.

13. Lassiter, *Power of the Pivot*, 2.

14. Elali, *Strategic Agility*, 5.

Modified from Elali[15]

- *Strategic sensitivity:* This is the ability to understand the internal and external environments, sense the changes, and look for potential opportunities.[16] Our eldest son, George, who I already mentioned has an exceptional level of resilience and has kept us awake many sleepless nights due to his many adventures, has demonstrated this determinant for years. When he was an undergraduate student at a respectable mid-western university in the USA, the International Marketing course during J-term decided to take a field trip to Hong Kong, Macau, and China. Our son was already visiting for Christmas and wanted to join his cohorts. The only available flight to Macau was through Manila, Philippines, with a one-hour connecting time. Needless to say, he missed the connection but was immediately able to negotiate access to a lounge, a relaxed layover, and demanding VIP accompaniment to the next connecting flight. Such a turnaround drama was actually an opportunity to explore yet another new country before heading to the final destination.

- *Leadership/team commitment:* The collectiveness of decision-making and buy-in of decisions and problem-solving strengthens leaders' abilities to shift directional strategies as deemed necessary.[17] Many leaders tend to adopt the route of victimizing themselves. They take the blame for something they were not responsible for, in an attempt to capture sympathy and establish a slip-away strategy. Many global leadership dilemmas remain un-tackled (e.g., Kennedy's assassination, Princess Diana's car accident . . .) only because the team lacked commitment toward the cause. When the team stands firm with the leader's decisions, mainly because they were partaking in that decision-making process, strategic agility is accomplished. The power of collective commitment is also seen in many religious groups, starting from the early Christian church and through many centuries of persecution until Christianity became the official religion of the Byzantine Empire in the fourth century.

- *Resource fluidity:* The flexibility to move resources around and attract even more resources offers sustainability and a competitive

15. Elali, *Strategic Agility*, 5.
16. Elali, *Strategic Agility*, 5.
17. Elali, *Strategic Agility*, 5.

advantage.[18] There is an old saying: *"When you are in the hole, stop digging."* This is the case for many entities during a crisis, when their resources are slowly depleting and they are seeking to replenish a leaking bucket. A leader must first be able to reallocate resources toward more fluid investments and close-down draining ones. For example, before the downfall of our Group of companies, I was heading a computer services business unit under the Group. One year prior to my departure, I proposed its dissolvement and transfer of assets to the Group. It was the right timing to preserve the integrity of that company, its employees and families, and transition out of the market. Unfortunately, the Group only lasted one year after acquiring the transferred assets.

These three determinants may enhance SS and offer superior performance in the form of competitive advantages. The ability to respond to a crisis through being agile, flexible, creative, and forward-looking, positions leaders—and their organizations—in the spotlight. Leading through times of crisis is becoming a rarity that stakeholders long to associate with, or even replicate. People want leaders who are differentiated in their strategies when a crisis hits.

Pivotal Power (PP)

The term "pivot" or "pivotal" surfaced in much of my literature review on agility. I always thought that the term indicated a stable stand-in-time point where other elements revolved around, only to discover that it actually meant a varying hinge point that could take any route or direction to fulfill the required movement. However, if the axis or joint is weak, it may break under the pressure of a swift alteration of direction. Hence, pivotal power (PP) requires a strong platform that allows leeway for wavering and changing directions. There are multiple shifts that leaders could adopt,[19] but the question is: *What are the right directional changes to adopt during a certain crisis?*

First, let us examine the definition of a pivot. It is a "person, thing, or factor having a major or central role, function, or effect."[20] Looking at this

18. Elali, *Strategic Agility*, 5.

19. Lassiter, *Power of the Pivot*, 3–4.

20. Merriam-Webster, *Pivot*.

definition and as a Christian, I can clearly state that the pivot of my life is Jesus Christ, my Lord. Yet through life, we tend to shift directions while remaining anchored to that pivot. Other elements may also be pivots in our lives, such as our parents, children, and best friends. While the pivot remains uncompromised, there are multiple directions that we could operate and adhere to, particularly in changing environments. For example, when I worked in the business world, I maintained my pivotal power with my faith by serving as a Gideon, offering the placement of New Testaments in schools, hospitals, and hotels. The role shifted when I joined the Bible Society. Same pivot, changed direction, different outputs, outcomes, and impact.

Once we realize our true pivotal power (PP), we can shift things around in our lives without compromising the core. For instance, once I realized that I was meant to work in the mission field, all the crises that rained on me then after did not matter. They were insignificant in comparison with the bigger picture, and all I had to do was shift some priorities around to endure the dilemmas. I recall one morning landing at the airport coming from Thailand and heading straight to one of the court cases to clear my name before heading to the UK the next morning. The pivotal hinges were working overtime, but the basic principles remained unchanged.

PP is the ability to shift operations to address changing circumstances. Whether the circumstances are acute or chronic, organizational leadership requires changing the course of action in multiple aspects. To illustrate, at any point in time in this decade, there are about 170 million migrant or expat workers shifting jobs around the globe.[21] If such workers were not able to shift their working habits from their home countries to their host countries, they would not be in demand. In our family, our youngest son, Michael Jr., is only 26, but is now transitioning into his fifth job assignment in a third host country. On average, this is one new team/supervisor every year for the past five years and three different labor markets and conditions, which can only be accomplished through his PP.

U.S. News did a piece on agile nations and their response to the CO-VID-19 pandemic, describing the pandemic as a deer crossing the road and the driver's ability to swerve and avoid the collision.[22] Every single sense in the body would become alert to the danger and work together to avoid the crash. Similarly, small businesses, organizations, multinationals,

21. Migration Data Portal, *Labour Migration*.
22. Reibstein and Bedi, *The Agile Nation*, 1.

governments, and communities at large exercised PP to avoid a head-on collision with a pandemic lockdown. Even hotel businesses, which were affected almost as much as the airline industry, pivoted toward hosting "quarantined" travelers, and in some cases such as New York City, housed homeless tenants to reduce the spread of the virus.

PP is not about size, structure, or age. It is about being flexible in changing the course and adopting new alternatives through our crisis response. The now ninety-year-old media-news guru, Rupert Murdoch, claimed: *"The world is changing very fast. Big will not beat small anymore. It will be the fast beating the slow."*[23] Organizational leaders should not worry about their size but rather about their pivotal abilities to move fast. Many large banks were slow to address the lockdown crises compared to more agile institutions, like PayPal and Intuit, who were forward-thinking and pivoted to support millions of customers.[24] It is not about size but rather about speed and flexibility.

PP may have salvaged our Group of companies had the organization shifted away from medical insurance toward general and life insurance industries. The health bills were skyrocketing while our insurance Group kept on acquiring large medical policies despite the obvious dangers. The main reason was the sheer size of the medical policy premiums, which added numbers and prestige to the portfolio, but lacked the profitability and sustainability for long-term continuity. The Group should have pivoted toward less risky insurance lines and directions, thereby sacrificing size for agility and flexibility. Bigger may sound exciting, but the bigger the operation is during a crisis, the higher the liabilities are in our responses.

In any crisis situation, a leader should immediately pose the question: *What are the alternatives?* When multiple coordinated suicide terrorist explosions rocked the transportation infrastructure of London, better known as the UK Tube Explosions of 2005, I was actually in the city trying to make my way to Heathrow Airport using public transportation. Watching people's faces glued to publicly exposed television screens on the streets, I sensed that something was wrong. The Breaking News banner revealed the crisis, and the options to get to Heathrow in time to catch my flight seemed hopeless. Just imagine the scene with me . . . a middle-aged Middle Eastern man rushing through the streets of London with a small suitcase after these multiple suicide explosions! Pivotal power came into action. My years of

23. Murdoch, *Quotes.*
24. Stubbs, *Agility,* 5.

experience traveling to the UK offered a variety of alternatives. In this case, it was a car ride to the busiest airport in the world rather than the usual bus or train ride that saved the day.

Deliberate Derailment (DD)

This is where the importance of timing, format, and context of our response counts. Changing pivotal directions due to changed strategies is required and legitimate in *leadership . . . in crisis,* but how would a leader know that the new course is better than staying within the set course? Unfortunately, many leadership derailments are uncontrolled, disastrous, and inadequate. In this section, we will tackle deliberate derailment (DD) as a response strategy rather than coincidental or reactive derailments as illustrated in the following narrative.

Derailment is defined as an expected leadership performance that does not meet up to its potential.[25] You bring in someone on your team with an impressive curriculum vitae and charisma, only to discover a few weeks later that their performance derailed from expectation. And when a person exhibits derailment under normal circumstances, it is highly unlikely that such a person would perform any differently, if not underperform, during a crisis.

Leadership derailment normally falls under three areas:[26]

1. *External factors*: When environmental changes impose a different set of rules, leaders are obliged to derail their roadmap in an attempt to adhere to the new realities.

2. *Leadership traits*: Some leaders under pressure simply choose to move away (distrust), against (manipulate), or toward (micromanage) their teams, none of which are healthy strategies.

3. *Leadership behaviors*: Whether an introvert or extrovert, such behaviors tend to predict how effective the conduct will be vis-à-vis the overall performance across jobs.

Examining the derailment of our Group of companies in the final few hours had similarities with the above three areas. The external environments were rapidly changing in several of the countries of operations,

25. Yost et al., *Successful Derailment,* 301–2.
26. Yost et al., *Successful Derailment,* 313–14.

without properly assessing these changes or their organizational impact. The leadership traits shifted from complete delegation to ultimate distrust and manipulation, thereby losing out on a lot of commitment levels. And the behaviors became selfish and defensive.

In this book's introduction, I mentioned the concept of the "Ostrich Syndrome Leader" who is usually unaware of, or uninterested in, the surrounding changing environments and their warning signals. An ostrich would typically stick its head in the sand when there is danger, believing that once its head was submerged in the sand and its sight, hearing, and smelling senses were numbed, the situation might go away. They usually end up dead due to their lack of sensemaking abilities during crises. Similarly, some leaders lack the proper sensemaking responses that are able to interpret realities and influence future processes, whereas they should be gaining an understanding of the vague situation.[27]

The following narrative from the Old Testament on David—the Warrior, King, Prophet, Psalmist, Leader, Shepherd—illustrates well an uncontrollable response and derailment path. In the second book of Samuel chapter 11, we witness a completely derailed illustration of this servant leader. He was indeed, a servant leader, a servant in his father's house. When the prophet Samuel came to anoint one of Jesse's sons, David was serving in his father's house. All his brothers were sitting around doing nothing. He was the only one tending to their household duties out of the eight brothers, and his father had almost forgotten about him when Samuel was going through the list of Jesse's sons.

David was also a servant in his enemy's (King Saul's) tent and palace. Even after being anointed as king, he was willing to be the king's servant. He played music for the disturbed King Saul and was one of Saul's armor-bearers. He was also a servant of his people as he fought Goliath single-handedly when no one dared to, and fought many other battles for his people. And he was a servant of God, wanting to build God's house and preserve the ark.

While he had an impeccable career path, David derailed big-time. It all began with the first verse of chapter 11 in 2 Samuel: "*. . . at the time when kings go off to war, David sent Joab out with the king's men and the whole Israelite army... But David remained in Jerusalem.*"[28] David should have been at war with his people, as it was the leader's duty to lead and not stay

27. Kalkman, *Questions in Crisis Response,* 650.
28. 2 Samuel 11:1 (NIV).

behind. Typically, the time when kings go off to war is Springtime, when the weather is appropriate for fighting, the ground is dry and not muddy, the harvest for each kingdom would be ripe and ready, and so getting the harvest was one of the main objectives for fighting. Hence, at the time when all kings went out with their armies to fight, David abandoned his leadership duties and remained behind rather than go to war with his chief of the army, Joab, the king's men and the whole army.

Remember, David was a great warrior, fought many battles, killing a lion and a bear, and slaughtering Goliath when he was still young. But in this new external environment, he sat at home instead of being on the battlefield, uninvolved in the service and mission. The servant leader was no longer serving in his father's house—he was now looking out for himself; not serving in the king's palace—it was time for others to serve him; not serving his people—he sent others to fight his battles; and not serving God.

Since there was no purpose, no vision in his life, David got bored, restless, woke up, and started walking on the roof ... and saw a beautiful woman bathing. The loss of purpose is the main reason for derailment. Unfortunately, David acted on this and took the first step toward temptation although he knew that the woman he lusted after was married, as Bathsheba was Uriah the Hittite's wife, who was one of David's strong fighters, fighting that day in the king's battles. Very simply, David's response to the changed environment was to take what was not his. He took something that belonged to one of his most loyal fighters. Married or not, it did not matter.

The result of that action was pregnancy, which was a consequence of derailment, and so the great King David attempted to cover-up the consequences of his behavior. What followed was a premeditated derailment to cover up the wrong behavior. David asked Joab to send for Uriah, and in a few days, Uriah appeared in front of the king, and when he did, David derailed the conversation and asked about how Joab was, how the soldiers were, and how the war was going. He then ordered Uriah to go to his home and rest, with the clear intention that when Uriah went home after a long and tiring trip, he would court his beautiful wife, Bathsheba, and the consequences of David's sin would be covered up. Instead, Uriah chose to sleep at the palace's door with his men; he did not go to his home and did not see his wife. The next morning when David asked him why he did not go home, Uriah answered: *"The ark and Israel and Judah are staying in tents . . ."* In the desert, on the battlefield, in spiritual warfare, *"How could I go to my house to eat and drink and lie with my wife? . . . I will not do such a thing!*"[29] Uriah refused one night with his own wife, associating with his colleagues on the battlefield. David tried again and delayed Uriah another day in Jerusalem. This time he invited him to his table and got him drunk. But David failed again, as Uriah did not go home.

The next part is repulsive, depicting the ultimate pit-bottom that David had reached. In the morning, when David found out that his second plan failed, he gave Uriah a letter to hand over to Joab which included the written execution orders of Uriah, hand-delivered by Uriah himself. And so it happened: Uriah died along with some of his colleagues so that the leader, David, could cover-up the consequences of his own sins. David's reaction to the lost battle was supposed to be that of anger, sadness at the loss of his men, punishment and reprimanding those responsible. But David's priorities for that battle were different. He secretly wanted to lose this battle, wanting some of his soldiers to die, and most importantly, he wanted to get rid of Uriah. David had broken more than 5 of the 10 commandments by then: Do not kill, commit adultery, steal, covet your neighbor's wife, and do not lie!

The supposedly derailed response to the crisis had a temporary happy ending. Uriah the Hittite was dead and his widow, Bathsheba, mourned her man. When the mourning period was over, David had her brought to his household in a heroic act for the king to marry the widow of his loyal soldier. And by this heroic act, David would have covered up the consequence of his derailment, until he was confronted by the prophet Nathan through another narrative found in chapter 12. It was then that David realized his wrong-doing and assumed responsibility for his behavior. But the interesting part about this story was that the consequence of the sin—the child conceived through this derailment—died.

Comparing the above biblical narrative to the three areas that cause a derailment, we deduct the following. First, the external factors that usually guided kings in that era to go to war changed for David. Instead of doing exactly what he was trained and groomed to do, he derailed from it, thereby allowing other external factors to impose new realities. Second, his leadership traits were completely compromised due to the derailed path. He distrusted his entourage, manipulated his closest comrades, including the chief of the army, and micromanaged the tiniest details of his tactics.

---

29. 2 Samuel 11:11 (NIV).

Third, his leadership behaviors lacked integrity and honor, justifying poor performance only to protect his derailed course of action.

Alternatively, Deliberate Derailment (DD) is the ability to bounce back through the leader's response to a crisis. Three strategies may enhance the success of deliberate derailments: reframing the new course, drawing on other people, and emphasizing lessons earned.[30] There is no doubt that any derailment is a painful process and leaders would attempt to avoid it. But it may also be an inevitable strategy to avoid becoming insignificant, as in the case of our bankrupted Group of companies, as the organization could not reframe nor draw on its people or lessons learned. Let us look at these three strategies in detail:

1. *Reframe derailment:*[31] This is related to the organizational culture and/or the leader's upbringing. If the culture was focused on a growth mindset and success criteria, leadership choices for reframing derailments could potentially always succeed. Personally, I am a strong advocate of the self-fulfilling prophecy (SFP) concept. I have experienced it in my own career and journey, that when we choose a path we so much want to succeed, and put all our energy and efforts toward the new set of goals, we may end up succeeding. Of course, we have to keep in mind that we cannot expect success in our SFP if 90 percent of the external factors are outside the leader's control. There should be a good ratio of controllable factors in the environment for the SFP to succeed.

2. *Draw on others:*[32] This challenges the leader to withdraw some dependence from the support network rather than undertake the entire process of the DD. Seek the advice and coaching of other seasoned leaders before you dispatch on a new course. The leader's response to a crisis should always be well-balanced, a calculated risk, and supported by main stakeholders. This is not about democratic or consultative leadership; as in crisis response, we do not have the luxury of taking time to consult around and get some soundings. It is best to have a coaching and mentoring system in place, where advice on the response could be drawn promptly and in a timely manner.

---

30. Yost et al., *Successful Derailment,* 315.
31. Yost et al., *Successful Derailment,* 315.
32. Yost et al., *Successful Derailment,* 316.

3. *Capture the lessons:*[33] Usually, unplanned derailments are caused by past failures, career setbacks, or traumas. However, these are also valuable lessons where a leader could identify some personal limitations s/he may not be aware of, or some blind spots in the decision-making process. Such learning requires humility and acknowledgment that these weaknesses present themselves as learning lessons rather than obstacles. Another important area is knowing which factors are outside the leader's control. Rather than trying feebly to control uncontrollable factors, it is best to recognize them and work through the controllable factors to minimize their impact on the response.

Adopting a DD strategy as a response to a crisis situation, leaders would be sending out the message that they may know the consequences that could arise from a crisis if the team or organization remained on its current route, and offer an alternative proactive course that could potentially lead to persistence and growth.

To close this chapter, it is important to emphasize the value of our response to a certain crisis. Several aspects may affect our response, including the timing, format, and context of the response. Three response approaches were addressed: (1) Strategic Swiftness, which is the ability to modify or reinvent strategic directions due to environmental changes, (2) Pivotal Power, which requires shifting operations to address changing circumstances, and (3) Deliberate Derailment, the skill to bounce back through the leader's response to a crisis. The next chapter will continue to discuss the combined impact of agility, flexibility, and change management on *leadership . . . in crisis.*

Recommended action points:

- Be prepared to adopt varying strategic directions based on new realities stemming from external environmental changes.

- Identify and anchor yourself to the true pivotal powers in your life.

- Be ready to deliberately derail your course of action to better fit crisis demands.

---

33. Yost et al., *Successful Derailment,* 316–17.

Chapter VIII

Practice Agility, Flexibility, and Change Management

The greatest danger in times of turbulence is not the turbulence
—it is to act with yesterday's logic.

(PETER DRUCKER)[1]

ON OCTOBER 7, 2019, while taking a quick shower following my gym time, I noticed a lump in the lower part of my body. It was an interesting finding, but did not alarm me in any way. The next day, I called a friend who is also a medical doctor and now serves on our board; he examined me that afternoon and assumed that the lump might have been caused by an in-flammation or a trauma, hence should take some anti-inflammatory drugs for a few days.

In the meantime, I was about to host an international conference with multiple speakers and media attention, so did not pay too much atten-tion to the matter. Unfortunately, a week after the conference, my father fell and broke his hip, so I was tending to him at the hospital and decided to conduct further investigation of this lump—since I was "stuck" at the hospital. Two weeks had passed since taking the anti-inflammation drug, so I was advised to conduct an ultrasound at the Emergency Room, which also failed to identify the source of this strange growth. Hence, I booked an appointment with a specialist in that same hospital.

1. Drucker, *Quotes.*

Following the examination, the physician put me on antibiotics, but was more or less sure that the lump was a tumor and that I needed to do body screening simultaneously while taking the antibiotics. This was all happening when my schedule was already overwhelmed, the country was going through civil riots and unrest, and my father was hardly recovering from his hip-replacement surgery . . . I just did not have time for it. Thankfully, the full body CT scan was clear, but the MRI indicated a growing tumor that needed further exploration.

By that time, I decided to take this issue more seriously and contact a leading medical expert to follow-up on my case. I was given an exceptional appointment on November 4, having explained that I would be traveling the next day to the UK for some important global meetings. That morning, while waiting in the car for my wife to accompany me, I heard her scream and tumble down the staircase. Tassoula had slipped on the wet floor, nose-dropped and landed on her left eyebrow, bursting her left eyelid open—and later we discovered that she fractured her arm too! Blood spurted out as she screamed in horror, thinking that her face was bashed. I immediately ran to her rescue, cleaned the wound, and assured her that it was only a deep cut just above her eyelid that needed stitching.

I couldn't believe it. This was happening within an hour of my consultation, an elderly father recovering from hip surgery, and now my wife needing urgent medical attention. What else could happen? My reaction under such circumstances was to stay calm and focused. Having cleaned up her wound, I accompanied her to the car and drove straight to the hospital where my appointment was scheduled. On the way, I remembered that we have an acquaintance and close friend of my brother-in-law, who is also an ophthalmologist, working in that same hospital and is specialized in reconstructive eye surgery. I called him just in time, as he was heading to another hospital, and explained the situation. It took a few minutes to stitch my wife's left eyelid.

Then we headed to my scheduled appointment—my wife wearing dark sunglasses and explaining to everyone that she had fallen earlier that day. It was not for another few days that her entire left bruised face became painted with blue, purple, and yellow, and her arm was put in a sling-shot! The specialist examined me and reviewed all the screening tests, and recommended that I conduct a surgical removal of the tumor, run a pathology, and then deal with the outcome, which could be anything from a benign to a malignant or lymphatic growth. He cleared me to travel the next day for our global meetings in the UK, but scheduled the surgery for the coming week.

I have always been healthy and sportive, stretching my body and mind to the limits of endurance and strength. But this was uncharted territory for me. Should I worry and focus all my energy on finding an immediate solution to this crisis? Or should I be flexible and agile to accept and adapt patiently to the new realities? In a crisis situation, leaders tend to seek full control of the situation although many aspects are beyond their control. This was my case, as in the instance of many similar patients who wait until their pathology results are out before they can understand *what* they are dealing with and *how*. I would like to label this phase as the discovery-to-diagnosis (D2D) phase. We discover a certain crisis but are unable to act upon it until we have a clear picture of the diagnosis, then leaders are able to address the crisis with the proper tools.

The D2D period is usually accompanied by anxiety, irrational responses, or pacifism. None of these reactions are healthy during the D2D crisis phase. Simply worrying or remaining anxious about the multiple possible outcomes of the diagnosis drains energy and clouds judgment. Best to maintain some objectivity despite the unknown factors until the time comes when the actual scope and size of the crisis are revealed. Sometimes leaders tend to assume the outcome and respond prematurely and irrationally to the crisis. This is simply a risk-taking approach that could lead to unwarranted results, even opposite to the desired ones. The third reaction of pacifism is a laissez-faire approach where leaders give up and let the flow take over. For such leaders, the final destination may be very different from what they may have wished for.

In my medical case, I was worried but maintained some objectivity, attended normal office hours, went to the gym regularly, planned ahead business-as-usual, took the planned trip to the UK, and participated with full engagement in the global meetings. One day prior to the surgery, I gathered the senior management team and informed them of the *discovery*, and that I would be taking the rest of the week off following the surgery. The next day, around noon, I was admitted to the hospital for a half-day surgery. I was my usual self, joking with the anesthesiologist about some of my bad sporting habits such as scuba diving, and even setting myself on the operating table in the OR. Thirty minutes later I was in the recovery room, feeling the pain of the incision but overwhelmed with hunger. I was finally fed, then the surgeon passed by, checked my wound, and discharged me in the early evening.

"Now we wait for the pathology results" were his final words. Waiting for the *diagnosis* is like waiting for a verdict. How does one cope with unknown looming turbulence hovering over the horizon? Being flexible during a crisis is key to staying focused on important matters. As Peter Drucker noted, we have to address upcoming turbulence with a new and changed mindset. The time I spent in the D2D phase was an opportunity to reflect on some of the bad habits and unhealthy practices I had accumulated over 30+ years of organizational leadership. So, the waiting time was used to analyze and assess some of the things that needed to change.

A few days later, the phone rang. It was the surgeon's office and he wanted to see me to check on my incision and share the results. The pathology results were out and the diagnosis was that it was a malignant tumor, but the cell types were localized and completely removed surgically. It was a 95 percent curable situation, and I was given a choice to increase that percentage to 99 percent through what my surgeon called "a shot" of chemotherapy. Three weeks later, I took that "shot" and have been in remission, observation, and monitoring mode for the last three years and counting.

In the weeks that followed, and mainly due to pandemic lockdowns and travel bans, I was able to rid myself of some unwanted 30 pounds (14 kilograms) over six months through regular exercising and adopting an intermittent fasting diet on my own, which suited my lifestyle, and have been able to maintain the ideal body weight ever since. In addition to the changed health style, I completed two book manuscripts and developed and implemented weeks of capacity-building training materials for online and physical workshops. Furthermore, my personal accomplishments were crowned with professional development through coaching a handful of emerging leaders in several countries. The D2D reflections were well-invested.

D2D is a window that *leadership . . . in crisis* fails to capitalize on. I have personally missed the D2D window of opportunity many times in my personal and professional journeys. In this chapter, we will revisit the concept of agility as the ability to be aware of the surrounding circumstances, alert to the available alternatives, and quick in the responsiveness process. Flexibility is also required to navigate through uncertain landscapes toward the shores of safety. And we will explore some tools for managing change through a changed mindset. I will also introduce the concept of Wisdom

Quotient (WQ) which I researched a few years ago. Let us commence by examining the various aspects of agility.

The multiple facets of agility

As noted in the previous chapter, agility is the capacity to implement change quickly and flexibly.[2] Several researchers proposed different facets of agility. Dr. Evans Baiya mentioned six organizational dimensions of agility: *financial, organizational, learning loop, leadership, people-factor,* and *supply chain.*[3] The combination of all these factors can improve the chances of penetrating through a crisis. Financial flexibility and slack finances are always a welcomed tool when a crisis is looming, similar to a horizontal malleable organizational structure. Both the learning abilities of the organization and its leadership style can contribute positively to its agility. And the leniency of its supply chain coupled with its people skills are essential for its survival.

The focus of this chapter is mainly on agility in the D2D phase. How can leaders apply multi-disciplines of agility when the discovery of the crisis is made and the diagnosis is still yet to come? I want to focus on two aspects. The first is *leadership agility*. In my medical case, I kept the matter private until the time came when the senior management team had to step in, take on new responsibilities, and uphold the decision-making process. A leader must recognize the timing when there is a need to relinquish control and delegate to qualified team members. My S-curve was a day before the surgery, while still in the D2D phase and requiring all the support of the team.

The second is the *learning loop* facet, which creates a learning organization and culture. What did I learn from my temporary crisis? I learned that my rapid-paced lifestyle could immediately come to a standstill; that despite my healthy and athletic patterns, our bodies are vulnerable; that regardless of our intellectual and cognitive abilities, a tiny tumor could turn our world upside down. It is also important to mention the *people-factor agility*, a prerequisite to the other facets. Issues such as empowerment and delegation are necessary for an agile organization.[4] I am so fortunate to

2. Lassiter, *Power of the Pivot*, 2.
3. Baiya, *Agility is Key,* 3.
4. Baiya, *Agility is Key,* 3.

have such dedicated people surrounding me. They represent the best version of my leadership.

Combining learning and agility is the ticket to surviving and thriving through crisis. Three additional facets are introduced by Yost and colleagues.[5] The first is the *learnable* practice; the leader's behavior should always be seeking new knowledge and innovation, and asking the question: *What can I learn from the crisis?* The second is the *self-reinforcement* aspect; leaders must look at the positive emotions resulting from the crisis in the form of gratitude, encouragement, and sustainability: *What was positive about this crisis?* And the third is the *catalytic* facet; leadership practices and behaviors in crises can become viral, scalable, and infect others positively: *Who else can learn from this crisis?*[6]

I experienced all three facets in my short medical condition. I have learned valuable and lifetime lessons from the crisis, particularly in the D2D phase. It offered me positive emotions and reinforcement that eventually affected my lifestyle and rid me of several bad habits. But most importantly, it transmitted a strong message of hope to cohorts. I recall one of the senior managers sharing, after I broke the news, how I had inspired him through continuing with the international conference, and then flying to the UK for global meetings—all within the D2D rollercoaster ride.

During one of my recent visits to Cyprus, I had dinner with the founder and retired CEO of SAT-7 Christian Satellite television, Terry Ascott. He gave me a copy of his biography book in which he shared a story from his experience under the section heading: Keep on Keeping on![7] It goes something like this. While he was on a farm, he witnessed an unborn chick trying to break out from its shell by pecking it with its little beak, breaking one piece at a time, trying to get out. Terry was tempted to help that little chick with his finger by peeling some of the shell. The farmer immediately interfered and explained that the chick had to do this task by itself, as any external help may hinder the chick's future survival. That little repetitive action to break from the shell was a lifelong lesson for the newborn chick.

Within those multiple facets of agility, leaders should be able to capitalize on such concepts by slowly pecking their way through a crisis—each at their own pace. There is no right or wrong facet, dimension, or aspect of agility. The more important concept to keep in mind is to adopt what is

5. Yost et al., *Successful Derailment*, 303.

6. Yost et al., *Successful Derailment*, 303.

7. Ascott, *Dare to Believe*, 35.

most relevant for leadership and organizational growth, particularly when one discovers the turmoil and is in a waiting mode until the full picture unfolds through a complete diagnosis. The advice is to use that time wisely and effectively to enhance leadership agility. Let us move on to explore the notion of flexibility.

The flex in flexibility

I still love to drive stick-shift cars, although they have become old-fashioned in many countries. Shifting gears based on the landscape of the road allows the driver to get the optimal power of the vehicle. Gears could also serve as a slowing-down mechanism when heading down a slope, where the shift gear serves as a protective pull-back force rather than an accelerating one. The flexibility offered by manual shifting gears is now being completely duplicated by modern automatic transmissions through advanced technologies, such as Tiptronic—all with the purpose of utilizing the vehicle to its utmost capacity.

This type of flexibility is necessary when navigating through uncharted crisis territories. We need that ability to shift gears and flex our motion toward common goals. In the opening story when my wife slipped and burst open her eyelid, any rigid motion or one-sided decision would have led to a win-lose or lose-win situation. For example, if I simply catered for her injury and ignored the opportunity to uphold my appointment with this famous surgeon [for a very legitimate reason], there could have been a lost opportunity; or if she told me to go on my own and that she would take a taxi to the ER at the closest hospital, I would have felt guilty and worried about her unknown state at the time, including the quality and safety of her treatment. By flexing our priorities and thinking ahead of the options—which is not always easy to do when in a panicking crisis situation—we both managed to achieve our goals and be there for one another.

Flexing and shifting are required tools in any crisis response. The flex—bend, stretch, or arch—instituting flexibility provide learning agile leaders with different utensils to use and apply. Brian Lassiter mentioned 14 strategic shifts that organizational leaders could adopt and implement to survive a crisis.[8] These include shifting:

---

8. Lassiter, *Power of the Pivot*, 3–4.

1. *Communication methods:* When in a crisis, people need consistent information and updates received through a friendly medium. Memos and more formal communication channels are not recommended, as stakeholders need to feel the confidence in the voice tone, the assurance that despite the challenges, there is still hope for recovery. Within the recent pandemic crisis, many leaders chose to record short videos and stream them as new communication methods. In my medical case, I called for an urgent senior management team meeting and explained the D2D situation face-to-face, thereby decreasing any speculation and eliminating any form of despair in my tone and approach.

2. *Implementation of strategies and action plans:* While it is important to uphold our strategic plans even in times of crisis, we should apply flexibility in its implementation and provide room for shifting some of the action plans. During turbulent times, it is best to divide goals and action plans into smaller chunks. The team would be more concerned with how to deal with tomorrow's challenges rather than worry about next year's plans. I recall when going through the D2D phase, how I implemented short-term goals and checked off my list the tests I had to conduct, yet keeping in mind the medium-range goal of needing to travel to the UK for our global meetings, which I was cleared to make only one day prior to the travel itinerary.

3. *Approaches for stimulating innovation:* As per the chapter's opening epigraph, leaders should never attempt to deal with new instability using old rationale. New challenges require courageous and creative solutions. Using traditional approaches in unconventional situations is bound to fail. The leader's task is to initiate and stimulate an atmosphere of innovation, encouraging new and radical ideas for thinking outside the box. Most of us, human beings, were forced into lockdowns at various stages and intensities of the COVID-19 pandemic. While many home-stuck people went about their personal and professional lives as usual, others decided to creatively change their lifestyles. For example, my wife and I, now stuck in the same premises for weeks, decided to engage in daily exercise routines since there was no gym access, prepare daily activities, and do something special on weekends—but still at home. We sought to create parallel innovative lifestyles that served as temporary solutions.

4. *Resources toward core competencies:* Many organizations spend a lot of resources on extra-curricular activities. Management considers such expenses necessary for team morale. But in a crisis, it is empirical to shift resources toward feeding the core competencies and not the luxuries. Core competencies may contribute toward flexing through a crisis, whereas other competencies, regardless of their importance under normal conditions, may be considered extravagances. This was the criticism faced by AIG in 2008 when they used US government bailout $85 billion funds from their economic turnaround to pamper their executives at a retreat for only $440K.[9] Despite the insignificant amount, aligning resources toward core competencies was a national demand during that economic crisis.

5. *Sales and customer relationships:* Only during a crisis will a leader be able to identify and shift relationships toward customers that matter—those true partners. These are delicate relationships that can only be tested during our response phase. A value-free customer is merely seeking profitability and may move on to the next supplier when things get tough. But a value-based customer is the one who participates in both good and bad times, willing to underwrite losses for the better good during times of crisis. These are the types of customer or partner relationships that leaders should be shifting toward. For example, in the Group bankruptcy story of chapter 7, it was very easy to identify which partners were value-based and which ones were value-free.

6. *Stakeholder mix:* This is a more complicated task. It requires leaders to diversify their risks and their income streams. It also forces leaders to choose which stakeholders to prioritize during crisis times. In my crisis leadership workshops, I usually conduct a Stakeholder Analysis with the participants in order to emphasize that our primary and secondary stakeholders tend to shift during uncertain times. We can no longer depend on the traditional analysis that was conducted during normal uneventful times. Sometimes, a nurse at the hospital during a vulnerable moment may be much more impactful than a close family member. One of my friends ended up marrying the nurse that cared for him during a health crisis—an example of shifting stakeholders' interests. So, keep checking your stakeholder mix.

9. Lengell, *Bailout.*

7. *Use of technology:* Zoom, MS Teams, WhatsApp, Google meets, Skype, iMessage, i-everything . . . are just a few examples that have infiltrated our lives in the past few years. Educational institutions had to deal with their own Learning Management Systems (LMS), whether it was a free platform such as Moodle, a paid one such as BlackBoard, or a tailored one created specifically for the institution. Good technology is necessary to shift through a crisis, and *Techflexing* encourages the use of technology to foster flexibility and balance.[10] However, there is a dark side to all this, as many uninformed individuals use technology to transmit incorrect and inaccurate data that could be harmful. Such was the case with the social media battles of those with versus against COVID-19 vaccinations. A leader must confront such inaccuracies/heresies and ascertain the team and organization's strategic direction.

8. *Workforce capacity building:* There is nothing more valuable than investing in organizational capacity strengthening during crisis times. Being flexible enough to use every opportunity for additional learning for individuals, teams, and the entire workforce presents an opportunity for growth and development beyond the crisis phases. For example, during the first wave of coronavirus lockdowns, a couple of our team members requested permission to pursue online workshops that they had planned to undertake in the past but failed due to excessive workloads. This was a unique opportunity for them to explore and undertake such capacity building programs, and now they are 'showing-off' the results of their investments.

9. *Work environment, well-being, and safety:* We are now experiencing a new era, where mental and physical well-being is an elevated leadership requirement. While communities are still asked to maintain physical distancing, most *homo sapiens* are in dire need of physical human contact. The flexibility required here is a combination of working-from-home vs. office presence, support groups, flexible working hours, results-based appraisals, and occasional traditional gatherings (e.g., Christmas lunch, birthday celebrations . . .). Maintaining safety during a crisis is necessary and should supersede any other consideration. I recall a time when Lebanon was still at war some 32 years ago, but the team managed to go out for a late lunch and head safely home before the snipers took their positions! It was a needed activity.

---

10. Bassous, *Techflexing.*

10. *Team engagement:* The key to flex through a crisis is to exercise continuous team engagement, such as open communication, empowerment, and improved processes. To reiterate, *leadership . . . in crisis* can only be as effective as its weakest team member. Hence, it is crucial to ensure that all team members are fully engaged, supportive, and trustworthy to complete the tasks at hand. Similar to an athletic team, organizational teams must understand each member's weaknesses, strengths, and needs, align toward a common goal, and synergize efforts to achieve that goal despite the looming crises. My wife and I worked as a team amidst her burst eyelid, my mysterious tumor, and the multiple crises in the country where we lived to phase out the D2D effects.

11. *Focus on improving processes:* Every crisis offers a "down time" which can be invested in improvements and adopting new processes. Instead of focusing our efforts on unproductive or conventional solutions, a crisis situation may be the impetus required to rid ourselves of unwarranted practices and instead adopt new entrepreneurial ones. In fact, entrepreneurial skills could best be depicted when the challenges are unconventional. Magd and colleagues[11] conducted a study on entrepreneurial skills required during the "new normal" that combined resilience, agility, and entrepreneurship as capabilities needed during a crisis to yield effective results. Thinking through improved results could take place at any time interval or place, even in a waiting room of the doctor's office or hospital lounge.

12. *Supply chain and network:* The supply chain is usually a complicated process, as it includes multiple external players. We are dealing with numerous suppliers, partners, and dispensers—all with conflicting interests. The flexible response toward the balancing act of stakeholders' demands and needs is crucial for surviving the crisis. Any tilting of favoritism toward one of the supply network members may be fatal. I recall the final days of our Group of companies and how management was trying to balance the supply chain demands. Banks were demanding the reduction of their credit lines; suppliers were requesting shorter payment periods; and agents were holding back their dues . . . all in anticipation of how the crisis would unfold. Managing the

11. Magd et al., *Entrepreneurial Skills,* 105.

supply chain network is difficult yet necessary to flatten the curve of their conflicting demands.

13. *Resource management strategies:* Unfortunately, every looming crisis is accompanied by a serious shortage in resources. Apparently, the two come together as one package: crisis and shortage. There is an old saying that goes something like this: *When a cow tumbles, many slaughters appear on the scene.* Meaning, when there is a scent of cash-flow need, suddenly every loan-shark within a few miles appears and offers a hand. Beware of such bailouts, as they are very short-term and associated with high risks. The preemptive solution is to always carry reserves that you, the team, or the organization need to actually forget that they exist, except in a crisis situation. Such alternative resources could offer the organization the needed flexibility and possibly save the situation. If invested, these resources need to be available for liquidation at very short notice.

14. *Views on business continuity:* There are several lessons one can learn from unsuccessful crisis leaders, such as trying to solve the wrong problem, creating the wrong solution, failing to act promptly, or attempting to "buy" a solution.[12] However, what we need to keep in mind is the long-term sustainability of our teams and entities. The risks must be carefully weighed to ensure longevity and survivorship, moreover sustainability and growth. While many personal crises force us to think one day at a time, flexible leaders can overcome this instantaneous strategy by looking and planning ahead toward the possibilities still available. I would have never thrived beyond my medical incident if I was not attentive to the pressing needs yet focused on the far-fetched vision.

Having examined these 14 strategic shifts in flexible responses toward a crisis, the next section will discuss briefly how to manage change in our crisis response, with the acknowledgment that change management is a wide discipline that is beyond the scope of this book.

---

12. Flamholtz and Randle, *Navigate a Crisis*, 237.

The good in change

Change is good. In fact, there is no change in life that cannot be considered as good, despite the temporary appearance that it was bad. Any leader that enters and exits a crisis the same, without instigating any changes to their behaviors, styles, perspectives, and/or philosophies, may have lost an opportunity for growth and missed valuable lessons. Remember the refrain of this book . . . don't ask: *"When will all this end?"* but rather *"How will all this end?"* If we focus on the *"when"* it may seem that we have no intention to change ourselves but actually wait until the situation changes. But if the focus is on the *"how"* it is already assuming a changed mindset and will for transformation.

In general, human nature dislikes change. People tend to enjoy their routines, comfort zones, familiarities, habits, and lifestyles. For example, some people have a daily mundane habit of drinking a certain type of coffee from a specific coffee shop at an assigned time of the day. I used to find such behaviors humorous, especially when we were at a conference center with a huge buffet breakfast and multiple coffee aromas, and then I find a couple of people walking in with the Starbucks coffee cups because they *had to have a Starbucks* (ironically, many of these venues offer Starbucks coffee in their breakfast buffet!).

When a crisis hits, it upsets people's routines and forces certain behavioral changes. Some resist this change in the hope that things would return to their "normal"—although they may not realize that their "normal" may no longer be significant after the crisis. Others adapt to new prospects, change, and move forward within a new mindset. This is why change is always considered a good component, as maintaining the status quo does not always serve the purpose. In fact, we have to seek the "good" in any change process and accept the embedded "goodness" resulting from a certain crisis.

I have often asked myself . . . what is the embedded "goodness" that accompanied the D2D phase of my malignant tumor? In fact, can we find any good change resulting from sickness, wars, death, . . . ? There is no easy answer to this question, as the good resulting from change could only unfold years after our primary encounters and denials. I know in my case that those few weeks of D2D were a wake-up call to change many of my behaviors and lifestyle patterns that were hurtful and unhealthy. Change is always good.

So, if change is always good, how can we manage change during a crisis for our benefit? Let me begin with a definition for managing change. Change management is the process of constantly renewing the leader, team, and/or organization's *alignment, formation,* and *competencies* in lieu of the needs of fast-changing internal and external environments.[13] Based on this definition, when a crisis hits, the leader is faced with three areas that require her/his ability to adjust, adapt, and apply.

The first is the *alignment* of resources. During any crisis, the response should prioritize the use of resources and align human, financial, and capital assets toward safe shores. This realignment requires a clear vision as to the changed destination. Managing the change of use of resource allocation may not always be welcomed by stakeholders, but it is a necessary step to start the process of revisiting priorities. For example, when COVID-19 forced organizations to downsize, some leaders chose to lay off some of the staff in an attempt to reduce expenses. But other organizational leaders shared these concerns with all their staff and collectively chose to retain the workforce as it is, reducing their incomes by the same ratio to compensate for the gain earned by layoffs.

The second is the *formation,* or reformation of resources, mainly human resources. Such development requires a learning attitude. According to Mento and colleagues, *"change is not possible unless people are willing to change."*[14] Usually an organization does not resist change, but rather the pattern of behaviors of people inside the organization that promulgate this climate of resistance or insistence to change. Leaders and teams play an important role in initiating, and reducing resistance to, organizational change. A few years back, I was asked to do a preliminary consultancy evaluation of a medical hospital and propose changes to its structure that would meet the changing environment. During my [final] meeting with the President, I explained that such changes would probably be resisted by several individuals, which could result in a loss of about 20 percent of the medical cadre. The President took a few days to think about it before responding that he could not risk losing all these people. A few years later, that hospital closed most of its departments . . . because people were not willing to change.

The third is the *competencies* required to manage the change process. Several approaches characterize how change occurs. A *planned* change triggers from being unsatisfied with the organization's status and accordingly,

13. By, *Organisational Change Management.* 369–80.
14. Mento et al., *A Change Management Process,* 53.

all stakeholders engage in a top-down process of change management; *emergent* change is a bottom-up, continuous, open-ended change process; *contingency* change depends on the situation variables to determine organizational structure and performance; and *choice* change is a proactive management decision to implement organizational changes.[15] Each one of these approaches requires a different set of skills and competencies. For example, *contingency* change, which is normally associated with crisis, requires alert crisis leaders with sense-making abilities, resilience, and tolerance to withhold internal and external pressure. Such contingent leaders may have excellent competencies during a crisis, but may prove to be ineffective in a post-crisis era.

Regardless, *leadership . . . in crisis* should adopt the dynamic *emergent* type of change, bottom-up, as an effective model for enduring organizational change due to the following reasons. First, front-liners, who are the key players in *emergent* change, are in direct contact with the beneficiaries and stakeholders of the organization; they can know firsthand what the needed changes are as they transmit the needs of the beneficiaries to the organization, and how to go about initiating the process.[16] Second, a bottom-up change is a living system, a continuous process with actions and reactions that determine the course of change in lieu of the needs of fast-changing internal and external environments.[17] It may be easier to be flexible with changes occurring at the bottom level than coming from the top. Leaders should seek to work well with bottom-up changes because the model links the leader's behavior and the teams' behaviors and performance.

One final comment regarding the good in change. Leaders should be aware that change does not come about without a cost—as indicated in the example of the 20 percent loss of the workforce. Therefore, it is important that leaders understand the mental processes that team members go through when a change during a crisis is initiated. In its simplest form, each team member passes through these four phases at different paces—called the Change Curve. (1) Denial: *This is not happening . . . for sure s/he will revert from this action . . . it simply cannot be done . . .* , (2) Resistance: *I will do every possible to stop this nonsense . . . this is outrageous . . . someone should stop her/him . . .* , (3) Exploration: *Maybe these changes are not so bad . . . let's give her/him a chance and see . . . it seems to be going in the right*

15. By, *Organisational Change Management.* 369–80.

16. Harari, *Change from the Middle,* 29.

17. Gould, *Drive Change,* 17–19.

direction . . . , (4) Commitment: *This is working just great . . . thankfully we undertook this direction . . . I will do everything possible to make it work . . .*

We now move into the final part of this chapter, which explores a level of Wisdom Quotient (WQ) required for a leadership response navigating through times of crises.

The Wisdom Quotient (WQ)

Wisdom Quotient (WQ) is a concept I researched a few years ago based on certain leadership behaviors that did not add up or make much sense.[18] Traditionally, researchers have associated leadership success with levels of Intelligence Quotient (IQ) and Emotional Quotient (EQ), and later on focused on Multiple Intelligences (MI) introduced by Gardner in the 1980s. However, my research indicated that there should be a level of wisdom associated with decisions taken, particularly through a crisis, by weighing the consequences of these decisions and their impact on multiple stakeholders.

But what is wisdom? Historically, wisdom has been associated with age, maturity, accomplishments, experiences, and/or social status. Early biblical writings refer to King Solomon as being wise, and the Book of Proverbs is full of wisdom sayings. Nowadays, however, the reference to wisdom is not very common, as if this attribute was no longer faddy or a necessity in today's industries and generations. In trying to define wisdom, Brooks offers a good explanation relevant to *leadership . . . in crisis:*

> *Wisdom doesn't consist of knowing specific facts or possessing knowledge . . . It consists of knowing how to treat knowledge: being confident but not too confident; adventurous but grounded. It is a willingness to confront counterevidence and to have a feel for the vast spaces beyond what's known.*[19]

Brooks' definition of wisdom intelligence emphasized the ability of how to treat knowledge, and whether this knowledge stemmed from cognitive or emotional foundations. Leadership wisdom encompasses understanding self, others, and the context, harmonizing goal achievements within various viewpoints, and seeking the short- and long-term common good through balancing intrapersonal, interpersonal and extrapersonal interests.[20] Based

18. Bassous, *What about WQ?*.

19. Brooks, *The Social Animal*, 37.

20. Service, *Innovation Across Cultures*, 35.

on the analysis of leading in times of crisis scanned throughout this book, wisdom seems to be a vital part of crisis leadership. Accordingly, I have defined Wisdom Quotient (WQ) as *"the ability to collect objective data, process it cognitively and emotionally, weigh the consequences intellectually and socially, choose the appropriate course of action, and manage the implications positively."*[21]

Following are a few recommendations to help improve WQ during a crisis response:

- *Manage knowledge sensibly:* With such vast information available on hand, managing knowledge—and determining what constitutes knowledge—is challenging.[22] Leaders should use their cognitive abilities to separate fact from fiction during a crisis, and to dissect emotionally charged materials. Concurrently, they should utilize social and emotional skills to dig deeper into knowledge bases. For example, in a medical condition, people tend to post their symptoms on Google and receive multiple information—some quite disturbing. It is best to wait and seek expert opinion, particularly in the D2D phase, before managing this knowledge sensibly.

- *Take your time:* Wise decisions require time to articulate, formulate, and assimilate. Leaders should seek "wise" counsel from close and objective companions before engaging in important life-impacting/changing decisions. By taking time to reflect, they would be seeking the short and long term common good of all stakeholders.[23] Furthermore, timely decisions are wise decisions; hence, wisdom is best depicted in time/contextual decisions.

- *Choose wisely:* You may think that your high IQ—which may sometimes elevate you among your peers and may instigate a feeling of superiority—can shape your decisions. This is a myth. In fact, the "smarter" you are, the more you should contemplate your decisions and alternatives.[24] A leader must keep in mind that other people possess unique contributions too. I recall a funny story a few years back when one of our book centers was subjected to a water damage claim coming from a nearby neurology-treating center. I met with the

21. Bassous, *What about WQ?*, para. 18.
22. Brooks, *The Social Animal*, 37.
23. Service, *Innovation Across Cultures*, 32.
24. Kumar, *EQ more Important than IQ*, 1–3.

owner—a neurologist—to try and settle the claim, but he kept justifying that the water damage was caused by faulty piping in our premises and not the high-pressure pumps they use in their center for treating patients, mainly with Parkinson disease. After he finished his defense argumentation, I smiled and responded with irony that I did not realize he was also a practicing plumber, in addition to being a neurologist . . . and suggested we leave the decision to the insurance surveyor!

- *Seek a balanced outcome:* Wisdom intelligence involves the harmonization of outcomes. Whatever difficult decisions leaders need to take during crisis times, they should also keep the consequences in mind. For example, history ascertains that a decision to go to war is never a wise one; it is sometimes necessary, but not wise if we evaluate the outcomes and consequences. This can only be achieved through the understanding of one's self and others, as leaders seek the right balance.[25]

- *Understand the context:* The Contextual Intelligence Quotient (CIQ) measure attributes much to wisdom in taking action under uncertain or unknown conditions, such as in a crisis situation.[26] Leaders must put an effort into recognizing and appreciating the diversity of alternatives and reactions before making a final judgment. Wisdom intelligence requires a holistic and inclusive approach to problem-solving, not a reactive spontaneous one. This is usually difficult to uphold when prompt decisions are needed. But it is an invitation to always seek to understand the bigger picture prior to reacting instantaneously and possibly harming the outcome.

- *Uphold relational balances:* Since most decision-making processes involve consequences on people and their lives, a highly effective WQ leader should always seek to keep relations with all concerned stakeholders intact—or at least respectable.[27] An understanding of individual uniqueness is needed. For example, in my 35+ professional career, I have had to let go (release, fire, make redundant . . .) many employees, staff, contractual workers, and volunteers. Yet I have maintained an ultimate intact personal relationship with most of them even after the "breakup." Many are still in contact, visiting me occasionally, and

25. Rockstuhl et al., *Cross-Border Leadership Effectiveness*, 828.

26. Service, *Innovation Across Cultures*, 19–50.

27. Service, *Innovation Across Cultures*, 29–34.

some have become donors too! Social interaction, interpersonal skills, and relationships should not be sacrificed; avoid using excuses, such as our dignity, to prohibit continued positive interaction.[28]

- *Know your values and judgments:* Wisdom is best displayed in uncertain and complex circumstances, such as *VUCA—Volatile, Unexpected, Complex,* and *Ambiguous*—events. A leader who is unaware of—or has intentionally ignored—her/his value system and ethical standards may not make wise judgments. The starting point of WQ are the inherent values; losing our value system is like losing the compass for wisdom intelligence. As a practicing Christian, my values are clearly expressed in the Bible as I seek to make judgments based on the servant-leadership model of Jesus Christ.

The above recommendations may constitute a good starting point for wisdom intelligence measures of our response to crises. The wisdom factor is embedded in our abilities to weigh our decisions and assess their consequences and implications. Therefore, high IQ levels and strong EQ portrayals are sometimes insufficient if not accompanied by value-based wisdom, or intelligence based on WQ.

In concluding this chapter, the focus was on the impact of crises that required leaders to respond with agility, flexibility, changed mindset, and wisdom. The emphasis on how we react during the discovery-to-diagnosis (D2D) phase was emphasized, including the lost opportunities and wasted energy during this phase. The chapter examined the multiple facets of agility, mainly the *financial, organizational, learning loop, leadership, people-factor,* and *supply chain* dimensions. It also addressed the flex—bend, stretch, or arch—in flexibility through a variety of tools and strategic shifts that organizational leaders could adopt and implement to survive a crisis. This was further examined through the good in change and the required change management of *alignment, formation,* and *competencies* as necessary tools, and concluded with several recommendations that helped improve WQ for *leadership . . . in crisis.* In the next chapter, the process of leadership confrontation and having honest, transparent conversations is introduced.

---

28. McFarlane, *Multiple Intelligences,* para. 14.

Recommended action points:

- Invest resources and energies objectively, timely, and wisely during the D2D pre-crisis phase.

- Use leadership learning and agility strategies to survive and thrive through crises.

- Be a change agent by aligning resources, formulating capacities, and focusing competencies toward solutions.

Chapter IX

Embrace Confrontational Leadership

Truth carries with it confrontation. Truth demands confrontation;
loving confrontation, but confrontation nevertheless.

(FRANCIS SCHAEFFER)[1]

My home country, Lebanon, has been experiencing multiple crises since
2019. It all started with a simple proposal by the government to charge
20 cents per day for the use of WhatsApp messenger (that's 6 US Dollars
per month!) for all mobile users. People reacted with demonstrations
and riots against this naïve proposal. But what followed was unexpected,
just like opening a can of worms, the equivalent of multiple-dimensional
crises. The demonstrators demanded the resignation of the Minister of
Communication, but then the entire government resigned as a step toward
pleasing the protestors and igniting nationwide reforms and restoration of
confidence in the public sector.

Well, the reforms never took place; instead, an economic, monetary,
political, and security freefall was witnessed like never before. Multiple
crises were hitting the nation and its residents like strong sea waves, knock-
ing down several industries with every blow. A few weeks after the first
demonstrations, the banks started to put restrictions on cash withdrawals.
This was later accompanied by slow, then hyper, inflation. Unlawful unan-
nounced capital control measures were practiced, and those desperate to

1. Schaeffer, *Quotes.*

withdraw their money or transfer them abroad for educational, medical, or family reasons were subject to enormous haircuts, reaching up to 80 percent cuts on their deposits. Then in early 2020, the new government announced that it would be defaulting on its Treasury Bonds (Eurobonds) repayment schedule, without any plans to refinance or renegotiate with the investors. This automatically dropped the credit rating of the banking system—once considered an equal to the Swiss banking system—down to a D- rating.

Then came the pandemic, which forced an already faltering economy to shut down for months. During all this, none of the political players (I cannot call them "leaders"!) were confronting the realities or speaking the truth. Instead, they were throwing accusations against each other, hoping for some foreign bailout to appear out of nowhere, despite the fact that none of the reforms requested by the international community were even close to being started. To add insult to injury, in the summer of 2020, the biggest non-nuclear explosion in history, the Beirut Blast, left 200+ dead, 6,500+ injured, and 300,000+ people homeless. And at the time of writing this chapter, the juridical process to condemn anyone for the blast is still pending, and the country continues to suffer hyperinflation, political unrest, and civil commotion.

How could *leadership . . . in crisis* handle all these unexpected hurdles without getting knocked off their feet? When a leader looks at the totality of a crisis and tries to handle all its diverse aspects simultaneously, s/he may fail. However, when you divide it into manageable chunks and confront each one separately and successfully, while confronting stakeholders with truths and realities of the situation, a leader could potentially emerge on top of the crisis. For our operations in Lebanon, I had to do exactly that: be proactive and preemptive in addressing the monetary and economic conditions, communicate the realities with our local and international partners, continue to deliver programs and activities in a hybrid model despite the challenges, and champion unprecedented path-goals toward growth. This gave our organization the reputation that we could lead and be productive despite multiple crises.

These final two chapters offer what most leadership theories, philosophies, models, styles, and behaviors ignore: *Confrontational Leadership*. Confronting realities, addressing diversions, facing problems, and simply "biting the bullet" are no longer the fad or trend for leaders. Instead, diplomacy in leading organizations and ministries, compromising solutions, and overuse of tactical actions have completely diluted this basic leadership principle. Leaders these days prefer the 'popularity' scale rather than the 'reality' scale. They choose to procrastinate, dodge, sway, or ignore confrontations to gain approval ratings and enhance their 'popularity', while sacrificing the overall stakeholders' good over narrow interests and personal comfort. This is even more evident in times of crisis.

Dr. Habecker's book on *The Softer Side of Leadership* mentioned the importance of *confrontation* as the first and primary phase of four phases relating to—what he termed—*The Forgiveness Cycle*.[2] Highlighting the correlation of confrontation with expectation, he elaborated on the positive side of confrontation, such as catching people doing the right thing rather than when doing the wrong thing. This attitude toward *Confrontational Leadership* is the correct notion, a formative type of confrontation where people appreciate the confrontation as part of their personal and professional development. Despite the negative connotation of the word "confrontation," I will attempt to spin a positive meaning to the term and present this leadership model as a desirable one, particularly in faith-based organizations and Christian ministries.

In this chapter, we will examine the pillars of *confrontational leadership* as an ethical and moral requirement for leading in times of crisis. The first concept to address is the *invisible elephant in the room* principle— where did this concept come from, how do confrontational leaders tackle it, and some strategies to adopt. This is followed by developing an appetite to *manage difficult conversations*, having honest dialogues, and tools to help avoid conversations that could go wrong. The third and last pillar is the *accountability to whom* attitude, where many leaders feel they are beyond questioning and are only answerable to their selected referee(s). The role of effective governance is brought into this discussion, as many failed *leadership . . . in crisis* models are associated with bad governance. Let us start with the first.

Invisible elephant in the room

The notion of the "elephant in the room" can be traced back to at least a couple of centuries, although the phrase only caught traction in the past few decades. It usually referred to a controversial issue that all stakeholders were aware of, but no one wanted to address or bring out to the open. It is

2. Habecker, *Softer Side of Leadership*, 175–79.

about diverting the focus from the obvious problem—and solution—toward other not-as-important issues. According to the Cambridge dictionary, there is an elephant in the room when *"there is an obvious problem or difficult situation that people do not want to talk about."*[3] That is why I have added the term "invisible" because if the problem was made visible to all concerned, then there would be no reason to ignore it. But still, many leaders choose to ignore the obvious.

Confrontational leadership should seek to start the conversations regarding any serious situation with the aim of revealing it and having the discussions required to resolve it. This is not an easy task, as many leaders try to evade such confrontations, particularly during crisis times, claiming that it was not the right timing to address such issues. And ironically, the right timing never comes around. Many coalition governments, teams, and boards of directors behave in a similar manner. They seem to accept the lowest common denominator that brings them together, keep postponing the discussions of serious and fundamental problems to avoid the confrontation, and avert their eyes away from proactive identification of the "elephant in the room." Such behaviors may serve for a short while before the inevitable truth and reality catch up, followed by the eruption of the problem in everyone's faces.

I have been a firm believer and a practicing *confrontational leader* since my early career years. I have tackled controversial issues ranging from organizational ones, such as unproductive staff, ineffective board governance, and inefficient operations to personal confrontations, such as inappropriate relationships, unacceptable behaviors, and lack of purpose. And it has made me a bit unpopular in several circles. This is not common within an *Honor/Shame* worldview of my upbringing, but more of an *Innocence/Guilt* worldview of my educational and professional journeys.[4] I always seek to reveal controversial issues with individuals and teams, in the hope that we can achieve a common understanding of the elephant's problem-impact and possible solutions. My action is not always seen with a positive outlook, particularly within *Honor/Shame* communities, who prefer to have indirect rather than direct conversations that frequently lead to additional misunderstandings and do not resolve the issues at hand.

In their book entitled *Co-Charismatic Leadership: Critical Perspectives on Spirituality, Ethics and Leadership*, authors Simon Robinson and

3. Cambridge Dictionary, *Elephant in the Room.*
4. Blankenburgh, *Inter-Cultural Intelligence*, 18–24.

Jonathan Smith recite this well-known story about placing an elephant in a dark room and asking people to walk into the room and describe, through feeling their way in the dark, what they believe they are experiencing.[5] In other traditions, the story is told slightly differently but with the same moral outcome, when four blind men are asked to describe an elephant by touching it with their hands, each from a different angle, deriving their own conclusions. Each one comes up with a different interpretation of what they were experiencing, defining the "problem" based on their own perceptions, interpretations, and conclusions. These interpretations are usually diverse, and sometimes contradictory, because each person is describing the "problem" from their own angle without shedding light on the overall controversy. While the majority of the people involved may agree that there is something large and significant in the room, none are fully able to describe the totality of the problem.

In a crisis situation, if a leader fails to shed light on a controversy or a problem, team members will tend to "feel" their way in the dark, hold on to what they believe is the issue, and derive their own mini- or sub-conclusions. There are several reasons why people, in general, do not want to address the elephant in the room. *Fear* is a common reason, as no one likes to shake the boat; *comfort* is another, as humans tend to hold on to their comfort zones; *underestimation* of the gravity of the situation; and *indifference* toward the organization or the cause.[6] Confrontational leaders would seek the opposite effect: a transparent, integrated, and clear response. It is part of the sense- and meaning-making that leadership must engage in before, during, and after a crisis. This is intensely important in an increasingly complex and plural world.[7]

Confrontational leadership also resonates with courageous leaders who have taken risks or had bigger dreams for their establishments. Through multiple interviews, Merilee Kern was able to capture several leaders' reactions to crises.[8] To illustrate, one leader attributed his personal growth aspects to a previous crisis he had survived; another claimed that her resilience had enabled her to call out the "elephant in the room"; others emphasized vulnerability as a listening tool before sharing truths. If a leader lacked the courageous and confrontational skills required to address

5. Robinson and Simon, *Co-Charismatic Leadership*.

6. LaRue, *Elephant in the Room*, para. 1.

7. Fruchter, *Study of Leadership*, 171.

8. Kern, *Courageous Leader*, 25–27.

the "elephant in the room," the unchallenged problem may feed into the persistence of the fear culture, encouraged by unbalanced use of power and influenced by unwarranted parties, depicted in declined productivity, and could potentially lead to lower morale and disengagement.[9]

Many authors, researchers, and practitioners offer advice on the best approaches to address this "invisible elephant in the room." Skimming through these suggestions—varying from making sure it was a real elephant to ignoring that it exists—and based on my own experiences in *confrontational leadership* essential for *leadership . . . in crisis,* the following are five proposed recommendations that may help leaders in lessening the elephant-effect to insignificance.

1. *Acknowledge its presence:* The first step is to acknowledge that there is an "elephant" by spotlighting the problem. Since this is mostly an invisible controversy, the first task of a confrontational leader is to acknowledge that it exists before dealing with it.[10] Most stakeholders would probably deny the presence of the problem, citing other factors that may be causing the same end-effect. This was similar to the Lebanese politicians in the opening story, when they tried to attribute all sorts of conspiracy theories as to why the country was collapsing, instead of putting their finger on the wounds of corruption and bad governance. Their claims for months were suddenly faced with undeniable brutal realities, and it was already too late to initiate corrective measures.

2. *Establish a communication strategy:* Once the "elephant" has been identified and acknowledged, along with the impact that the controversy may bring about, leaders should encourage having open communication about it.[11] This will remove the taboos surrounding the invisibility of the "elephant" and foster open dialogue. When there is a serious issue facing a team, the leader must adopt open and transparent communication processes by encouraging people to speak and provide constructive feedback.[12] Each team member, from their own angle or perspective, may contribute to providing a solution to the crisis. The leader's task is to establish a clearly channeled communication

9. LaRue, *Elephant in the Room*, para. 2.
10. Daskal, *Deal with the Elephant*, para. 6.
11. Bradt, *Address the Elephant*, para. 13.
12. Daskal, *Deal with the Elephant*, para. 12.

strategy that recognizes all the voices that need to be heard. This was evident in several countries' response to the COVID-19 virus, where multiple (sometimes contradictory) voices were featured addressing the controversies associated with this pandemic.

3. *Be direct, honest, and thorough:* There is no need to maneuver around the "elephant" when all stakeholders are aware of its presence.[13] Best to be direct in naming the obstacle and making it public, spelling out the truth to the best of one's knowledge. The leader should express honestly in seeking the group's help in addressing the "elephant" and try to be thorough in finding solutions collectively. Unaddressed issues will continue to foster confusion and distract people from the main tasks, which are usually time-consuming and unproductive. For example, when we were dealing with the multiple crises in my home country, our teams met almost daily (physically or virtually) to discuss every possible aspect of the crises, such as increasing prices due to hyperinflation, working from home to reduce operational costs, or canceling some planned events. The best outcomes were always the collective decisions that tackled specific problems.

4. *Set a positive intention:* Confrontational leaders should specify their positive intention to understand the controversy, rather than an intention to reprimand.[14] This requires a humble yet firm spirit: *"There is a crisis no doubt, and we need to work together to overcome it."* This positive intention should stem from a need for corrective measures rather than one that places blame on shortcomings. It is unfortunate that many people view *confrontational leadership* with a negative connotation, insinuating that such leaders are always out to make trouble rather than crediting such leaders for the courage they possess in undertaking controversial issues. This negative connotation could be attributed to a "blamology" attitude that some leaders depict after they call the "elephant" by its name, rather than realigning the course of action they should seek to achieve with their stakeholders. Any leader who practices courage only to call out the invisible "elephant" without collectively seeking corrective measures is not applying *confrontational leadership* to its full extent.

---

13. Bradberry and Wolfe, *Elephant in the Room,* para. 6.
14. Chism, *The Undiscussables,* 13.

5. *Enlarge the room:* In a recent visit of the United Nations Secretary-General, António Guterres to the Middle East, and during his departing press conference, he mentioned the concept of the "invisible elephant in the room," probably referring to all the armed militias taking matters into their own hands. He then introduced a possible solution to this crisis by adding: *"When you have an elephant in the room, the best thing you can do is expand the room so that the elephant does not become a problem."*[15] This recommended approach was interesting and worth exploring. When a leader is dealing with an "elephant" standing in the middle of a limited room of resources, stakeholders, and capacities, taking all the area, reserves, and breathing space, enlarging or expanding the boundaries of the room may slowly diminish the space occupied by the "elephant." In other words, by slowly enlarging the room—its capacity, stakeholders, resources, players, and supplies—the controversy may lose its significance. The "elephant" could be resized compared to the new zones of reality.

Manage difficult conversations

In a podcast by Dr. Deborah Tannen under the title *Why conversations go wrong,* the linguist stated the following: *"There are so many things that could misfire. The pace at which you speak, how you get to the point, the rhythms, the intonation patterns."*[16] Conversations could always turn the wrong way, particularly during the last two years or so, when people had to dialogue virtually. Imagine if the topic was a controversial one; the room for misinterpretation and misunderstanding is elevated and augmented. Managing difficult conversations is an integral part of *confrontational leadership* and a skill required for leading through crises with varying emotions, differences in opinions, and higher stakes.[17]

Let me reiterate the scenario behind having these conversations. You are dealing with *leadership . . . in crisis,* handling multiple crises and conflicting stakeholders' demands, juggling resources, trying to balance inputs and outputs, and managing multi-tier relationships across organizations and communities. In the midst of all this, a staff member walks into

15. Guterres, *Elephant in the Room.*
16. Tannen, *Why Conversations Go Wrong.*
17. Priftanji, *Managing Difficult Conversations,* 1723.

your office requesting to work from home permanently as her children are home-schooled and she has no other option, even though the infrastructure to function 100 percent from home-offices is still not in place . . . How one manages this seemingly unimportant conversation, in light of the other bigger issues at hand, is one aspect of the confrontation saga.

In the following few paragraphs, we will attempt to look at the positive aspects of holding difficult conversations rather than avoiding them. Avoiding these conversations can lead to unhealthy relationships, worsening situations, and declining productivity.[18] Avoidance of truthful and honest conversations may resemble what physicians call "The Silent Killer," mainly referring to hypertension or high cholesterol levels affecting a person's health without feeling a direct effect.[19] It is important that leaders, particularly in crisis situations, have these difficult conversations without procrastination, as the longer they postpone the confrontation, the wider the gap for corrective measures will be. The following five tools may help in initiating and sustaining difficult conversations.

1. *Self-awareness and preparedness:* These types of conversations should never be done in a reactive instant or at the spur of the moment. They require preparation and being self-aware of the consequences that may arise from the conversation. This is not easy to keep under control, and it may cause some sleepless nights when your mind is racing through all possible scenarios of how the outcome might be—which is not a bad thing, since it can contribute to the preparedness mode. I have been through similar situations too many times, when my mind is reciting the dialogue back and forth. This may be draining yet allows the leader to develop all sorts of response mechanisms to the direction of the conversations. The self-awareness and the identification of one's own vulnerabilities can add value to the dialogue.[20] It also involves knowing what you want as an outcome and keeping the end in mind. Hence, confrontational leaders should never engage in difficult conversations when they are angry or compromised, as they would lose control of the dialogue.

2. *Contrasting the obvious:* In an attempt to foster an honest dialogue, sometimes the leader needs to divert the conversation to another topic

18. Priftanji, *Managing Difficult Conversations*, 1723.

19. Beer, *Boards Need Truth*, 51.

20. Beer, *Boards Need Truth*, 50.

of mutual interest before retreating back to the difficult conversation.[21] The tone of the discussion should always be positive, avoiding any allusions of cynicism, irony, or demeaning tones. I have often monitored conversations that went wrong; it was rarely about the content of the exchange and more about the tone, body language, and interruptive gestures. The outcomes of such exchanges resembled throwing the baby out with the bath water. No one seemed content after the conversation and the gap was widened, sometimes beyond reconciliation. Hence, stating something other than the obvious until the time is right to address the real issues is a technique that may take longer in a confrontational conversation, but may lead to better results.

3. *Use stories:* The use of stories, or anecdotes from past experiences, are excellent tools to de-personify the dialogue. Stories are the meaning we give to past events and the emotions and judgments connected to them.[22] However, I do not recommend commencing the conversation with a story, because the listener may be trying tediously to understand the meaning of the story without much clue as to the intended purpose. This may cause more confusion and broaden the misunderstanding. For example, if you needed to relinquish the services of an unproductive staff member, you should not start the conversation with how . . . *many years ago, you left your employer and how that has worked fine for you* . . . nor open the conversation with *"we are no longer requiring your services"* . . . Best to start the conversation from the points raised in the last staff appraisal, areas that needed development, then revert to a story of, for example, a previous staff member who left your employment and found her/himself much better off in another organization.

4. *Negotiate for a win-win outcome:* Dealing with people is one of the most difficult tasks of management, mainly because of misunderstandings and misperceptions. Add to it the complexity of having a difficult conversation—and during a crisis. Confrontational leaders should always seek a win-win outcome, where the results of the dialogue could be viewed favorably by both parties. One strategy to adopt is to motivate, rather than manipulate, the opponent.[23] In any type of ne-

21. Priftanji, *Managing Difficult Conversations*, 1723–24.

22. Priftanji, *Managing Difficult Conversations*, 1724.

23. Denny, *Communicate to Win*, 39–40.

gotiation, the use of manipulation is short-lived, whereas motivating the negotiators toward mutually-exclusive goals seems longstanding. The conversation should be directed in a way that results in exciting outcomes. This is not easy to achieve, as the conversational parties are usually armed with defensive arguments, comparative analyses, and transactional opinions, which may take some time to disclose, move aside, then restart the building process. I have had to go through this process multiple times with other senior leaders who had prepared their arguments, said them at the onset of the meeting, then moved on together toward more win-win outcomes. The key is to allow room for this expression; otherwise, they would still feel manipulated.

5. *Organizational positioning:* Does your organization—company, church, community . . .—encourage a culture where people can have honest yet difficult conversations? Some organizations foster this type of open communication and are commended for clearing the air when controversies arise.[24] On the other hand, there are many organizational cultures that nurture manipulative, lobbying, back-stabbing, contradictory, and parallel conversations. Many organizational leaders prefer the latter culture, as it offers the opportunity to manage difficult conversations to their benefit, as a Machiavelli strategy to "divide and rule." I consider such positionings to be unethical and un-Christian. A pastor once conversed with me that lobbying was a legitimate democratic practice. I responded candidly that lobbying required going behind the backs of "brothers and sisters in Christ" and presenting a hypocritic two-faced strategy. *Confrontational leadership* is all about face-to-face conversations, not behind-the-back lobbying.

Accountability to whom?

In my own research on factors that motivated workers in faith-based non-profit organizations, several participants in the research claimed that they felt a higher calling, a vocation, that motivated them to do their work effectively.[25] While this type of motivation is applauded, it should not be confused with accountability. Our calling may be related to pious reasons, but we should always be held accountable by our fellow humans—colleagues,

24. Sequeira, *VUCA Organizational Context*, 341–43.
25. Bassous, *Factors that Affect*, 375.

board of directors, supervisors, management teams . . . Unfortunately, in many Christian organizations, some tend to believe they are only answerable to God, thereby escaping any tangible cohort accountability.

Confrontational leadership tends to hold people accountable for their expected productivity, output, outcome, and/or impact, but a confrontational leader should always be accountable to another body of stakeholders. Otherwise, *confrontational leadership* may be associated with despotism— the power of holding everyone accountable but not being answerable to any authority. To ensure a healthy and balanced confrontation, we will examine a few principles behind the practice of line accountability, particularly in a crisis situation, and emphasize the crucial role of an effective governing board of directors in maintaining the equilibrium for *leadership . . . in crisis.*

Within every confrontational setting, leaders could have the following three options to act upon based on Dr. Habecker's book:[26]

1. *The "ignore it" option:*[27] This occurs when the leader chooses to ignore the controversy and just move on, in the hope that it will go away. I have always argued against this option for two reasons: (1) The problem rarely goes away without an effective confrontation, and (2) ignoring it or procrastinating the confrontation is a waste of time and resources. For example, many faith-based organizations are homing unproductive staff simply because their leaders choose to ignore the needed confrontation. My argument goes something like this: If this organization was your own sole-proprietorship, you might choose to leave one or 100 unproductive employee(s) in the organization, as you are free to do as you wish with your profits; but when you are a steward of resources, mainly from donations, in a nonprofit, faith-based, and/or ministry, then your responsibility is ten-fold to confront an unproductive staff, as these resources are not yours to waste.

2. *The compromise option:*[28] This is the go-in-between option where the problem is handled through a compromising effort of both parties. It requires negotiations, bargaining, and concessions before a settlement is reached. But should confrontational leaders accept a compromise when there is a fundamental controversy that may hinder the integrity and credibility of the organization? Compromises tend to become

26. Habecker, *Softer Side of Leadership,* 177–79.
27. Habecker, *Softer Side of Leadership,* 177–78.
28. Habecker, *Softer Side of Leadership,* 178.

precedents, and before you know it, a leader may be asked to compromise on another situation that was already compromised, thereby abolishing the main principles of *confrontational leadership*. In my opinion, there are no gray areas when it comes to dealing with organizational problems; it is either black or white. I recall in my early days when I joined the Bible Society working alongside my predecessor, who was a godly man and a grandfather figure to the staff. One staff member took advantage of his laissez-faire style and was completely unproductive, which prompted me to step in and confront her with the facts, which eventually led to a dismissal package. A few weeks later, the Chairman of the Board of Directors requested a meeting wanting to renegotiate the severance package on behalf of that staff. My predecessor could not say "no" but I could! I told the chairman that, with respect to his wishes, we would settle the extra amount from our own salaries and not from the organization, so as not to set a precedent. And we did, jointly.

3. *The "winner take all" option:*[29] In this option, there is a bragging winner and a sore loser. The result of the confrontation is bitterness on one side and self-glorification on the other. This is usually the case in several cultures that exhibit the *Power/Fear* or *Innocence/Guilt* worldviews.[30] But this option is not very evident in the *Honor/Shame* worldview, where such cultures tend to opt for a compromise, or even ignore the confrontation. I have witnessed several organizational leaders take this route, thinking that they were fulfilling their confrontational mandates. In fact, such behaviors create more animosity and disrespect rather than attempt to sort out the controversy. Many years ago, our international organization, governed by a global board, had to let go of its Director General (DG) in a very ruthless manner. Although the board was unhappy with the performance of the DG, they never addressed these under-performances nor their expectations. Overnight, the DG received a legal termination letter, with no option to discuss, revert, or appeal the case. The result of the "winner take all" is a temporary apparent victory; the long-term effect is something else, as few candidates were willing to step into the DG position as they witnessed the handling of the board, and the outgoing DG

29. Habecker, *Softer Side of Leadership*, 178.
30. Blankenburgh, *Inter-Cultural Intelligence*, 11–14.

went to a competitor organization, severed all communication and networking activities with all stakeholders of the previous employer.

There is a fourth option that I would like to introduce: *The reconciliation option,* which will be addressed in detail in chapter 10. This option challenges confrontational leaders to address the controversy, problem, or behavior in a manner that is constructive and beneficial for both individuals or entities. It does not want to ignore the matter, reach a compromise, or achieve a win-lose outcome; it seeks to acknowledge the problem, present the facts, and accomplish the ultimate longstanding good of the individuals or entities involved in the confrontation. The following eight steps, inspired by management guru Peter Drucker, may offer the antecedents for the *reconciliation option:*[31]

1. *Uphold integrity:* Any confrontation should maintain the integrity of all involved intact. The leader must ensure high ethical and moral levels of any confrontation, regardless of the issues being addressed.

2. *Know the facts:* Confrontations should never be held based on hearsay, informal grapevine communication, or simply gossip. The leader is responsible for getting all the objective facts necessary to engage in the reconciliation process.

3. *Declare your expectations:* It is best that expectations are declared from the onset of the interaction, which can easily diminish any misunderstanding. The leader should provide feedback regularly and ultimately during the confrontation.

4. *Display commitment:* Although confrontations are unpleasant instances, it is important to remind people of personal and professional commitments to the cause. The leader must be living that commitment first before expecting others to follow suit.

5. *Expect positive results:* Every confrontation should seek positive results for all stakeholders involved, despite the difficult conversations and truthful facts. The leader should focus on positive behaviors while calling out the trespasses.

6. *Take care of people:* All confrontations encompass people with feelings, families, burdens, priorities . . . The leader is tasked with caring for the person while condemning the behavior.

31. Cohen, *Principles of Success,* 60–61.

7. *Duty before self:* Duty toward the organization, stakeholders, and board of directors should supersede the personal comfort of the leader. S/he must undertake the painful steps required to confront and reconcile the results.

8. *Be at the frontline:* Confrontation should never be seconded or delegated to a sub; it is the leader's responsibility. The leader is the most qualified individual to conduct this difficult but necessary task.

One final note on the role of governance in the accountability saga: Effective board of directors, trustees, or managers are key to upholding a *confrontational leadership* culture. There are two aspects to consider. The first is the information and data shared with boards, and the second is their role. Boards need to hear the true situational analysis of their organizations. They are responsible for holding the leader accountable for the overall performance of the organization. Research has indicated that, when boards request leaders to conduct honest conservations within the organization and uphold accountability, the entire organizational performance is improved.[32] Having these honest confrontations throughout the organization is a healthy practice.

I have wondered about the Ravi Zacharias International Ministry (RZIM) Board of Directors. How did they react when they learned that their founder and president was also a co-owner of a female-staffed spa in several locations? What was their line accountability and how did they practice their governance? The board definitely did an outstanding job after the crisis was revealed, but they were unable to steer the accountability balance prior to the eruption of all the sexual-harassment accusations.

Second is the board's role, along with the senior management team, who are jointly responsible for enhancing a culture of accountability within the boundaries of the organization.[33] Such behaviors infiltrate the structure, encourage honest, healthy and reconcilable confrontations, and can survive crises with minimal effect. While there is a thin line between governance and management, as in the anecdote mentioned under *the compromise option* section, it is important to emphasize the board's role in setting direction, monitoring results, and holding leadership accountable against stakeholders' expectations. Simply put, the board is the pedal, brake, and

---

32. Beer, *Boards Need Truth*, 50–52.

33. Luciano et al., *Strategic Leadership Systems*, 690.

steering wheel of the organization.[34] Their governance is the ultimate level of accountability umbrella that encompasses the confrontation thermostat of the organization. Boards are asked to undertake their true role in the confrontational journey.

In the secular world, there are many examples of failed board roles in the past two decades. The Enron and WorldCom collapses are recent examples. Bernard Madoff's Ponzi scheme is another. The 2008 economic depression bailouts are yet another. If boards of directors fail to uphold their confrontational accountable roles, particularly during crisis times, the snowball effect of failed organizations would plunge with a domino effect.

To conclude, this chapter underlined the provocative concept of *confrontational leadership* as a prerequisite for *leadership . . . in crisis*. Three main pillars were discussed. Recognizing and identifying the "invisible elephant in the room" as the first step in the confrontational journey, including the five strategies that may shed light on this "elephant." Managing difficult conversations when confronting cohorts or partners as a necessary evil that leaders should undertake. And holding all stakeholders accountable for their performance with a consolidation purpose as the ultimate canopy for consolidatory outcomes. The next chapter unfolds the detailed tools of confrontation, construction, and consolidation.

Recommended action points:

- Be prepared to tackle the "elephant in the room" in your personal and professional journeys.

- Equip yourself with the necessary tools to conduct difficult conversations, particularly in crisis situations.

- Adopt the *reconciliation option* with relevant stakeholders as a preferred confrontational tool and accountability process.

---

34. Nordberg, *Corporate Governance*, 7.

Chapter X

Adopt a Proactive Confrontational Leadership Model

Not only so, but we also glory in our sufferings, because we know that suffering produces perseverance; perseverance, character; and character, hope.

(ROMANS 5:3-4)[1]

MY WIFE AND I have shared multitudes of amusing stories about parenting three boys, who are two years apart, and transitioned into teenage years with a 3-year overlap (you can also imagine the financial burden when they transitioned to university level!). Most of the time, these stories were funny, revolving around hiking, camping, sports, music . . . One of the stories was about how we brought home a Dalmatian puppy. The classic movie, *101 Dalmatians,* had been re-released, and the boys, who were enjoying their early childhood, were just intrigued by this movie. So, we finally put our courage together and got them a puppy from one of our friends. We ingeniously named her "Spotty" (very creative) and I built her a wooden doghouse, painted it white, and splattered black spots on the doghouse. Spotty was also special, because she was heterochromatic: one blue eye and one black eye. All the neighborhood wanted to come and see the dog and the doghouse, and our boys acted like proud parents in front of their friends, although most of the work for caring for Spotty was on the parents' shoulders, as usual.

1. Romans 5:3-4 (NIV).

Five years into this project, and as my boys were now reaching the phase of growing children, we conducted a "science" project by breeding Spotty with a brown spotted Dalmatian. Ten puppies were born after six weeks, seven survived, four were black-spotted and three were brown-spotted. We placed Spotty and the puppies in the garage for a few weeks. It was a scene when the puppies would pop their heads over the short fence to greet our boys coming from school. And again, all the neighborhood wanted to come and see the puppies. However, keeping and caring for the puppies was a very tedious job, so we finally agreed with the boys that we would only keep two puppies and give away the other five. It was a difficult phase with lots of crying, but we finally ended up with Spotty and the two pups: Bernie, a brown-spotted male, and Spunky, a black-spotted female. The backyard was now dedicated to these three dogs, who were extremely friendly and only barked if there was a serious situation.

It was a Saturday afternoon when my youngest son, Michael Jr., who was probably 10-years-old at that time, and myself were at home. We heard the sound of pebbles being thrown and bouncing off the kitchen backdoor in the backyard where the dogs resided. I opened the kitchen backdoor but could not see who was throwing pebbles at the dogs. My son was angry at these inconsiderate passersby, but we couldn't do much. This kept repeating (as the stone-throwers were probably not aware that anyone was home) until I decided to take action. With the next pebble landing in our backyard, I jolted the kitchen backdoor open, ran through the yard, jumped over the garden fence, and chased the two kids down the road for about 50 yards/meters before they ran out of breath and stopped, feeling scared and threatened by a crazy adult going out of his way to chase some kids playing around.

"What are you doing?" I yelled at the two breathless boys. *"Why are you throwing rocks at our dogs? Over and over? What did they ever do to you?"* Suddenly I saw two ladies a little bit ahead, trotting their way to the scene. Apparently, they were the two boys' mothers, taking a promenade walk on our back street, while their sons were teasing our dogs (and us) by throwing pebbles and then disappearing, over and over again. I calmed down and explained to the two mothers what had been going on for the last 30 minutes. They immediately apologized for their sons' behavior, reprimanded the boys, asked them to apologize to me (and Michael Jr. who had now caught up with me), and went on their way.

Here is the gist of the story. From the moment I took action and until we got back home, Michael Jr. was repeating this phrase with pride: *"That's my father . . . that's my father."* Although we were alone, the two of us, father and youngest son, it was one of the proudest moments of my life. A crisis that was teasing and provoking my son, and I took action to resolve it. *"That's my father."*

And it is my genuine hope that throughout the anecdotes and experiences shared in this book, we realize, acknowledge, and declare the One who accompanies us through all our crises: *"That's my Father . . . That's my Heavenly Father."* *That's my Father* who has sustained me this far . . . *That's my Father* who helped me overcome this crisis . . . *That's my Father* who cares for my every need . . . *That's my Father* who I can depend on, seek, and find. *That's Him.* This *Father* portrayed Himself to humanity through His Son, Jesus Christ, who lived as a human amongst us, being similar to us in every aspect except sin.

We are now at the final episode of this journey, where everything comes together. This entire book is focused on research, theory, experience, and practice. Setting those aside, we now focus on the leadership model that changed history, that of Jesus Christ. This chapter provides several scenarios of probable team-members' lagging performance, particularly during crises, based on the leadership model of Jesus Christ, and how he addressed such situations. We will be examining the four reactions that people usually adopt when faced with overwhelming crises: *Disloyalty, Denial, Doubt,* and/or *Disappointment*—the 4D's. We will then explore how a leader should be tackling these unfortunate reactions through a confrontational approach that *leadership . . . in crisis* should examine, and hopefully adopt through challenging the 4D's with 3C's: *Confront, Construct,* and *Consolidate.* But first, let us examine the context in which Jesus Christ deployed his leadership model.

The context

Hundreds of articles, research, and books have focused on the leadership style, model, and philosophy of Jesus Christ.[2] From the mere few pages of the synoptic and John's Gospels, scholars, theologians, philosophers, researchers, and practitioners have produced a wealthy library of leadership theories, all revolving around Jesus Christ's few years of historic life. No

2. Nsiah, *Leading as Jesus Led,* 103.

other person has attracted so much attention from the academic, educational, and even business worlds[3]—not because of what happened during Jesus Christ's short earthly life span, but due to the consequential aftermath that changed history. Here is how Jesus Christ led his people in preparation for the ultimate crisis.

I. He invested in people

The three years that Jesus Christ spent in selecting and developing his leadership team were part of a formation program in crisis management that eventually transitioned into a succession plan.[4] The verb "teach" appeared some 60 times and the word "disciple" is mentioned 261 times in the four gospels and the book of Acts.[5] Not only did Jesus Christ teach in words, but also in deeds, providing the ideal role-model leadership style that was expected of his followers. His teaching method was a common-knowledge process, using parables, examples, and relational one-on-one tutoring.[6]

Accordingly, Jesus Christ earned the global title: "The Great Teacher."[7] This recognition did not only come from his followers, but also from those who did not follow his teachings; even his foes. He invested in his people by ensuring that his vision, mission, and focus were transmitted regularly in words and works. His equipping and empowering styles translated into a powerful movement that was hundred-fold more effective post-crisis and upon his succession. This great teacher taught his followers using the following techniques:

1. *He invited people to walk with him.* [8] He allowed his people to share his life, eating, socializing, and interacting with him. Teaching his people went beyond the formal setting and more toward informal learning.

2. *He invited people to do and become something.*[9] He clearly invited his people to action, crisis management, and to glory. Working toward an altruistic goal made his people feel valued and worthy.

3. Roberts, *Leadership of Jesus*, 1–5.
4. Gray, *Formation and Transitions*, 9–10.
5. Foster, *Discipleship*, para. 1.
6. Ward, *Facilitating Human Development*, 12–14.
7. Ward, *Developing Christ-like Leaders*, 9.
8. Ward, *Developing Christ-like Leaders*, 10.
9. Ward, *Developing Christ-like Leaders*, 10.

3. *He walked with his people toward a changed lifestyle.*[10] He challenged the social structure of the time and accepted a humble, simplistic life. Living in humility with his people set a precedent for his followers and successors.

4. *He felt compassion and expressed his feelings to his people.*[11] He penetrated the formal and social structures by establishing intimate emotional bonds with his learners. Expressing his emotions and empathy brought him closer to his people.

5. *He responded with care and respect to the people's questions.*[12] He never turned away inquirers, seekers, or doubters. Listening to their concerns and challenges strengthened the bond with his people.

6. *He put his people to work in active learning projects.*[13] He engaged in teaching and learning through doing things—a scholarly-practitioner model. Learning through experience and apprenticeship intensified the transfer of knowledge.

7. *He reoriented his people in their cultural relationships.*[14] He established new platforms for intercultural reconciliation with the other communities. Enlarging the scope of accepting the other who is different globalized his teachings and earned him the title of a global leader.

II. He organized his people

A closer reading of the gospels reveals an organizational leadership structure that he established to overcome crisis situations. This is a rarity with charismatic leaders, as in the case of Jesus Christ, as such leaders tend to possess strong influential skills but may lack organizational rigor. Evidence of Jesus Christ's charisma trace back to his astonishing encounter with learned men at the early age of 12 and throughout his three-year change mandate.[15] Yet with his charismatic leadership and very short tenure, he was able to organize his people in a sustainable form to overcome the crisis.

10. Ward, *Developing Christ-like Leaders,* 10.
11. Ward, *Developing Christ-like Leaders,* 10.
12. Ward, *Developing Christ-like Leaders,* 10.
13. Ward, *Developing Christ-like Leaders,* 10.
14. Ward, *Developing Christ-like Leaders,* 10.
15. McCulloch, *Two Problems of Charisma,* 15–20.

The main purpose of this organizational leadership would be to establish a core group that would eventually be called to lead others.[16] While most people recognize the vital role of the 12 disciples, Jesus Christ recognized various capacities within his team and organized his people accordingly. He also viewed people in terms of their needs rather than his own.[17] This enabled him to allocate roles and distribute responsibilities accordingly. Following are components of his organizational skills:

- *The 12 disciples:* This constituted the *core team* that Jesus Christ hand-selected, trained, served, and nurtured.[18] They witnessed his leadership and recorded his everyday behavior. Eventually, they became the pillars of the mission and took over the mantle in the post-crisis phase, including establishing a team-member succession plan with the nomination and selection of Matthias in Acts chapter 1.

- *The inner circle:* From within this team, Jesus Christ entrusted a small group—Peter, James, and John—to bear witness to special encounters. In recognizing their capacity to go the extra mile, he invested in these three individuals who would, in the succession plan, assume key crisis leadership roles. Jesus Christ acknowledged their value and motivation to serve his mission.[19]

- *The base assembly:* These were the appointed 72 (or 70) with a specific mandate mentioned in Luke chapter 10. They will later serve as the assembly to select a replacement disciple in Acts chapter 1 and in the organization of the early church in Acts chapter 6. Jesus Christ was preplanning the potential growth of people, even during the crisis, to equip them for future responsibilities.[20]

Other formats of informal groups were organized around the formal structure, such as the group of women who were catering to Jesus Christ and the disciples, the treasurer (Judas the Iscariot) who attended to the financial needs, and various community leaders who viewed Jesus Christ's mission favorably, such as council members Nicodemus and Joseph of Arimathea (John chapters 3 and 20). In organizing his people, Jesus Christ

---

16. Sánchez, *Lessons in Leadership*, 23.

17. Low, *Moving Mountains*, 56.

18. Slear, *Level-Five Leader*, 25.

19. Low, *Moving Mountains*, 58.

20. Low, *Moving Mountains*, 60.

treated them as equals although he was able to know and identify differences and gaps in capacities.[21] His earthly legacy represents the largest organization known to humanity today, which has withheld multitudes of crises over time and throughout the world.

The 4D's

Effective *leadership . . . in crisis* requires effective learning, as learning is an integral part of leadership.[22] People are prone to mistakes and will commit many blunders in their personal and professional journeys. The key is to learn from mistakes during crises and move on, rather than become hostage by these blunders. Having examined the context that accompanied the investment incurred and organization depicted in the leadership model of Jesus Christ, let us now observe how people reacted at the onset of the crisis and what caused, and still causes, the 4D's.

Despite investing in and organizing his people, Jesus Christ confronted a recognizable failure ratio at the end of the three-year formation program. Separate incidents with individuals and the team put to question the effectiveness of investing, teaching, equipping, empowering, organizing, and developing people when a crisis was impending. And although a few incidents were recorded, there could have been other members sharing the same dispositions yet remaining anonymous. At the very end of his earthly mission, Jesus Christ encountered a most discouraging setback from his entrusted entourage when the crisis was at its peak. This supposedly "failed" *leadership . . . in crisis* consisted of the following 4-D's perspectives: *Disloyalty, Denial, Doubt,* and *Disappointment.*

I. Disloyalty

Disloyalty is defined as the *"quality of not being loyal to a person, country, or organization"*; it can also refer to unfaithfulness toward a person or cause.[23] In organizational leadership, loyalty refers to the allegiance a person has for the leader, team, and/or organization. It is usually the success indicator of the leadership cause. Once a team's loyalty is jeopardized, particularly in a

---

21. Low, *Moving Mountains*, 58.

22. Covrig, *Lessons in Leadership Development*, 15–16.

23. Oxford Languages, *Disloyalty.*

crisis, the entire mandate is at risk of falling apart. Loyalty, or lack of, is associated with the authenticity and ethical behavior of the leader.[24] A leader who could express the cause in an authentic manner and illustrate ethical behavior is bound to yield stronger loyalty amongst the team members— which was evident in Jesus Christ's leadership. Loyalty is highly correlated with organizational success; the stronger the organizational culture's association with loyalty, the better the results.[25]

Disloyalty is the reverse, negative side of organizational leadership success. I have witnessed several behaviors of disloyalty in my 35+ years of leadership, even from my closest cohorts. For example, when I was working in our Group of companies, our Executive Manager, who was nurtured throughout his professional life within the organization, starting from humble beginnings to the executive level, decided to leave. While this was a legitimate and expected career move, his manner and choice of departure portrayed a level of disloyalty. His departure was announced in a local newspaper window ad and not through a face-to-face meeting, and he transitioned toward our fiercest competitor.

Similarly, after three years of loyal service in the team and as treasurer, Judas the Iscariot turned against the leader and betrayed him. This disloyalty was stemmed from a human desire to establish an earthly institution with sustainable physical resources. Moreover, the love of money is the root of many evils. The price of disloyalty was 30 pieces of silver, worth buying a small plot of land. The main factors behind disloyalty are usually related to money or power.

II. Denial

Denial is the active *"refusal to acknowledge a person or a thing."*[26] Denying a leader's influence and status is quite detrimental; similarly, denying people's resistance to change is damaging. Some leaders, when facing a crisis, take actions that their teams may not feel comfortable with, and may resist. Unfortunately, many leaders tend to deny that such resistance to change exists, and move forward without consideration of these change-phobics.[27] Conversely, team members may deny the authority and authenticity of their

24. Keselman and Saxe-Braithwaite, *Authentic and Ethical Leadership,* 154–56.

25. Alimudin et al., *Effect of Spiritual Leadership,* 85.

26. Merriam-Webster, *Denial.*

27. Kerfoot, *Immunity to Change,* 422–23.

leader's decision-making processes. This can take several formats, from denying receipt of the instructions to intentionally sabotaging the decisions.

Denying a leader's legitimate standing undermines the entire organization and/or cause. *"She is not my boss"* or *"He does not represent us"* are examples of current days' denial processes phrases. In the past few years, there have been a lot of programs, activities, and funding allocated to the Middle East and North Africa (MENA) region in the area of trauma healing. Attempts to align the efforts and synergize the ministry have failed so far. What is worse are all the efforts to deny and eliminate the other, as if they were non-existing. Denying a person, leader, organization, ministry, or pastor's well-meaning effort is hurtful and damaging to the overall morale of the institution.

After assuming many leadership positions within the team, a proactive member, always ready to take the initiative and the first to recognize Jesus Christ's deity, Peter, under pressure, denies knowing the leader. This denial was caused by a reactive chain of events that reversed the initial objective behind the plan—to stay close to the leader during the crisis. Unable to protect the leader, Peter's denial added insult to injury. While Peter's denial was a result of fear and cowardness, many people today knowingly deny Jesus Christ as the savior of humanity, which is a sad reality.

III. Doubt

Doubt is *"to believe that something may not be true or is unlikely . . . to have no confidence in someone or something."*[28] To me, this is worse than disloyalty or denial. To doubt the capacity of a leader to find the right solutions during a crisis is destructive. Doubt has always accompanied relationships—man and wife, parents and children, managers and staff, politicians and constituencies, ministers and congregations ... It can become a fictitious monster, transmitting an array of uncertainty and ambiguity in an organization.[29] Unfortunately, the "doubters" sometimes earn more attention than the respondents, particularly in a crisis, when uncertainty levels are high and the environment is complex and changing rapidly. Doubt is a killer of team unity and can affect the team spirit indefinitely.

I do not keep count of how many times various team members had questioned and doubted decisions I had to take during a crisis. My

28. Merriam-Webster, *Doubt.*

29. Hawkins and Edwards, *Monsters of Doubt,* 29.

argument was and will continue to be the same: *Look at the bigger picture before questioning the matter.* But it is a fact that not all team members have access to the bigger scenario. Therefore, *leadership . . . in crisis* needs to realize that doubt is a natural companion when leading in crisis times, and should contribute more time in communicating the bigger picture to lessen doubters' fears. While my team had questioned and doubted my decisions during certain crises, they have also recognized the ultimate common-good outcome resulting from those decisions in the post-crisis phases, some claiming: *"We never really doubted your decision."* But deep down inside, I know that they did doubt, and that is okay and legitimate.

After bearing witness by 10 other members of the team, Thomas challenged the leader and his team members by doubting Jesus Christ's prophecies and the team's eye-witness account. This doubting attitude originated from a pragmatic realistic-pessimistic stance and a drive to differentiate Thomas from the team, now that the leader was no longer around. High standards of evidence were required to change this doubter's decision. We encounter such doubters every day of our lives who challenge our precepts and question our decisions.

IV. Disappointment

Disappointment is defined as *"sadness or displeasure caused by the non-fulfilment of one's hopes or expectations."*[30] This is probably the less intense of the 4D's but the most generalized reaction. Team members may vary in their disappointment levels toward the leader and the format in which they express their dissatisfactions. Disappointment simply indicates a difference in alignments between expectations. When expectations are aligned, disappointment disappears. Unethical leadership practices usually lead to disappointments and dissatisfaction.[31] Some levels of disappointment are beyond repair, just like breaking a clay jar, whereas most other milder disappointments are mendable. The good thing about disappointment is that it can turn around very quickly.

My youngest son was disappointed that Saturday afternoon when I could not take action to halt the perpetrators who were throwing pebbles at our dogs in the backyard. It took a couple of minutes of proactive crisis management to turn the situation around. The situation turned from

30. Oxford Languages, *Disappointment.*
31. Keselman and Saxe-Braithwaite, *Authentic and Ethical Leadership,* 154.

disappointment to admiration. People are continuously disappointed with their leaders: *she did not get the raise she expected; he was hoping to work from home all five working days; assigning a project lead to Tamar rather than Sam* ... Leaders can allow moments of disappointment to linger until they reveal a plan that could lead to a turnaround situation and respectful acceptance of the outcome.

Despite having accompanied Jesus Christ for 3 years, lived, ate, and walked with him, observed his miracles as eye-witnesses, all the disciples were disappointed with the outcome of this journey (including the two disciples of Emmaus). It was only a few days earlier when they were disputing amongst themselves who would sit on his right and left side. However, during the crisis phase, they all went and hid in the upper room, afraid to go out, be seen, or be associated with the leader. Today, we can notice similar disappointment patterns with several so-called "Christian leaders" who have not upheld their promises to their followers.

The 3C's

As I mentioned in the introduction of this book, I like confrontations; despite the lost opportunities encountered in my professional tenure due to confrontational positions, I prefer it anytime, any day, over lukewarm diplomatic compromises. However, as human beings, we avoid confronting people, especially those closest to us. We fear that *confrontation* may result in losing those dearest to us, so we avoid it. We tend to procrastinate in the hope that the crisis or problem will go away by itself, but it rarely does. In fact, some of my best friends and supporters are those I confronted—and even clashed with—over matters in the past. And I look back with a smile over the discussions we had that led our relationship to transition to the next level, the *construction* level. Now that each party has expressed their stances and cleared the air, it is time to construct our expectations and social contracts based on these new paradigms. There is no turning back to the era of non-confrontations. And this is topped off with a *consolidation* factor that unites outlooks and aligns efforts.

How did this leader handle these seemingly team-disruptive 4D's failures that occurred within a short span of crisis days following years of team building? Jesus Christ attempted to reconcile, using the 3C's, with each person/incident. With Judas' *disloyalty*, Jesus Christ was not given the opportunity to reconcile with him as he (Judas) took his own life in remorse.

But with Peter's *denial*, John chapter 21 described how he reinstated Peter's confidence and leadership responsibilities by asking him, three times (ironically, the same number that Peter is recorded denying Jesus), to take care of His sheep. With Thomas' *doubt*, Jesus attended to his cognitive level and reconciled with him using his (Thomas') preset standards, which were no longer necessary. And with the disciples, Jesus Christ appeared to them several times, empowered them with the gift of the Holy Spirit, and turned their *disappointment* into admiration, courage, and bearers of the Good News to the entire world.

The 3C's provide *leadership . . . in crisis* with the necessary tools to wrestle the 4D's that summarize how countless people may react in uncertain times. Leaders working with teams during *VUCA—Volatile, Unexpected, Complex, Ambiguous*—contexts should absorb the 4D's retorts and embrace a lifestyle of internal self-confrontation and external confrontations of real situations.[32] Through understanding the team and their approaches, *leadership . . . in crisis* should learn, adopt, practice, and disseminate the 3C's: *Confront, Construct,* and *Consolidate*.

I. Confront

The proactive action of positive confrontation is the first necessary step in the reconciliation process. It requires creating an environment—an organizational culture—that enables and promotes the channeling of energies toward adopting the new realities.[33] Confrontation should not be limited between a leader and a team member, but should also include cohort healthy confrontations to enable internal competition and creativity. A word of caution: *Confrontation should never be misinterpreted as an invitation for hostile clashing, conflict or blowing off steam.* It is about dialoging through a two-way communication about the controversy or problem with the aim of reducing its impact.

It is interesting that the gospel narratives of Jesus Christ's confrontations in at least two of the incidents mentioned in the 4D's, predate the actual incidents. For example, with Judas' *disloyalty*, Jesus confronted Judas during The Last Supper by telling him: *"What you are about to do, do quickly."*[34] He confronted Judas based on the latter's intention to disown his

---

32. Sequeira, *VUCA Organizational Context*, 341.

33. Essawi, *Value Confrontation Leadership*, 47.

34. John 13:27 (NIV).

master. Same with Peter's *denial*, when, in the same setting, he told him: *"Truly I tell you, this very night, before the cock crows, you will deny me three times."*[35] Peter responded by denying the denial and patronizing the confrontation: *"Even though I must die with you, I will not deny you."*[36] This is a fundamental lesson on the need to conduct a self-confrontation prior to confronting others. As for Thomas' *doubt* and the disciples' *disappointment*, Jesus Christ confronted both incidents/people head-on by repeating the phrase *"Peace be with you"*[37]—rather than *Shame on you*—in an intentional constructive confrontation. He further challenged Thomas by adding *"Put your finger here; see my hands. Reach out your hand and put it into my side. Stop doubting and believe."*[38] What a powerful lesson in upholding positive confrontations.

II. Construct

After confrontation, leaders are tasked with the duty of reconstructing the relationship to its aspired level. Leaving the process at the confrontation level may be subject to different interpretations and misinterpretations. Therefore, it is necessary to construct the relationship and expectations based on a common aligned understanding. This requires conversations that should be conducted safely, constructively, and non-defensively.[39] Leaders should avoid reverting back to the confrontational problem during this phase and focus on rebuilding new precepts of commonality. The ultimate goal is to empower and motivate associates by overlooking the past and moving forward.

In my opinion, the best illustration of the construction factor in history was how Jesus Christ dealt with the 4D's. It is logical to exclude Judas' *disloyalty* from the list, but there is something to say about the way Judas' successor was consequently chosen. The construction criteria were already in place for succession: Someone who had accompanied the Lord from the time of his baptism and witnessed his resurrection.[40] Peter's *denial* construction was more direct. There was no blame or reverting back to the

35. Matthew 26:34 (NRSV).
36. Matthew 26:35 (NRSV).
37. John 20:19 (NIV).
38. John 20:19 (NIV).
39. Beer, *Boards Need Truth*, 50.
40. Acts 1:21–22.

denial incident, but rather a clear mandate of what needs to be done in the present and future: *"Take care of my sheep."*[41] By these directives, Jesus Christ reinstated Peter to his original mandate. Constructing Thomas' *doubt* was equally personal and emotional, having confronted Thomas with the facts of his pierced hands, feet, and side. There is no account that shows Thomas actually doing that, touching the wounds, as the initial confrontation was more than sufficient. And the *disappointed* disciples were constructed and empowered with the same mission of Jesus Christ: *"As the Father has sent me, I am sending you."*[42] Restoring them to the required status that changed history.

III. Consolidate

The consolidation, or reconciliation, phase is a necessity for proper closure. The phrase "to consolidate" is usually derived from financial transactions and entries, used by two vendors to consolidate their accounts, making sure that they have the same figures and expectations. Relationships require the same type of consolidation. *"Are we good?"* is a common colloquial way to express this action. The page is turned, and there is no turning back or recalling any of the controversies, with the exception of the lessons learned. Consolidation requires *leadership . . . in crisis* to empower their learnable team members, relinquish some control mechanisms, and encourage servant leadership.[43] Reconciling with people who had expressed 4D's reactions prerequisites a servanthood heart.

With the servant leadership model in mind, let us examine one last time how Jesus Christ consolidated with his entourage. As already mentioned, Judas passed the opportunity to consolidate with the Lord, although the Bible includes many similar narratives where reconciliation was possible with *disloyal* people, such as King David's illustration in chapter 7. Scared and depressed Peter who went back to his old fishing job following his *denial* incident became the spokesperson of the early church, challenging cultural barriers and authorities through his sermons, just because Jesus Christ shared with him the keywords: *"Follow me."*[44] Insecure *doubting* Thomas, having admitted the deity of Jesus Christ, *"My Lord and my*

41. John 21:16 (NIV).
42. John 20:21 (NIV).
43. Paas et al., *Antecedents of Servant Leadership*, 639–41.
44. John 21:19 (NIV).

God,"[45] became the apostle who traveled all the way to the Far East with the Good News message. Jesus Christ's next words to Thomas were profound: *"Because you have seen me, you have believed; blessed are those who have not seen and yet have believed."*[46] A message to all Christian believers of all times and ages. And the frightened and *disappointed* disciples were consolidated and given the Great Commission to go to all nations.[47] Early church history indicated that 11 of the 12 apostles were martyred for their faith, and only one survived old age, banished to Patmos Island. Such was the power of the consolidated mission.

Leadership . . . in crisis implications

Adopting the implementation of the 3C's to counter the 4D's is not an easy task. I have failed many times in perpetuating these approaches. Some leaders and organizations cannot accept such behaviors amongst their team members, even during a crisis, yet the leadership lessons from Jesus Christ's life indicate that reconciliation is possible.[48] This leader's legacy is based on the highest level of ethical values, humble leadership, and global reach, yet provides the opportunity for a second chance by not giving up on people. This leader exemplified level-five leadership as demonstrated through his passion, vision, mission, goals, plan, and recruitment of the right people despite their weaknesses.[49] Second chances are, therefore, legitimate and necessary for personal and organizational development.

The most important lesson is not to give up on people, regardless of the gravity of their failures. Jesus Christ was able to transform the 4D's perspectives from failure to success. He transformed (1) Judas' *disloyalty* into personal remorse, regret, and consequential events, (2) Peter's *denial* into an eloquent public speaker and champion of the mission, (3) Thomas' *doubtful* attitude into an evidenced factual proof of his claims, and (4) the disciples' *disappointment* into the largest mission in history. With the exception of Judas, people were always reconciled to the leader and adopted his mission with the same rigor. Organizational leaders are asked to reconsider their policies and procedures when it comes to people's behaviors in

45. John 20:28 (NIV).
46. John 20:29 (NIV).
47. Matthew 28:19–20.
48. Bergant, *Follow the Leader*, 31.
49. Slear, *Level-Five Leader*, 24–25.

times of crisis, using the 3C-4D model below continuously and repeatedly. *Confront, Construct,* and *Consolidate* any behavior or team reaction during a crisis that may be regarded as *Disloyal, Denial, Doubt,* and *Disappointment.* That's real *leadership . . . in crisis.*

FIGURE 7

3C-4D Leadership in Crisis Model

I recently came across a satirical comic-strip cartoon portraying the dilemmas of refugees trying to cross the high seas on a raft toward developed countries, moving from one crisis (their homelands) through another (their rough journeys) toward the unknown (a host country). The cartoon shows a small boat full of refugees being confronted by border patrol police pointing their guns at the vulnerable boat. A young refugee is calling out to the border patrol naïvely saying: *"Don't worry, we are not here to steal your country."* He received an answer from border patrol police: *"Why not, we stole yours!"* This is an ironic reminder of the centuries of colonialism and how humanity should be given a second chance. Simply to say that most of us have, at some point in the past, reacted within the 4D's perspectives toward other leaders during a crisis, and were thankfully reciprocated with the 3C's.

Jesus Christ never gives up on people. He gave second chances to his people and continues to do so to date. Being humble, serving, and reconciling, he was able to develop—not penalize—his people. Jesus Christ did not present his people with a five-year plan or long-term objectives when he called them to drop their fishing nets and follow this man from Nazareth.[50] He simply invited people to follow his leadership model, a path he was willing to take before asking others to join. He never gives up on people; neither should we!

This final chapter penetrated to the core of *leadership . . . in crisis* by presenting the leadership model of Jesus Christ. First, we looked at the context in which he invested in and organized his people. Then came the reaction to the crisis through the team's 4D's responses: *Disloyalty, Denial, Doubt,* and *Disappointment,* to which the leader proactively responded with the 3C's: *Confront, Construct,* and *Consolidate.* Looking at the leadership implications, it is vital that we adopt the *3C-4D Leadership in Crisis Model* by understanding people's uncertainties in times of crisis, aligning expectations, and moving forward. Now we conclude with a recap on whether leadership is really in crisis.

Recommended action points:

- Invest in and organize your team members to be better equipped when facing a crisis.
- Understand the dynamics of the 3C-4D model to enhance your leadership in crisis skills.
- Try to offer people around you a second chance.

50. Copeland, *Why lead?*, 11–12.

Conclusion: Is Leadership in Crisis?

THIS BOOK HAS EXAMINED multiple leadership models and illustrations, ranging from those that depicted failed crisis leadership to others that are exemplary in approaching uncertainties. *Leadership . . . is in crisis* if it loses its authenticity, influence, and meaningfulness during *volatile, unexpected, complex,* and *ambiguous* events. Monitoring leadership behaviors that suddenly altered because of changing external environments, derailed away from their principles and value systems, avoided confronting crucial and vital matters, and/or evaded effective stakeholders' accountability are some of the signs that *leadership . . . is in crisis*. Scores could be written about such ineffective practices from a global perspective, as no country, culture, community, or organization could claim preeminence from this "pandemic."

Leadership . . . in crisis presented an alternative pathway to enhance performance and uphold *accountable, healthier,* and *courageous* leadership models. It offered substitutes to the current situation and extended a helping hand to communities consisting of new and emerging leaders who are in dire need of high-performing, reliable, and trustworthy leaders in today's world. Operationalizing crisis leadership at a mediocre level is no longer a viable option. We must seek to raise the bar, escalate the ceiling, and advance the quest for leadership to regain its respected stance.

This book attempted to contribute to this quest. Following are some of the principles, tools, and notions discussed to achieve the aspired level of *leadership . . . in crisis*. Finding the sources of our *resilience* to build that wall is essential for achieving a bird's-eye view and realizing that every crisis has an end, offers new learning opportunities, and develops stronger leaders. Crises are windows of opportunities that may enable leaders who have access to verified information to capitalize on their resources in a sustainable manner and create new avenues and renewed mindsets. Looking beyond a crisis' immediate uncertainties offers several ideal meaningful opportunities and learning lessons.

Maintaining and increasing our *stamina* levels is achieved through discovering what motivates us, going on our pace and accelerating our speed, replenishing energy levels, and completing the task. Such stamina levels are crucial for *leadership . . . in crisis* through preserving energy and balancing task-people orientations. Regulating operations during a crisis is necessary for sustaining the team through continuous communication and reallocation of tasks. But stamina also requires an accelerated pace to address growing needs and make difficult decisions.

Leadership *agility* is dependent on three double-lettered abbreviations: SS, PP, and DD. *Strategic Swiftness* offers an opportunity to shift personal or organizational directions and capitalize on competitive advantages; *Pivotal Power* allows leaders to alter courses of action while remaining anchored to the base; and *Deliberate Derailment* proposes options for derailing the pathway based on changed external factors, leadership traits, and behaviors. Agility, flexibility, and change management also present a D2D window, allowing leaders to objectively assess internal and external environments during the discovery-to-diagnosis phase of any crisis.

Confrontation in leadership is required to address crisis situations. This is accomplished through tackling the invisible elephant in the room, managing difficult conversations, and being accountable to an effective governing body. *Confrontational leadership* offers a reconciliation option as a win-win positive alternative. Jesus Christ adopted a *confrontational leadership* model to achieve reconciliation with the team. While the reactions to the crisis were attributed to the 4D's—*Disloyalty, Denial, Doubt,* and *Disappointment*—the leader approached these reactions with the 3C's—*Confront, Construct,* and *Consolidate.* The *3C-4D Leadership in Crisis Model* stems from the need to understand people's uncertainties in times of crisis, align expectations, and move forward.

So, what's next? This book only scratches the surface of the corrective measures needed to lead in diverse and complex situations. The COVID-19 pandemic crisis that penetrated the globe and enforced a "new normal" on leadership presented multitudes of excelling models for *leadership . . . in crisis,* but there were also many examples of failed leadership during this phase. This book has attempted to prepare new, emerging, and seasoned leaders to enhance their leadership tools in pre-crisis stages, discern the times, and tackle the "next normal" effectively. What's next? *Leadership . . . in . . . !*

Bibliography

"Blending Resilience and Sustainability." Strategic Direction 31, no. 1 (January 2015): 6–8.

"Brand agility in time of crisis." Daily Financial Times (Colombo, Srilanka). June 9, 2020. https://www.ft.lk/Opinion-and-Issues/Brand-agility-in-time-of-crisis/14-701321.

"The Chairman of Nissan Has Been Arrested in Tokyo. Here's Why." Fortune. November 19, 2018. https://fortune.com/2018/11/19/nissan-chairman-carlos-ghosn-arrest/.

Agnes, Melissa. "Becoming Crisis Ready: Transforming Today's Uncertainties into Strategic Opportunities." Public Management, May 1, 2019.

American Psychological Association. "Building your resilience." January 2012. https://www.apa.org/topics/resilience.

Anne Mcelvoy and Alice Hart-Davis. "Charge up on Energy; The Key to Success Is an Ability to Bounce Back from Fatigue. Here Is Our Guide to Raising Those Stamina Levels." The London Evening Standard (London, England), November 15, 2005.

Ansell, Chris, and Arjen Boin. "Taming Deep Uncertainty: The Potential of Pragmatist Principles for Understanding and Improving Strategic Crisis Management." Administration & Society 51, no. 7 (August 2019): 1079–1112.

Arasy Alimudin, Dahlia Septian, Agus Dwi Sasono, and Ani Wulandari. "Effect of Spiritual Leadership to Organizational Culture and Employee's Loyalty." Jurnal Terapan Manajemen Dan Bisnis 3, no. 2 (October 1, 2017): 76–86.

Ascott, Terence. Dare to Believe! Stories of Faith from the Middle East. Eugene: Resource Publications, 2021.

Baiya, E. (2020). Why agility is key to companies surviving the pandemic. https://www.fastcompany.com/90516862/why-agility-is-key-to-companies-surviving-the-pandemic.

Bassous, Michael. "IQ, EQ, … but what about WQ?" Wordpress. September 18, 2013. https://mbassous.wordpress.com/2013/09/18/iq-eq-but-what-about-wq/.

Bassous, Michael. "Techflexing: The new era of time-management." Wordpress. March 4, 2014. https://mbassous.wordpress.com/2014/03/04/techflexing-the-new-era-of-time-management/.

Bassous, Michael. "What Are the Factors That Affect Worker Motivation in Faith-Based Nonprofit Organizations?" Voluntas: International Journal of Voluntary and Nonprofit Organizations 26, no. 1 (February 1, 2015): 355–81.

Beer, Michael. "Boards Need Truth (Whether They Want It or Not)." NACD Directorship, May 2020, 50–53.

Bennett, Janet. Cultivating intercultural competence: A process perspective. In D. Deardorff (Ed.), The SAGE handbook of intercultural competence. Thousand Oaks: Sage, 2009.

Bergant, Dianne. "Follow the Leader!" America, April 4, 2005.

Bernard, Larry C, Michael Mills, Leland Swenson, and R Patricia Walsh. "An Evolutionary Theory of Human Motivation." Genetic, Social, and General Psychology Monographs 131, no. 2 (May 2005): 129–84.

Bernstein, Jonathan and Bonafede, Bruce. Manager's Guide to Crisis Management. New York: McGraw Hill Professional, 2011.

Bhaduri, Raka "Leveraging Culture and Leadership in Crisis Management." European Journal of Training and Development 43, no. 5/6 (April 2, 2019): 554–69.

Blankenburgh, Marco. Inter-Cultural Intelligence: From surviving to thriving in the global space. Dubai: Knowledgeworkx, 2014.

Bloomberg, Michael. "Quotes." 2022. https://www.azquotes.com/quote/928534

Boin, Arjen., Kuipers, Sanneke, and Overdijk, Werner. "Leadership in Times of Crisis: A Framework for Assessment." International Review of Public Administration 18, no. 1 (April 2013): 79–91.

Borgida, Eugene and Mobilio, Lynne. "Social Motivation." American Psychological Association, Encyclopedia of Psychology 7 (2000): 347-350.

Bradt, George. "How Leaders Can Address the Elephant(s) in the Room." Forbes. August 7, 2013. https://www.forbes.com/sites/georgebradt/2013/08/07/how-leaders-can-address-the-elephants-in-the-room/?sh=54713a8d5660.

Brooks, David. The Social Animal: The Hidden Sources of Love, Character, and Achievement. New York: Random House, 2011.

Burns, James M. Leadership. New York: Harper & Row, 1978.

By, Rune. "Organisational Change Management: A Critical Review." Journal of Change Management 5, no. 4 (December 1, 2005): 369–380.

Cambridge Dictionary. "Culture." 2022. https://dictionary.cambridge.org/dictionary/english/culture.

Cambridge Dictionary. "Elephant in the Room." 2022. https://dictionary.cambridge.org/dictionary/english/an-elephant-in-the-room.

Cappiello, Dina. and Weber, Harry (2010), "BP accused of withholding 'critical' spill data." The San Diego Union-Tribune. August 19, 2010. www.sandiegouniontribune.com/sdut-bp-accused-of-withholding-critical-spill-data-2010aug19-story.html.

Carlin, John. Invictus. Nelson Mandela and the Game that made a Nation. New York: Penguin Books, 2008.

Cateora, Philip et al. International Marketing (18th ed). New York: McGraw-Hill, 2020.

Center for Creative Leadership. "4 Unexpected Lessons Learned from Hardships & Adversity." 2020. https://www.ccl.org/articles/leading-effectively-articles/4-lessons-learned-from-hardship-adversity/.

Chism, Marlene. "The undiscussables: How to address the elephant in the room." SmartBrief. March 4, 2019. https://www.smartbrief.com/original/2019/03/undiscussables-how-address-elephant-room.

Cohen, William. "Drucker And Principles Of Success: Lessons That Are Still the Basis of Leadership Success." Leadership Excellence 35, no. 5 (May 2018): 58–61.

Copeland, Adam J. "Why Lead? Discipleship as Leadership." The Christian Century, November 13, 2013.

Covey, Steven. The 7 Habits of Highly Effective People (First Fireside Edition). New York: Simon & Schuster, 1990.

Covrig, Duane M. "Lessons in Leadership Development from the Master Student." The Journal of Applied Christian Leadership 5, no. 1 (Winter 2011): 13–17.

D'Souza, Anthony. *Empowered Leadership: Your Personal Guide to Self Empowerment.* Atlanta: Haggai Institute, 2001.

Daskal, Lolly. "How to Deal with the Elephant in the Room." Lead from Within. November 14, 2016. https://www.inc.com/lolly-daskal/how-to-deal-with-the-elephant-in-the-room.html.

Demiroz, Fatih, and Naim Kapucu. "The Role of Leadership in Managing Emergencies and Disasters." European Journal of Economic & Political Studies 5, no. 1 (Summer 2012): 91–101.

Den Hartog, House, et al. "Culture Specific and Cross-Culturally Generalizable Implicit Leadership Theories: Are Attributes of Charismatic/Transformational Leadership Universally Endorsed?" The Leadership Quarterly 10, no. 2 (January 1, 1999): 219–56.

Denny, Richard. *Communicate to Win (2nd Ed.).* UK: Kogan Page, 2009.

Dezenhall, Eric and Weber, John. *Damage Control: The Essential Lessons of Crisis Management.* Westport: Prospecta, 2011.

Dimino, Kimberly, Kathleen M. Horan, and Carolene Stephenson. "Leading Our Frontline Heroes Through Times of Crisis with a Sense of Hope, Efficacy, Resilience, and Optimism." Nurse Leader 18, no. 6 (December 1, 2020): 592–96.

Dmiroz, Fatih, and Naim Kapucu. "The Role of Leadership in Managing Emergencies and Disasters." European Journal of Economic & Political Studies 5, no. 1 (Summer 2012): 91–101.

Dotlich, David L., Peter C. Cairo, and Stephen H. Rhinesmith. "Leading in Times of Crisis." Leading in Times of Crisis - Business Book Summaries 1, no. 1 (September 7, 2009): 1–11.

Drucker, Peter. "Quotes." 2022. https://quotefancy.com/quote/887806/Peter-F-Drucker-The-greatest-danger-in-times-of-turbulence-is-not-the-turbulence-it-is-to.

Effah, Bernard et al. "The Managerial Leadership and Energy (E=mc2) of Kumasi Polytechnic." Developing Country Studies, 4, 23 (2014): 93-104.

Elali, Wajeeh. "The Importance of Strategic Agility to Business Survival During Corona Crisis and Beyond." International Journal of Business Ethics and Governance (IJBEG). 2021. https://ijbeg.com/index.php/1/article/view/64.

Essawi, Mohamad. "Assessment of Value Confrontation Leadership." Conflict Resolution & Negotiation Journal 2013, no. 1 (March 2013): 44–52.

Ferraro, Giulia. "After the Crisis: The Role of Resilience in Coming Back Stronger." Connections (18121098) 19, no. 4 (Fall 2020): 97–107.

Finton David. *Cognitive-Economy Assumptions for Learning.* In: Seel N.M. (eds) Encyclopedia of the Sciences of Learning. Boston: Springer, 2012.

Flamholtz, Eric, and Yvonne Randle. "How Entrepreneurial Leaders Can Navigate a Crisis Successfully: Lessons and Hypotheses." International Review of Entrepreneurship 19, no. 2 (April 2021): 225–72.

Fleming, Renée, Ingo Titze, and Rachelle Fleming. "The FlemIngo Stance: Resistance Training in Breath Management." Journal of Singing 78, no. 1 (September 2021): 83–86.

Foley, R. A., and M. Mirazón Lahr. "The Evolution of the Diversity of Cultures." Philosophical Transactions: Biological Sciences 366, no. 1567 (April 12, 2011): 1080–89.

Forbes, B.C. "Quotes." 2022. https://quotefancy.com/quote/1190688/B-C-Forbes-In-the-race-for-success-speed-is-less-important-than-stamina.

Foster, Roster. "Discipleship in the New Testament." Society of Biblical Literatur.e. Teaching the Bible. 2010. https://www.sbl-site.org/assets/pdfs/tbv2i7_fosterdiscipleship.pdf

Fox, Tom. "Realistic optimism." Executive Leadership 27, no. 3 (March 2012): 8.

Frandsen, Finn, and Winni Johansen. "Advice on Communicating During Crisis: A Study of Popular Crisis Management Books." International Journal of Business Communication 57, no. 2 (April 2020): 260–76.

Frankl, Viktor. *Man's Search for Meaning (4th Ed)*. Boston: Beacon Press, 1992.

Fruchter, Dasi. "In the Study of Leadership, Spirituality Is the Unexpected Elephant in the Room [Review Essay]." Public Administration Review 75, no. 1 (January 2015): 171–74.

Galinsky, Adam D, William W Maddux, Debra Gilin, and Judith B White. "Why It Pays to Get inside the Head of Your Opponent: The Differential Effects of Perspective Taking and Empathy in Negotiations." Psychological Science 19, no. 4 (April 2008): 378–84.

Gerdeman, Dina. "Leadership under Fire." Harvard Business School. October 4, 2017. https://hbswk.hbs.edu/item/5-leaders-forged-in-crisis-and-what-we-can-learn-from-them.

Gibbs, Alexandra. "Why HSBC chose to move on from being 'the world's local bank." CNBC, August 17, 2016. https://www.cnbc.com/2016/08/17/why-hsbc-chose-to-move-on-from-being-the-worlds-local-bank.html.

Gould, B. "Drive Change or Cultivate It?" The Antidote 3, no. 4 (June 1, 1998): 23–25.

Gray, Katherine. "Generation to Generation. Jesus, Formation and Transitions in Leadership." Health Progress (Saint Louis, Mo.) 95, no. 4 (July 2014): 8–13.

Greimel, Hans. "Nissan takes control of Mitsubishi with Ghosn as chairman." Automotive News Europe. October 20, 2016. https://europe.autonews.com/article/20161020/ANE/161029998/nissan-takes-control-of-mitsubishi-with-ghosn-as-chairman.

Guidestar. "Ravi Zacharias International Ministries, Inc." January 2022. https://www.guidestar.org/profile/13-3200719.

Guo, Chao and Bielefeld, Wolfgang. *Social Entrepreneurship: An Evidence-Based Approach to Creating Social Value*. San Francisco: Jossey-Bass, 2014.

Guterres, António. "Press Conference." December 2021. https://middleeast.in-24.com/News/516968.html.

Habecker, Eugene. *The Softer Side of Leadership: Essential Soft Skills that Transform Leaders and the People they Lead*. Oregon: Deep River Books, 2018.

Hackman, J. Richard. and Oldham, Greg. *Work Redesign*. Boston: Addison-Wesley, 1980.

Haley, Dennis. "Leading in a Crisis." Personal Excellence 14, no. 6 (June 2009): 14.

Hammer, Mitchell, Gudykunst, William, and Wiseman, Richard. "Dimensions of intercultural effectiveness: An exploratory study." International Journal of Intercultural Relations 2, no. 4 (1978): 382–393.

Harari, Oren. "Leading Change from the Middle: With These 11 Rules, You Don't Have to Be Top Brass to Lead Profound Change in Your Company." Management Review, February 1, 1999.

Hassanzadeh, Maryam et al. (2015). "Developing Effective Global Leadership." Journal of Educational and Social Research 5, no. 3 (2015): 14–24.

Hawkins, Beverley, and Gareth Edwards. "Managing the Monsters of Doubt: Liminality, Threshold Concepts and Leadership Learning." Management Learning 46, no. 1 (February 2015): 24–43.

Herzberg, Frederick. *Work and the Nature of Man*. London: Staples, 1966.

Higgs, Malcolm. "How Can We Make Sense of Leadership in the 21st Century?" Leadership & Organization Development Journal 24, no. 5 (August 1, 2003): 273–84.

Hunter, Bill, George P. White, and Galen C. Godbey. "What Does It Mean to Be Globally Competent?" Journal of Studies in International Education 10, no. 3 (January 1, 2006): 267–85.

Institute of Government. "Coronavirus: how different countries supported the unemployed." January 10, 2022. https://www.instituteforgovernment.org.uk/coronavirus-support-workers-comparison.

J. Lukas Thürmer, Frank Wieber, and Peter M. Gollwitzer. "Management in Times of Crisis: Can Collective Plans Prepare Teams to Make and Implement Good Decisions?" Management Decision 58, no. 10 (December 1, 2020): 2155–76.

Johnson, John. "Getting and staying involved: What motivates volunteers in a non-profit organization." Ph.D. dissertation, Capella University, 2007.

Jori Pascal Kalkman. "Sensemaking Questions in Crisis Response Teams." Disaster Prevention and Management: An International Journal 28, no. 5 (June 3, 2019): 649–60.

Joshua Paas, Rob F. Poell, and Saša Batistič. "The Elephant in the Room: Exploring the Motivational Antecedents of Servant Leadership." Leadership & Organization Development Journal 41, no. 5 (June 15, 2020): 637–52.

Juan Manuel Menéndez Blanco. "What Is behind Grit? Developing Stamina for Your Organization." Development and Learning in Organizations: An International Journal 35, no. 6 (February 24, 2021): 11–13.

Kadey, Matthew. "7 of the Healthiest Fruits You Can Eat for Better Performance" December 24, 2018. https://www.runnersworld.com/nutrition-weight-loss/a24784787/healthiest-fruits/.

Kahn, Richard and Kellner, Douglas. Global Youth Culture. ResearchGate. 2004. https://www.researchgate.net/publication/240595521.

Karnazes, Dean. Utlramarathon Man: Confessions of an All-Night Runner. NY: Penguin, 2006.

Kaschner, Holger. "Effective Crisis Decision-Making." Journal of Business Continuity & Emergency Planning 11, no. 1 (January 1, 2017): 27–36.

Kaur, Sandeep. "Does Grit Have a Significant Impact on Mental Well-Being?" Indian Journal of Health & Wellbeing 12, no. 1 (January 2021): 1–9.

Kennedy, John. "Remarks of Senator John F. Kennedy, Convocation of The United Negro College Fund, Indianapolis, Indiana." April 12, 1959. https://www.jfklibrary.org/archives/other-resources/john-f-kennedy-speeches/indianapolis-in-19590412.

Kerfoot, Karlene M. "Denial and Immunity to Change: It Starts with the Leader." Nursing Economic$ 27, no. 6 (November 2009): 422–23.

Kern, Merilee A. "How To Be a Courageous Leader in the Post-Pandemic Era: 3 Must-Have Traits for Courageous Leadership in Today's Workplace." Personal Excellence 25, no. 7 (July 2020): 24–27.

Keselman, David, and Marcy Saxe-Braithwaite. "Authentic and Ethical Leadership during a Crisis." Healthcare Management Forum 34, no. 3 (May 2021): 154–57.

Kets de Vries, Manfred F.R., and Elizabeth Florent-Treacy. "Global Leadership from A to Z: Creating High Commitment Organizations." Organizational Dynamics, March 22, 2002.

Klann, Gene. (2003). *Chapter 2: What Is Crisis Leadership? In Crisis Leadership.* Center for Creative Leadership. 2003. https://www.ccl.org/wp-content/uploads/2020/03/crisis-leadership-center-for-creative-leadership-guidebook.pdf.

KnowledgeWorks. "Inter-Cultural Intelligence." 2022. https://www.knowledgeworkx.com.

Koehn, Nancy. "Real Leaders Are Forged in Crisis." Harvard Business School. April 3, 2020. https://hbr.org/2020/04/real-leaders-are-forged-in-crisis.

Kouzes, James and Posner, Barry. *Leadership: The challenge (3rd Ed.).* San Francisco: Jossey-Bass, 2002.

Kraft, Dave. *Leaders who Last.* Wheaton: Crossway, 2010.

Kumar, T. (2012). "Is EQ more important than IQ." Golden Research Thoughts 2, no. 6 (2012): 1-3.

LaRue, Paul. "How to Talk About the Elephant in the Room." Connection Culture Group. September 16, 2018. https://www.connectionculture.com/post/how-to-talk-about-the-elephant-in-the-room.

Lassiter, Brian. "The Power of the Pivot: Organizational Agility is Key to Survival." Performance Excellence Network. May 26, 2020. https://www.performanceexcellencenetwork.org/pensights/the-power-of-the-pivot-organizational-agility-is-key-to-survival-may-2020/.

Law, Terry. and Gilbert, Jim. *The Hope Habit: Finding God's Goodness when Life is Hard.* FL: Charisma House, 2010.

LeMoine, Sarah, Kristen Greene, Kathleen Mulrooney, and Katrina Macasaet. "You Matter: Promoting Professional Resilience During Collective Crisis." Zero to Three 41, no. 1 (September 2020): 53–58.

Lengell, Sean. "AIG followed bailout with $440K retreat" The Washington Times. October 8, 2008. https://www.washingtontimes.com/news/2008/oct/08/aig-followed-bailout-with-440000-retreat/.

Leonard, H. Skipton. "Leadership Development for the Postindustrial, Postmodern Information Age." Consulting Psychology Journal: Practice & Research 55, no. 1 (Winter 2003): 3–14.

Lewis M. Paul. *Ethnologue: Languages of the world, (16th ed.).* Dallas: SIL International, 2009.

Lexico. "Glocal". 2022. https://www.lexico.com/definition/glocal

Library of Congress. "Leadership." June 2021. https://www.loc.gov/books/?all=true&q=leadership.

Low, Kim Cheng Patrick. "Moving Mountains - The Vital Art of Persuasion from Jesus." Leadership & Organizational Management Journal 2010, no. 3 (September 2010): 55–63.

Luciano, Margaret M., Jennifer D. Nahrgang, and Christine Shropshire. "Strategic Leadership Systems: Viewing Top Management Teams and Boards of Directors from a Multiteam Systems Perspective." Academy of Management Review 45, no. 3 (July 1, 2020).

Luu, Trong Tuan. "Worker Resilience during the COVID-19 Crisis: The Role of Core Beliefs Challenge, Emotion Regulation, and Family Strain." Personality and Individual Differences 179 (September 1, 2021).

MacShane, Denise. "Marathon Man: Stamina growing, pace lacking." London: The Observer, 2000.

Magd, Hesham, Siraj K Kunjumuhammed, and Ravi Thirumalaisamy. "Entrepreneurial Skills in the New Normal: A Review of Literature." Global Business and Management Research: An International Journal, July 1, 2021.

Mandela, Nelson. "Quotes." 2022. https://www.brainyquote.com/quotes/nelson_mandela_378967.

Martin, Andre and Ernst, Christopher. "Leadership, learning and human resource management: Exploring leadership in times of paradox and complexity." Corporate Governance, Journal 5, no. 3 (July 2005): 82–94.

Maslow, Abraham. Higher and Lower Needs, Understanding Human Motivation. Cleveland: Howard Allen, 1948.

McCarthy, Mary K. "'I Didn't Train for This': Take Cues from Elite Athletes to Maintain Stamina during the COVID-19 Crisis: We Can Train Ourselves to Develop Mental Toughness to Get Us through Challenging Times." OBG Management, June 1, 2020.

McCarty, Melissa. "Stamina and Energy." Massage Magazine, no. 170 (July 2010): 74–78.

McCulloch, Andrew. "Jesus Christ and Max Weber: Two Problems of Charisma." Max Weber Studies 5, no. 1 (January 1, 2005): 7–34.

McFarlane, Donovan A. "Multiple Intelligences: The Most Effective Platform for Global 21st Century Educational and Instructional Methodologies." College Quarterly 14, no. 2 (January 1, 2011).

McGregor, Douglas. The Human Side of Enterprise. Boston: McGraw-Hill Book Company, 1960.

Mendenhall, Mark E., B. Sebastian Reiche, Allan Bird, and Joyce S. Osland. "Defining the 'Global' in Global Leadership." Journal of World Business 47, no. 4 (October 1, 2012): 493–503.

Mendenhall, Mark, et al. Global Leadership: Research, Practice, and Development (3rd Ed). New York: Taylor & Francis, 2018.

Mento, Anthony J., Raymond M. Jones, and Walter Dirndorfer. "A Change Management Process: Grounded in Both Theory and Practice." Journal of Change Management 3, no. 1 (March 2002): 45.

Merriam-Webster. "Culture". 2022. https://www.merriam-webster.com/dictionary/culture.

Merriam-Webster. "Denial". 2022. https://www.merriam-webster.com/dictionary/denial.

Merriam-Webster. "Doubt". 2022. https://www.merriam-webster.com/dictionary/doubt.

Merriam-Webster. "Pivot" 2022. https://www.merriam-webster.com/dictionary/pivot.

Migration Data Portal. "Labour migration." February 18, 2022. https://www.migrationdataportal.org/themes/labour-migration.

Millikin, John P. "The Global Leadership of Carlos Ghosn at Nissan." Thunderbird International Business Review 47, no. 1 (January 2005): 121–37.

Mitchell, George E., Hans Peter Schmitz, and Tosca Bruno-van Vijfeijken. Between Power and Irrelevance: The Future of Transnational NGOs. New York: Oxford University Press, 2020.

Mitut, Iulian. "The Role of Leadership in the Management of Crisis Situations." Romanian Economic and Business Review 6, no. 3 (Fall 2011): 20–33.

Moral Stories. "The Rabbit and the Turtle" 2022. https://www.moralstories.org/the-rabbit-and-the-turtle/.

Morwood, James. The Pocket Oxford Latin Dictionary. Oxford University Press, 2012.

Murdoch, Rupert. "Quotes." 2022. https://www.brainyquote.com/quotes/rupert_murdoch_173446.

Niccolò Machiavelli. *The Prince*. Evergreens. London: Alma Books, 2013.

Nordberg, Donald. *Corporate Governance: Principles and Issues (1st Ed.)*. UK: Sage Publications, 2011.

Northouse, Peter. *Introduction to Leadership: Concepts and Practice (3rd Ed.)*. Thousand Oaks: SAGE Publications, 2015.

Nsiah, Gabriel. "Leading as Jesus Led: Christ Models of Leadership." Open Journal of Leadership 2, no. 4 (2013): 103-105.

Olympics. "Marathon man Akhwari demonstrates superhuman spirit." October 19, 1968. https://olympics.com/en/news/marathon-man-akhwari-demonstrates-superhuman-spirit.

Oxford Languages. "Disappointment." Google's English dictionary. 2022. https://languages.oup.com/google-dictionary-en/.

Oxford Languages. "Disloyalty." Google's English dictionary. 2022. https://languages.oup.com/google-dictionary-en/.

Parisi, Bill. "Maximizing Your Athletes' Acceleration." Coach and Athletic Director, December 1, 2008.

Pasmore, Bill et al. "Turning Crisis into Opportunity: Preparing Your Organization for a Transformed World." Center for Creative Leadership. 2020. https://www.ccl.org/articles/white-papers/turning-crisis-into-opportunity/.

Pink, Daniel. *Drive: The Surprising Truth about what Motivates us*. New York: Riverhead Books, 2009.

Prewitt, Vana. "Integral Leadership for the 21st Century." World Futures: The Journal of General Evolution 60, no. 4 (2004): 327–333.

Price David. *Atlas of world cultures*. London: Sage, 1990.

Priftanji, Dorela, John D Hill, and Daniel M Ashby. "Managing Difficult Conversations." American Journal of Health-System Pharmacy 77, no. 21 (November 2020): 1723–26.

Proverbicals. "The library of proverbial wisdom." 2022. https://proverbicals.com/chinese

PWC. "Global Crisis Survey 2021: Building resilience for the future. March 2021. https://www.pwc.com/gx/en/crisis/pwc-global-crisis-survey-2021.pdf

Reibstein, David and Bedi, Suneal. "The Agile Nation." U.S. News. April 13, 2021. https://www.usnews.com/news/best-countries/articles/2021-04-13/ag...y-becomes-the-most-powerful-factor-to-survive-in-a-changing-world.

Reynolds, David. "The Dunkirk Delusion: From Our Finest Hour to the Coronavirus Crisis." New Statesman, May 22, 2020.

Richard Hu. "COVID-19, Smart Work, and Collaborative Space: A Crisis-Opportunity Perspective." Journal of Urban Management 9, no. 3 (September 1, 2020): 276–80.

Roberts, David Bryte. "A directed content analysis of the leadership of Jesus among his twelve disciples using the framework of the situational LeadershipRTM model." ProQuest Dissertations, 2012.

Robinson, Simon. & Smith, Jonathan. *Co-Charismatic Leadership: Critical Perspectives on Spirituality, Ethics and Leadership*. New York: Peter Lang, 2014.

Rockstuhl, Thomas, Stefan Seiler, Soon Ang, Linn Van Dyne, and Hubert Annen. "Beyond General Intelligence (IQ) and Emotional Intelligence (EQ): The Role of Cultural Intelligence (CQ) on Cross-Border Leadership Effectiveness in a Globalized World." Journal of Social Issues 67, no. 4 (December 1, 2011): 825.

Rogers, Eileen M. "Optimism or Positivity." Leadership Excellence 26, no. 5 (May 2009): 19.

Rogers, Eileen M. "Realistic Optimism." Personal Excellence 14, no. 2 (February 2009): 7.

Rubenstein, Herb. "The Evolution of Leadership in the Workplace." Vision (09722629) 9, no. 2 (April 2005): 41–49.

S.M. Riad Shams, and Rajibul Hasan. "Capacity Building for Transnationalisation of Higher Education: Knowledge Management for Organisational Efficacy." European Business Review 32, no. 3 (February 25, 2020): 459–84.

Sánchez, Patricia Datchuck. "Lessons in Leadership." National Catholic Reporter, April 29, 2011.

Schaeffer, Frances. "Quotes." 2022. https://quotefancy.com/quote/1402202/Francis-Schaeffer-Truth-carries-with-it-confrontation-Truth-demands-confrontation-loving.

Sequeira, Arminda Sá. "Leadership in a VUCA Organizational Context: Are We Ready for a Paradigm Change?" Proceedings of the European Conference on Management, Leadership & Governance, January 2019, 340–48.

Service, Robert W. "Leadership and Innovation Across Cultures: The CIQ--Contextual Intelligence Quotient." Southern Business Review 37, no. 1 (January 2012): 19–50.

Slater, Susan. "When the Tide Goes Out: Leading People in the Difficult Times." Journal of the Quality Assurance Institute 23, no. 2 (April 2009): 15.

Slear, Sharon. "Jesus the Level-Five Leader." Momentum (0026914X) 40, no. 2 (April 2009): 24–25.

Sparrowe, Raymond T., and Robert C. Liden. "Two Routes to Influence: Integrating Leader-Member Exchange and Social Network Perspectives." Administrative Science Quarterly 50, no. 4 (December 1, 2005): 505–35.

Stafford, S., & Taylor, J. (2016). Transnational Education as an Internationalisation Strategy: Meeting the Institutional Management Challenges. Journal of Higher Education Policy and Management, 38(6), 625–636.

Stern, Eric. "Preparing: The Sixth Task of Crisis Leadership." Journal of Leadership Studies 7, no. 3 (September 22, 2013): 51.

Stubbs, Rocky. "Agility: The Key to Surviving a Crisis." Forbes Financial Council. June 25, 2020. https://www.forbes.com/sites/forbesfinancecouncil/2020/06/25/agility-the-key-to-surviving-a-crisis/?sh=22162d761382.

Svartengren, Magnus, and Therese Hellman. "Study Protocol of an Effect and Process Evaluation of the Stamina Model; a Structured and Time-Effective Approach through Methods for an Inclusive and Active Working Life." BMC Public Health 18, no. 1 (August 29, 2018): 1070.

Tannen, Deborah. "Why Conversations Go Wrong." 2021. Hidden Brain. https://hiddenbrain.org/podcast/why-conversations-go-wrong/.

Taylor III, Alex. "How would Ghosn fix GM?" CNN Money. July 10, 2006. https://money.cnn.com/2006/07/10/news/companies/8381630.fortune/index.htm.

Taylor, Sully. "Creating Social Capital in MNCs: The International Human Resource Management Challenge." Human Resource Management Journal 17, no. 4 (November 1, 2007): 336.

The Economist. "What is the economic cost of covid-19?" January 7, 2021. https://www.economist.com/finance-and-economics/2021/01/09/what-is-the-economic-cost-of-covid-19.

The Jesuits. "About Us." 2022. https://www.jesuits.org/about-us/the-jesuits/.

TMH Business Coaching & Consulting. "If you chase two rabbits, you will not catch either one: Focus on one goal at a time." June 20, 2020. https://tmhbusinesscoaching.com/

if-you-chase-two-rabbits-you-will-not-catch-either-one-focus-on-one-goal-at-a-time/.

Topel, Fred. "How Did Forrest Gump Run So Far and Long?" May 9, 2021. https://www.cheatsheet.com/entertainment/how-did-forrest-gump-run-so-far-and-long.html/.

UAE. "Fact Sheet." 2022. https://u.ae/en/about-the-uae/fact-sheet.

UNESCO Universal Declaration of Cultural Diversity, Adopted by the General Conference of the United Nations Educational, Scientific and Cultural Organization at its thirty-first session on 2 November 2001.

Veil, Shari R. "Mindful Learning in Crisis Management." Journal of Business Communication 48, no. 2 (April 2011): 116–47.

Viktor E. Frankl Quotes. BrainyQuote.com, BrainyMedia Inc, 2022. https://www.brainyquote.com/quotes/viktor_e_frankl_160380.

Ward, Ted W. "Developing Christ-like Leaders." Common Ground Journal 10, no. 1 (Fall 2012): 9–11.

Ward, Ted W. "Facilitating Human Development." Common Ground Journal 10, no. 1 (Fall 2012): 12–14.

Warren, Rick. "Quotes". 2022. https://quotefancy.com/quote/899898/Rick-Warren-The-secret-of-endurance-is-to-remember-that-your-pain-is-temporary-but-your.

Wikipedia. "Mass-Energy Equivalence" 2022. https://en.wikipedia.org/wiki/Mass–energy_equivalence.

Wills, Stefan and Barham, Kevin. "Being an International Manager." European Management Journal 12, no. 1 (March 1994): 49–58.

Winnard, Julie, Adcroft, Andy, Lee, Jacquetta, and Skipp, David. "Surviving or Flourishing? Integrating Business Resilience and Sustainability." Journal of Strategy and Management 7, no. 3 (August 12, 2014): 303–15.

Winnard, Julie, Lee, Jacquetta, and Skipp, David. "Putting Resilient Sustainability into Strategy Decisions – Case Studies." Management Decision 56, no. 7 (July 9, 2018): 1598–1612.

Wolfe, Nicole and Bradberry, Travis. "How to Address the Elephant in the Room." TalentSmartEQ. 2021. https://www.talentsmarteq.com/articles/How-to-Address-the-Elephant-in-the-Room-1619550111-p-1.html¬/.

Wong, Paul. "Viktor Frankl's Meaning Seeking Model and Positive Psychology." In A. Batthyany & P. Russo-Netzer (Eds.), Meaning in existential and positive psychology. April 2014), New York: Springer.

Wood, Roy. "Crisis Leadership." Defense AT & L, July 1, 2013.

World Vision. "5 Global Crises the world can't ignore in 2021." 2020. https://www.wvi.org/fragile-context/context/5-crises-the-world-can%27t-ignore-in-2021.

Yost, Paul, DeHaas, CodieAnn., and Allison, Mackenzie. Learning Agility, Resilience, and Successful Derailment. UK: Oxford University Press, 2021.

YouTube. "Pizza maker in Chicago uses oven to 'toss' face shields for front-line medical workers" April 17, 2020. https://www.youtube.com/watch?v=WhBgHpkHsjA.

Yu, Howard, Boutalikakis, Angelo, and Shan, Jialo. "Surviving a Crisis – Why Preparation is Key to Resilience." International Institute for Management Development. 2021. www.imd.org.

Zamoun, Khaled and Gorpe, Tevhide Serra. "Crisis Management: A Historical and Conceptual Approach for a Better Understanding of Today's Crises." Intechopen. June 27, 2018. https://www.intechopen.com/chapters/60813.

BIBLIOGRAPHY

Zamzow, Aaron. "The Five Best Ways to Improve Firefighter Stamina: When You Set out to Build Your Stamina, You Work to Increase the Amount of Time That You Can Perform at the Peak of Your Abilities." Firehouse Magazine, January 1, 2021.